attacking with
with
1 e4

by John Emms

EVERYMAN CHESS

Published by Everyman Publishers plc, London

First published in 2001 by Everyman Publishers plc, formerly Cadogan Books plc, Gloucester Mansions, 140A Shaftesbury Avenue, London WC2H 8HD

Reprinted 2001, 2003

British Library Cataloguing-in-Publication Data
A catalogue record for this book is available from the British Library.

ISBN 1 85744 267 9

Distributed in North America by The Globe Pequot Press, P.O Box 480, 246 Goose Lane, Guilford, CT 06437-0480.

All other sales enquiries should be directed to Everyman Chess, Gloucester Mansions, 140A Shaftesbury Avenue, London WC2H 8HD
tel: 020 7539 7600 fax: 020 7379 4060
email: dan@everyman.uk.com
website: www.everyman.uk.com

The Everyman Chess Opening Guides were designed and developed by First Rank Publishing.

EVERYMAN CHESS SERIES (formerly Cadogan Chess)
Chief advisor: Garry Kasparov
Commissioning editor: Byron Jacobs

Typeset and edited by First Rank Publishing, Brighton.
Production by Book Production Services.
Printed and bound in Great Britain by The Cromwell Press Ltd., Trowbridge, Wiltshire.

CONTENTS

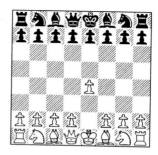

BIBLIOGRAPHY

Books

Encyclopaedia of Chess Openings volumes A-E (Sahovski Informator 2001)
Nunn's Chess Openings, Nunn, Burgess, Emms and Gallagher (Everyman 1999)
Closed Sicilian, King (Everyman 1997)
Winning with the Closed Sicilian, Lane (Batsford 1992)
Beating the Anti Sicilians, Gallagher (Batsford 1995)
Bishop's Opening, Harding (Batsford 1976)
Vienna Game, Lane (Everyman 2000)
Play the Open Games as Black, Emms (Gambit 2000)
The Ultimate King's Indian Attack, Dunnington (Batsford 1997)
Play the French, Watson (Everyman 1996)
The Complete French, Psakhis (Batsford 1992)
Opening Preparation, Dvoretsky and Yusupov (Batsford 1994)
Easy Guide to the Panov-Botvinnik Attack, Aagaard (Everyman 1998)
The Ultimate Pirc, Nunn and McNab (Batsford 1998)
A Killer Chess Opening Repertoire, Summerscale (Everyman 1999)
Modern Defence, Speelman and McDonald (Everyman 2000)
The Scandinavian, Emms (Everyman 1996)
The Complete Alekhine, Burgess (Batsford 1992)
New Ideas in the Alekhine, Burgess (Batsford 1995)

Periodicals

Informator
ChessBase Magazine
The Week in Chess
Chess
British Chess Magazine

INTRODUCTION

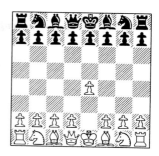

This is a book aimed for those who want a opening repertoire based on 1 e4. Moreover, this is an openings book for those who have neither the time nor the inclination to learn reams and reams of the latest modern opening theory. When possible, I've deliberately avoided recommending variations which require massive memorisation, or variations where the assessment changes at every super-grandmaster tournament. No main line Najdorfs, Dragons, Spanish Openings and Petroffs here!

In general I've opted for 'opening systems', in which learning the major ideas is just as important as learning the actual variations. Even though I've often steered away from main lines, I've made sure that I've chosen openings with some pedigree. Many of my recommendations have been played at one time or another by world class players (even World Champions).

I have, however, resisted the temptation for an 'all-in-one' solution. For example, the King's Indian Attack can be played against virtually every defence to 1 e4, However, it's generally thought that it's at it most effective when played against the French Defence; it's my choice here, but *only* against the French. I've opted for a good variety of systems, ones which will give you practice in a wide num-ber of positions (it's generally thought to be good for your chess to familiarise yourself with different types of openings, rather than sticking to just one).

I've paid particular attention to the psychological aspect when choosing these opening systems. I've endeavoured to come up with lines which make Black feel uncomfortable (I've often drawn on my own experiences for this). I've also avoided virtually all of Black's gambits, even if they are considered incorrect at the highest levels. It's just not most players' cup of tea to win an early pawn and then try and grovel out into an ending. Playing White should be more fun than that!

Sometimes, within an opening, I've given White more than one choice of variation. I've generally done this when there is little to pick between two or three lines, or when I've decided that a particularly sharp line needs a good back-up if something new is discovered for Black. Certain lines will favour certain players: you can make your own choices.

I've opted for a 'variation by variation' approach; I still believe that this is the best way of studying a new opening. I've also tried to paint as realistic picture as possible; I'll certainly say when a particular line is scoring well for White, but I'll also give the best defences for Black. If Black plays the best moves he may equalise – that's just chess for you. But even so, I've strove to ensure that Black has no easy way to reach a dull equality. Even the equal positions here give White good chances to play for the win!

I won't go into the specifics of the repertoire here. This can be discovered as you turn the pages.

Finally I would like to thank all those who have helped me in some way or another with this book. Special thanks go to Jonathan Rowson for some thoughts and recommendations.

John Emms
Kent
June 2001

CHAPTER ONE

Attacking the Sicilian: The Closed Variation

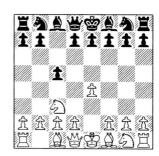

1 e4 c5 2 ♘c3

The Closed Sicilian is a solid and, at the same time, aggressive way of meeting 1...c5. It's true that White builds up slowly in the opening, but the overall aim is an eventual attack on the black king (I admit that, technically speaking, this could be said about any opening; after all, the eventual aim is always checkmate!). Seriously though, the Closed Sicilian is the perfect weapon for players wanting a heavyweight battle, but not having the time or inclination to study the main lines of the Open Sicilian. Indeed, even some of the most seasoned professional players are getting fed up of trying to find the faintest of edges against the Najdorf, Dragon, Scheveningen, Sveshnikov etc, and are turning their attention elsewhere.

The Closed Sicilian has a good pedigree; advocates include former World Champion Boris Spassky and England's top two, Michael Adams and Nigel Short. Unlike some anti-Sicilians, there's no easy way for Black to reach dull equality; even if Black plays the best moves a tense struggle will certainly lie ahead.

While researching the Closed Sicilian for this book, it's become apparent to me how logical White's moves are. It's certainly more important to learn the ideas than the con-crete lines (although both would be ideal!), even though I'm presenting the variations in a structured way. A final point is that there is still much uncharted territory and ample opportunity for players to express new ideas in this opening.

Main Line 1:
Black fianchettoes the king's bishop

1 e4 c5 2 ♘c3

This move is important. White wants to fianchetto his king's bishop, but before he does so he eliminates the possibility of Black playing 2...d5 (2 g3 d5 is playable for White, but that's outside our repertoire!).
2...♘c6

Other black options will be studied later in this chapter.
3 g3 g6

Black's most popular and successful way of dealing with the Closed Sicilian is to follow suit with his own fianchetto. The bishop on g7 will have a great influence over events in the centre and on the queenside.
4 ♗g2 ♗g7 5 d3

The above is the normal move order to reach this position, but are there others, for example 1 e4 c5 2 ♘c3 g6 3 g3 ♗g7 4 ♗g2 ♘c6 5 d3.

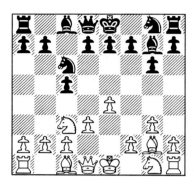

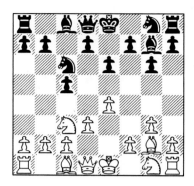

Now we will concentrate on Black's three main choices from this position:

A: 5...e6

B: 5...♖b8

C: 5...d6

Before moving onto Black's main moves, let's take a brief look at other possibilities for Black.

a) 5...♘f6 is likely to transpose to Variation C1 after 6 ♗e3 d6.

b) Likewise, 5...e5 will transpose to Variation C2 after 6 ♗e3 d6.

c) 5...b6 is unusual, but quite playable. White should continue as normal with 6 ♗e3. Hort-Toran Albero, Palma de Mallorca 1969, continued 6...♗b7 7 ♕d2 d6 8 ♘h3 ♕d7 9 0-0 e6 10 ♖ae1 ♘ge7 11 ♗h6 0-0 12 ♗xg7 ♔xg7 13 f4 f5 14 ♘g5 and Black's slightly weak kingside gave White the advantage.

A)

5...e6

With this move Black delays committing the d-pawn with ...d7-d6 and prepares to develop with ...♘ge7. This line often simply transposes to 5...d6 variations, but here we concentrate on Black refraining from playing an early ...d7-d6, as in some lines Black looks to gain from this by playing ...d7-d5 instead and thus saving a tempo with this central counterattack.

6 ♗e3!

It must be said that 6 f4 is also very possible, but in the main I'm recommending playing the Closed Sicilian with an early ♗e3 and ♕d2. The reasons for this are threefold: firstly, I believe lines with ♗e3 and ♕d2 to more direct and aggressive than those with an early f2-f4; secondly, there is less theory for the white player to learn and lastly, I think lines with ♗e3 and ♕d2 are easier to play.

More often than not, White will later offer the exchange of bishops with ♗e3-h6, thus weakening Black's control over the dark squares on the kingside. Indeed this is one of White's key ideas here.

6...♘d4!?

Black occupies the all-important d4-square. The knight is actively placed here and it certainly prevents White from playing d3-d4 in the near future. The knight is also reasonably secure on d4, being protected by both the bishop on g7 and the pawn on c5. However, the d4-square isn't an outpost in the strictest sense of the word – White can fight for its control by moving the c3-knight and playing c2-c3.

Other possibilities for Black include:

a) 6...d6 transposes to Variation C4. In fact this move is Black's most popular choice and may well be Black's best option.

b) 6...♕a5!? 7 ♕d2 (7 ♘ge2 ♘d4 8 0-0 ♘e7 9 ♘c1 d6 10 ♘b3 ♕c7 looks okay for

Black) 7...♘d4 8 f4 ♘e7 9 ♘f3 d6 10 0-0 transposes to Variation C43.

c) 6...♘ge7?! 7 ♗xc5 ♕a5 8 ♗e3 ♗xc3+ 9 bxc3 ♕xc3+ 10 ♗d2 ♕c5 11 ♘e2 and Black has no compensation for losing his dark-squared bishop, Jansen-Langer, Budapest 1999.

d) 6...b6 7 ♕d2 ♗b7 8 ♘ge2 ♘ge7 (8...♘d4? 9 ♗xd4 cxd4 10 ♘b5 d5 11 ♕b4! is very unpleasant for Black) 9 ♗h6 0-0 10 h4 f6 11 ♗xg7 ♔xg7 12 0-0-0 ♘d4 13 f4 h5 14 ♘xd4 cxd4 15 ♘e2 e5 16 g4 hxg4 17 h5 and White had a very strong attack, Medina Garcia-Benko, Siegen Olympiad 1970.

7 ♘ce2!

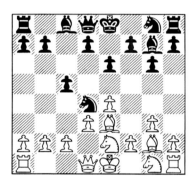

With this surprising move White immediately makes use of the unprotected state of the c5-pawn in order to challenge the d4-knight.

7...♘e7

Or:

a) 7...d5 8 c3 ♘xe2 9 ♘xe2 dxe4 10 ♗xc5! exd3 11 ♘f4 d2+ 12 ♕xd2 ♕xd2+ 13 ♔xd2 ♘f6 14 ♖ad1 ♘d7 15 ♗d6 ♗e5 16 ♗xe5 ♘xe5 17 ♖he1 ♘d7 18 ♔c1 and White has a terrific lead in development, Barczay-Uhlmann, Trencianske Teplice 1979.

b) 7...♘xe2 8 ♘xe2 ♗xb2 9 ♖b1 ♗g7 (9...♕a5+? loses to 10 ♗d2 ♕xa2 11 ♖xb2 ♕xb2 12 ♗c3) 10 ♗xc5 and the exchange of the c5-pawn for the b2-pawn is favourable for White. Black can now grab a pawn with 10...♕a5+ 11 ♗b4 ♕xa2, but following 12 c4

White has excellent compensation.

c) 7...b6 8 ♗xd4! cxd4 9 e5 ♖b8 10 f4 f6 11 ♘f3 fxe5 12 fxe5 ♕c7 13 ♘exd4 ♗xe5 14 ♕e2 ♗xd4 15 ♘xd4 ♕c5 16 ♘b3 ♕g5 17 0-0 and Black was simply overrun in Spassky-Hjartarson, Belfort 1988.

8 c3 ♘xe2 9 ♘xe2 d6

Black can also protect the c5-pawn with 9...b6. Following 10 d4 cxd4 we have:

a) 11 ♗xd4 e5! 12 ♗e3 ♗b7 looks equal, but not 12...0-0?! 13 ♕d6! ♗b7 14 0-0 ♖c8 15 ♖fd1 ♖c7 16 a4 ♘c6 17 b4 ♖e8 18 ♕d3 ♕a8 19 a5 bxa5 20 b5, which was very good for White in P.Kovacevic-Peev, Pancevo 1989.

b) 11 ♘xd4 ♗b7 12 0-0 0-0 13 f4 f5 14 e5 ♗xg2 15 ♔xg2 g5 and I prefer White, Bronstein-Korzubov, Minsk 1983.

10 d4

White was also slightly better after 10 ♕d2 0-0 11 h4 ♘c6 12 d4, as in Smyslov-Renter, Parnu 1947, but the text move looks more direct.

10...cxd4 11 ♘xd4 0-0 12 0-0

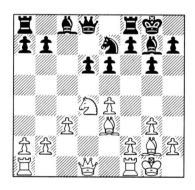

12...a6 13 ♕d2

White has an easy plan and a comfortable edge; the d6-pawn is vulnerable and White can increase the pressure along the d-file. King-Domont, Swiss League 1999, continued 13...♕c7 14 ♗h6 e5 15 ♗xg7 ♔xg7 16 ♘c2 ♗e6 17 f4 f6 18 ♘e3 ♖ad8 19 ♔h1 ♕c5 20 ♖ad1 a5 21 f5 ♗c4 22 ♖f2 gxf5 23 exf5 and White eventually won.

B)

5...♖b8!?

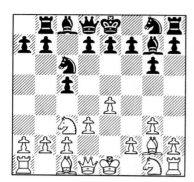

With this move Black delays showing his hand on the kingside and immediately prepares for the ...b7-b5-b4 push. This will gain important space on the queenside, force the white knight away from c3 and increase the scope of Black's dark-squared bishop. It must be said that 5...♖b8 has little independent value and usually transposes to lines considered later. Here we will look at possible deviations for Black.

6 ♗e3

Once again preparing ♕d2 and incidentally attacking the c5-pawn.

6...♘d4!?

Once again occupying the d4-square. Alternatively:

a) 6...d6, transposing to Variation C3, is Black's most obvious choice.

b) 6...b5!? 7 ♕d2 (7 ♗xc5 b4 8 ♘a4!? ♕a5 9 b3 is an interesting looking exchange sacrifice) 7...b4 8 ♘d1 d6 9 ♘e2 once again leads us to Variation C3.

7 ♘ce2!?

Following the same recipe as in Variation A. 7 ♘ge2 or 7 ♕d2 are likely to transpose to Variation C3.

7...♘xe2 8 ♘xe2 ♗xb2 9 ♖b1 ♗g7

9...♕a5+? once again loses to 10 ♗d2 ♕xa2 11 ♖xb2! ♕xb2 12 ♗c3.

10 ♗xc5

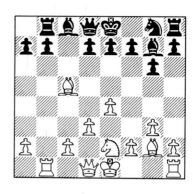

10...d6

10...♕a5+?! 11 ♗b4 ♕xa2 12 c4 once again gives White immense compensation for the pawn. After 10...d6 11 ♗d4 ♗xd4 12 ♘xd4 ♗d7 13 f4 (Sarfati-Rogers, Wellington 1988) Rogers gives 13...♕c7 14 ♕d2 ♘f6 as being equal. However, White could deviate earlier, keeping the dark-squared bishops on with 11 ♗e3 or 11 ♗b4, in either case with a slight edge for White.

C)

5...d6

This sensible move is Black's most popular choice. Black opens a diagonal for the c8-bishop, but other than this, he keeps all options open as to how he will develop both on the kingside and queenside.

6 ♗e3

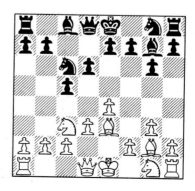

6 f4 is also very playable, but as I've said

before, we are mainly concentrating on ♗e3 lines for this repertoire.

Now Black must make an important choice. The main options are:

C1: 6...♘f6
C2: 6...e5
C3: 6...♖b8
C4: 6...e6

Others possibilities include:

a) 6...♕a5 7 ♕d2 ♘d4 8 f4 ♘f6!? (8...e6 transposes to C43) 9 h3 0-0 10 ♘f3 ♘xf3+ 11 ♗xf3 ♖b8 12 g4 b5 13 0-0 and White will push his pawns on the kingside, Arwanitakis-Mitter, Graz 1999.

b) 6...♘d4 is another transpositional move: 7 ♕d2 ♖b8 (7...e5 8 f4 transposes to C22) 8 ♘ge2 b5 transposes to Variation C32.

c) 6...b5 7 e5! ♕d7 (7...♗b7 8 exd6 exd6 9 ♘xb5 ♘ge7 {Ljubojevic-Miles} and now Miles gives 10 ♘e2 with an advantage to White) 8 exd6 exd6 and now:

c1) 9 ♘ge2 ♘ge7 (9...b4 10 ♘d5 ♗xb2 11 ♖b1 ♗g7 12 c3 gives White an edge – Romanishin) 10 d4 b4 11 ♘e4 0-0 12 ♗h6 c4 13 ♗xg7 ♔xg7 14 d5 ♘e5 15 f4 ♘g4 16 h3 ♘h6 17 g4 and White has a clear plus, Romanishin-Torre, Indonesia 1983.

c2) 9 ♗f4!? ♘ge7 (9...b4 10 ♘e4 ♗xb2 11 ♖b1 ♗e5 12 ♗xe5 dxe5 13 ♕f3 is good for White) 10 ♘xb5 0-0 11 ♘xd6 ♗xb2 12 ♖b1 ♕e6+ 13 ♘e2 ♗c3+ 14 ♔f1 ♗g7 and Black has insufficient compensation, Lebredo-R.Hernandez, Bayamo 1984.

d) 6...h5!? is an adventurous move. Black aims to activate his h8-rook with ...h5-h4. A good reply to this is 7 h3!, which prevents a black piece coming to g4 and prepares to answer ...h5-h4 with g3-g4.

C1)
6...♘f6

A very sensible move, one of the first that springs to mind. Having said that, on my database this move is actually less popular than 6...♖b8, 6...e5 and 6...e6.

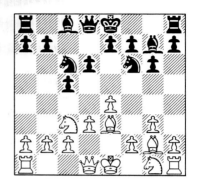

Black develops the knight to its most aggressive square, prepares to castle and throws in the positional threat of ...♘g4. On the other hand the knight blocks the g7-bishop and thus loosens Black's control over d4. Another point, which may work in White's favour, is that the knight on f6 (compared to e7) is more vulnerable to a kingside pawn assault by White. In fact, instead of the usual ♕d2, I believe White should aim for a slow pawn assault on the kingside.

7 h3

Preventing at once any annoyances with ...♘g4, while preparing a later assault with g3-g4. Now Black has two ways of playing.

C11: 7...e5!?
C12: 7...0-0

C11)
7...e5!?

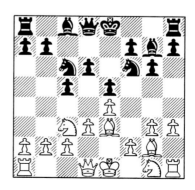

It may seem like a sweeping statement, but I've always thought that ...♘f6 and ...e7-e5 don't really mix that well in the Closed Sicilian, and I'm not alone in this belief. On the other hand, none other than Garry Kasparov has played this move, so it certainly deserves some respect, and it's true that White is already committed to h2-h3 and ♗e3.

8 ♘ge2

One of the points of Black's play is that 8 f4 can be met by the annoying 8...♘h5! 9 ♘ge2 ♘d4, which looks quite pleasant for Black.

8...0-0 9 0-0 ♘d4

More recently two of Adams' opponents has played the inventive 9...b5!?. After 10 ♘xb5 (10 f4 b4 11 ♘d5 ♘xd5 12 exd5 ♘d4 13 fxe5 ♘xe2+ 14 ♕xe2 ♗xe5 is fine for Black) 10...♖b8 we have:

a) 11 a4 a6 12 ♘a3 ♖xb2 13 ♘c4 ♖b8 14 f4 exf4 15 ♘xf4 ♘a5 (Adams gives 15...♘e5 16 ♘xe5 dxe5 17 ♘d5 ♘xd5 18 exd5 ♕d6 19 ♕d2 ♗d7 as unclear) 16 ♘d2! ♗d7 17 ♖a2 with a roughly level position, Adams-Kasparov, Linares 1999.

b) 11 ♘ec3 a6 12 ♘a3 ♖xb2 13 ♘c4 ♖b8 14 ♗g5 h6 (14...♗e6!? 15 ♘d5 ♗xd5 16 exd5 ♘e7 looks unclear) 15 ♗xf6 ♗xf6 16 ♘d5 ♗g7 17 ♖b1 ♖xb1 18 ♕xb1 and White had the tiniest of edges in Adams-Topalov, Dos Hermanas 1999.

10 f4 ♖b8

Or 10...♘xe2+ 11 ♘xe2 exf4 12 ♘xf4 ♗d7 13 ♕d2 ♗c6 14 ♔h2 ♘d7 15 c3 and White has the straightforward plan of doubling rooks on the half-open f-file, promising him some advantage, Kuijf-Sunye Neto, Amsterdam 1983.

11 ♕d2 ♘e8 12 ♖f2 b5 13 a3 a5 14 ♖af1 b4 15 axb4 axb4 16 ♘d1 ♘xe2+ 17 ♕xe2 ♗a6 18 f5

Ostojic-Memic, Wiesbaden 1994. In the diagrammed position White's extra space on the kingside guarantees him some advantage, so black players would do well to take a second look at 9...b5!?.

C12)

7...0-0 8 f4

Naturally ♕d2 is also possible, but the idea of ♗e3-h6 is less enticing when Black hasn't weakened his dark squares by moving the e7-pawn.

8...♖b8

Black follows the logical plan of expansion on the queenside by preparing ...b7-b5-b4. After 8...e5 9 ♘ge2 (9 ♘f3 ♘h5! targets the g3-pawn) 9...exf4 (9...♘h5?! 10 f5! ♘f6?! 11 g4! was clearly better for White in Jurkovic-Voitsekhovsky, Pardubice 1995, but of course Black's play here was pretty awful) 10 ♘xf4 ♖b8 11 0-0 b5 12 a3 a5 13 ♕d2 b4 14 axb4 axb4 15 ♘ce2 ♗b7 16 ♖f2 ♖a8 17 ♖af1 ♖a2 18 b3 White can hope to take advantage of the semi-open f-file, Moldovan-Nevednichy, Bucharest 1995.

9 ♘f3 b5 10 0-0 b4 11 ♘e2 a5

An important alternative here is 11...♘d7!?, freeing the g7-bishop and attacking the b2-pawn. Now 12 ♖b1 is answered by 12...♕a5 and 12 c3 ♗a6 13 ♖f2 bxc3 14 bxc3 ♕a5 was fine for Black in Tischbierek-Van Wely, Antwerp 1998. Instead I prefer 12 ♕c1!?, for example 12...a5 13 g4 ♕b6 14 f5 ♘d4 15 ♘exd4 cxd4 16 ♗h6.

12 g4 ♗a6

Or 12...♘e8 13 ♖b1 ♘c7 14 f5 ♘b5 15 h4 a4 16 h5 a3 17 b3 ♘bd4 (King prefers 17...♘c3 18 ♘xc3 bxc3, intending ...♘b4) 18 ♕d2 ♘xf3+ 19 ♖xf3 ♘e5 20 ♖g3 ♗b7 21 ♖f1 ♖c8 22 hxg6 hxg6 23 ♗h6 ♔h7 24 ♖h3 and Black has no good answer to White's inevitable attack, Berg-Dinstuhl, Richmond 1994.

13 f5 a4 14 ♘f4 c4 15 ♖f2 ♘e5 16 g5

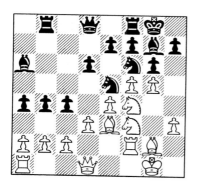

We are following Iuldachev-Tisdall, Jakarta 1997, which continued 16...♘fd7 17 d4 c3 18 b3 ♘xf3+ 19 ♕xf3 ♗b7 20 ♕g4 ♖a8 21 ♖af1 ♖a5 22 h4 and White had an impressive looking kingside attack.

C2)

6...e5

This move is one of Black's most solid options available. Immediately he takes a vice-like grip on the d4-square and thus rules out for a long time the possibility of d3-d4. On the other hand, some players might be averse to blocking the long diagonal and hence restricting the affect of the g7-bishop

on the queenside. Nevertheless, a study of the diagram quickly points to the fact that White's main pawn break is f2-f4, a move which will allow the g7-bishop back into the game. In view of this, it's really no surprise that White still often angles for the exchange of dark-squared bishops with ♕d2 and ♗h6.

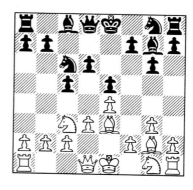

7 ♕d2

7 f4 will tend to reach the same position as the main line after 7...♘ge7 8 ♘f3 0-0 9 0-0 ♘d4 10 ♕d2.

Now Black has two main choices:

C21: 7...♗e6
C22: 7...♘ge7

7...♘d4 8 f4 ♘e7 9 ♘f3 0-0 10 0-0 transposes to Variation C22.

C21)
7...♗e6

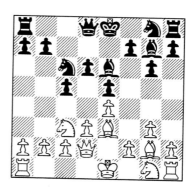

Delaying the development of the kingside and thus ruling out ♗h6 for the time being.

8 f4 exf4

Another possibility is 8...♘d4 9 ♘d1!? (to chase the knight away with c2-c3) 9...exf4 (9...♘f6? 10 fxe5 dxe5 11 c3! wins a pawn for White) 10 gxf4 ♘e7 11 c3 ♘dc6 12 ♘f3 0-0 13 0-0 ♔h8 (intending ...f7-f5) 14 ♘g5 ♗c8 15 ♘f2 f6 16 ♘f3 f5 17 ♘h1! (planning ♘g3) 17...♗e6 18 ♘g3 ♖c8 19 ♘g5 ♗g8 20 h4 h6 21 ♘f3 and White had a useful edge in the game G.Giorgadze-San Segundo, Vigo 1994.

9 ♗xf4 ♘d4

9...h6!? is a little played but interesting idea. Black prevents ♗h6 and prepares ...g6-g5 and ...♘ge7-g6. Following 10 ♘f3 ♘ge7 11 0-0 ♕d7 12 ♘d1?! d5! 13 ♕f2 g5! 14 ♗e3 d4 15 ♗d2 ♘g6 Black was fine in the game Neumeier-Loginov, Oberwart 1994. However, 12 ♘d1 was a little too accommodating in my mind. I prefer 12 ♗e3! (preparing d3-d4) 12...♘d4 13 ♖ab1 g5 14 a3.

10 ♘f3 ♘xf3+ 11 ♗xf3 ♕d7

12 0-0

12 0-0-0 ♘e7 13 ♗h6 ♗e5 14 ♖de1 0-0-0 was equal in the game Sturua-Loginov, Borzomi 1984.

12...0-0-0 13 ♖ab1 ♘e7 14 b4!

White has a useful attack on the queenside, M.Buckley-Mirzoeva, World Girls Under-18 Championship, Oropesa del Mar 1999.

C22)
7...♘ge7

The normal square for the g8-knight in this system. With this move Black prepares to castle and blocks neither the g7-bishop nor the f-pawn.

8 f4

Naturally White can also play for the immediate exchange of bishops with 8 ♗h6!?, but in comparison to Variation C44 (6...e6 7 ♕d2 ♘ge7 8 ♗h6), Black is much better placed here. In effect he is a tempo ahead, because in the other line Black usually plays ...e6-e5, increasing his dark-squared grip once the bishops have been exchanged. For this reason I believe it's better for White to delay ♗h6 until later. Nevertheless, 8 ♗h6 is still playable, for example 8...0-0 9 ♗xg7 ♔xg7 10 f4 ♘d4 11 ♘f3 ♗g4! 12 0-0 and now:

a) 12...♕d7? (Ljubojevic-van der Wiel, Tilburg 1983) 13 fxe5! ♘xf3+ 14 ♗xf3 dxe5 15 ♗xg4 ♕xg4 16 ♕f2 and White wins a pawn (Van der Wiel).

b) 12...♗xf3! 13 ♗xf3! ♕b6 14 ♘d1?! c4 15 ♔h1 cxd3 16 ♕xd3 ♖ac8 17 c3 ♘xf3 18 ♖xf3 f5! was very good for Black in Narayana-King, Calcutta 1993. King suggests 14 ♖ab1 as an improvement for White, after which the position looks roughly equal.

8...♘d4

Black can also try to do without this move, for example 8...0-0 9 ♘f3 ♖b8 (9...♘d4 10 0-0 transposes to the main line) 10 0-0 and now:

a) 10...b5 11 fxe5! ♘xe5 12 ♘xe5 ♗xe5 13 d4 (13 ♗h6!?) 13...cxd4 14 ♗xd4 b4 15 ♘d5 and I prefer White.

b) 10...exf4 11 ♗xf4 f5?! (it looks tempting to strike back on the kingside but White's pieces are better placed to exploit the open space; 11...b5 looks stronger, after which I would carry on with 12 ♗h6) 12 ♗h6 b5 13 ♗xg7 ♔xg7 14 ♖ae1 and the black king is a little bit exposed, the consequence of ...f7-f5 and the exchange of dark-squared bishops. The conclusion of A.Ledger-Duncan, British

League 1997 is quite instructive: 14...b4 15 ♘d5! fxe4 16 dxe4 ♗g4 17 ♘g5 ♕d7 18 ♘f6! ♖xf6 19 ♖xf6 ♔xf6 20 ♕f4+ ♗f5 (20...♔g7 21 ♕f7+ ♔h6 22 ♕xh7+ ♔xg5 23 ♕h4 is mate.) 21 exf5 ♕xf5 (21...gxf5 22 ♕h4 White's attack is decisive.) 22 ♕xd6+! ♔xg5 23 ♖f1 ♕xf1+ 24 ♔xf1 ♖b6 25 ♕f4+ 1-0.

9 ♘f3 0-0 10 0-0

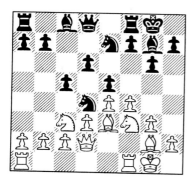

Now we have a further split:

C221: 10...♗g4
C222: 10...exf4

Other possibilities are:

a) 10...♖b8!? (preparing ...b7-b5) 11 ♘d1 b5 12 c3 ♘xf3+ 13 ♗xf3 b4 14 fxe5 (14 ♘f2 exf4 15 ♗xf4 ♘c6 16 ♗h6 bxc3 17 bxc3 ♗xh6 18 ♕xh6 ♕f6 19 ♕f4 ♕e5 was a little better for Black in Niebling-Ivanchuk, Frankfurt 1998) 14...bxc3 15 bxc3 ♗xe5 16 ♗h6 ♗g7 17 ♗xg7 ♔xg7 18 d4 ♕b6 19 ♘e3 ♗a6 20 ♖f2 cxd4 21 cxd4 ♘c6 22 ♖d1 and the idea of ♘d5 gives White a pull, Frost-Fantin, York 2000.

b) 10...♕b6!? (this looks a bit one dimensional, but in fact it has useful nuisance value) 11 ♖ab1 ♗d7 12 a3 ♖ac8 13 ♔h1 a6 14 f5!? (a typical sacrifice; 14 ♖f2!?, keeping the tension, is another possibility) 14...gxf5 15 ♗h6 f6 16 ♘h4 fxe4 17 dxe4 ♖f7 18 ♗xg7 ♔xg7 19 ♘d1 c4 20 ♘e3 ♕c6 21 c3 ♘b3 22 ♕e2 and White has enough compensation for the pawn, An.Rodriguez-Spangenberg, Buenos Aires 2000.

C221)
10...♗g4 11 ♘h4!?

11 ♖f2 is the solid approach:

a) 11...♘xf3+ 12 ♗xf3 ♗xf3 13 ♖xf3 exf4 14 ♗xf4 d5 15 ♖e1 ♕d7 16 ♗h6 ♖ae8 17 ♗xg7 ♔xg7 18 ♕f4 gave White an edge in Hort-Ostojic, Hastings 1967.

b) 11...♕d7 12 ♖af1 exf4 13 ♗xf4 ♘xf3+ 14 ♗xf3 ♗xf3 15 ♖xf3 b5 16 ♗h6 b4 17 ♗xg7 ♔xg7 18 ♘d1 and I prefer White, Short-Nataf, FIDE World Championship, New Delhi 2000.

11...♕d7

Or 11...exf4!? and now:

a) 12 ♗xf4 ♕d7 13 ♖f2 b5 14 ♗h6 ♖ae8 15 ♖af1 b4 16 ♗xg7 ♔xg7 17 ♘d1 ♗xd1! (eliminating the knight, which would otherwise influence White's attack from e3) 18 ♕xd1 d5 19 c3 bxc3 20 bxc3 ♘dc6 21 ♕f3 d4 22 ♕f6+ ♔g8 23 c4 (Romanishin-J.Horvath, Balatonbereny 1993) and now King suggests 23 ♘f3.

b) 12 ♖xf4!? ♗e6 13 ♖f2 d5 14 ♗h6 (the same old story; off come the bishops and Black's kingside is weakened) 14...♖c8 15 ♗xg7 ♔xg7 16 ♖af1 f6 17 exd5 ♘xd5 18 ♘e4 and White is slightly better, Liljedahl-Spassky, Gothenburg 1971.

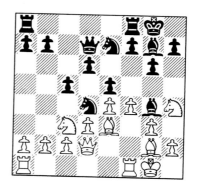

This position is ripe for further investigation. Possibilities include:

a) 12 ♖f2 f6 and now:

a1) 13 fxe5?! releases the tension much too soon, giving Black unnecessary counter-play on the half-open d-file; 13...dxe5 14 ♘b1?! b6 15 c4 ♖ad8 16 ♘c3 g5! was good for Black in Orlov-Lerner, St Petersburg 1997.

a2) 13 ♖af1 (preparing f4-f5) 13...exf4! 14 gxf4 f5! and Black has equalised.

a3) 13 f5!? (Black always has to be wary of this positional sacrifice) 13...gxf5 14 ♖af1 fxe4 15 dxe4 and White has reasonable com-pensation for the pawn.

b) 12 f5!? gxf5 13 ♗h6 ♘g6?! (13...fxe4 looks more resilient) 14 ♗xg7 ♔xg7 15 h3 ♘xh4 16 gxh4 f4 (16...♗h5 17 ♕g5+ ♗g6 18 exf5 f6 19 ♕g4 is good for White) 17 hxg4 ♕xg4 18 ♖f2 ♔h8 19 ♘d5 ♕xh4 20 c3 and White went on to win, Todorcevic-Velikov, Marseille 1990.

c) 12 ♖ae1!? looks interesting, for example 12...f6 13 f5!? gxf5 14 ♘d5!? fxe4 15 ♘xe7+ ♕xe7 16 dxe4

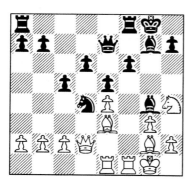

and White will follow up with c2-c3, fol-lowed by ♘f5. White's position is easy to play and I believe he has more than enough compensation for the pawn.

C222)
10...exf4

Releasing the tension in the centre is probably Black's most reliable course of ac-tion.

11 ♗xf4

White recaptures with the bishop and keeps alive the possibility of ♗h6. 11 gxf4 f5! puts an immediate block on White's kingside ambitions.

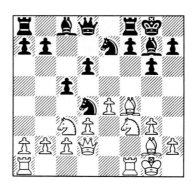

11...♘xf3+

Or 11...♗g4 12 ♘xd4 ♗xd4+ (12...cxd4? 13 ♘b5! a6 14 ♘xd6 g5 15 ♘xb7 ♕b6 16 ♗d6 ♕xb7 17 ♕xg5 was very good for White in Fahnenschmidt-Gauglitz, German Bundesliga 1994) 13 ♔h1 and White has a comfortable edge. He can play ♗h6, answer-ing ...♖e8 with ♗e3, followed by doubling on the f-file.

12 ♖xf3 ♕b6!

I believe this was originally played by the Hungarian Grandmaster Lajos Portisch in a game against Bent Larsen. White would love to double on the f-file, but this annoying move prevents this plan, at least for the time being. Now White must simply protect the b2-pawn.

13 ♖b1 ♗e6 14 ♗e3!?

Alternatively:

a) 14 ♗g5?! (this simply loses time) 14...♘c6 15 ♗e3? ♘e5 16 ♖ff1 ♘g4! 17 ♗f4 c4+ 18 ♔h1 cxd3 19 cxd3 ♗d4 20 h3 ♘e3 21 ♖fe1 ♘xg2 22 ♔xg2 ♕c6 and Black's bishop pair promise him an advantage, Lar-sen-Portisch, Rotterdam 1977.

b) 14 ♗h6 (exchanging the bishops looks logical) 14...♖ae8 15 ♗xg7 (15 ♔h1!?) 15...♔xg7 16 ♔h1 f6 17 a3 d5 18 b4 cxb4 19 ♖xb4 ♕c7 20 ♘b5 ♕d7 21 ♘d4 ♗g8 with an unclear position, Adams-Kramnik, FIDE World Championship, Las Vegas 1999.

14...♘c6 15 ♖ff1

The Hungarian GM Forintos gives this prophylactic move in *ECO*. White takes the sting out of ...♘e5 or ...♘d4. In a way 15 ♖f2 looks more natural, as White keeps the option of doubling rooks on the f-file. However, after 15...♘e5! White has to expend another tempo with 16 h3, as 16 b4? ♘g4! 17 bxc5 ♗xc3 18 cxb6 ♗xd2 19 ♗xd2 ♘xf2 20 ♔xf2 axb6 results in a winning position for Black.

15...♘d4

Or 15...♘e5 16 b4!? ♕c7 17 ♘b5 ♕c6 18 bxc5 dxc5 19 a3 a6 20 ♘c3, followed by ♘d5.

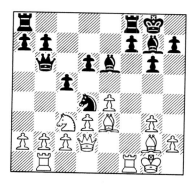

After 15...♘d4 A.Ledger-Emms, British League 2000, continued 16 a3 ♖ac8 17 ♘d1 ♗a2 (17...f5!?) 18 ♖a1 ♗e6 (or 18...♗b3 19 ♖c1) 19 ♖b1 ♗a2 20 ♖a1 and a draw was agreed, as it's difficult for White to make any progress.

Instead of 16 a3, White could try 16 ♖f2!?, an interesting loss of tempo now that ...♘e5 is no longer possible. White can consider following up with a2-a3 and b2-b4, while with c2 protected, White has the option of ♗h6. If Black's queen leaves b6 (to take the sting out of b2-b4) White goes back to the older plan, for example 16...♕c7 17 ♗h6 b5 18 ♖bf1 b4 19 ♘d1 and White fill follow up with c2-c3.

C3)

6...♖b8

A very flexible continuation. Black refuses to commit himself at all on the kingside and immediately begins preparations for a queenside offensive with ...b7-b5-b4.

7 ♕d2 b5

7...e6 transposes to Variation C42.

8 ♘ge2

White blocks neither the f-pawn nor the dark-squared bishop with f2-f4, so White keeps both plans of f2-f4 and ♗e3-h6 available.

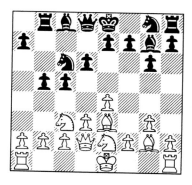

Now Black has an important choice: whether or not to occupy the d4-square.

C31: 8...b4
C32: 8...♘d4

C31)

8...b4

Here we look at variations where Black, in general, refrains from playing ...♘d4.

9 ♘d1 e5

Clamping down on the d4-square is Black's most solid option, but there is also something to be said for keeping the long diagonal free of obstacles.

a) 9...a5 10 0-0 ♗a6 11 f4 ♕c8 (11...♕c7!?) 12 ♖b1 ♘f6 13 ♘f2 0-0 14 ♗h3 ♕c7 15 g4 c4 16 g5 ♘d7 17 ♘g4 b3 18 axb3 cxd3 19 cxd3 ♖xb3 20 ♘c1 ♖b7 21 f5 and White has a strong kingside attack, Van Putten-Middelburg, Dutch League 1996. The rest of the game is attractive: 21...♗d4 22 ♘h6+ ♔g7 23 f6+ exf6 24 ♗xd7 ♕b6 25 gxf6+ ♔h8 26 ♘g4 ♗xe3+ 27 ♘xe3 ♖xd7 28 ♔h1 ♘b4 29 ♖f3 ♕d4 30 ♘c2! ♘xc2 31 ♕h6 ♖g8 32 ♕xh7+! 1-0.

b) 9...e6 10 0-0 ♘ge7 11 ♗h6! (White sticks to the main plan of exchanging bishops) 11...0-0 12 ♗xg7 ♔xg7 13 f4 e5 14 f5! f6 15 ♘e3 ♘d4 16 ♖f2 ♗d7 17 ♖af1 g5 18 h4 h6 19 ♘c1 ♗e8 20 c3 and White has a healthy space advantage on the kingside, Ramik-Belunek, Czech League 1999.

c) 10...h5!? prevents ♗h6 ideas, but slightly weakens the kingside. White should now head back to f2-f4 plans. 10 h3! ♘f6 11 f4 ♕b6 12 ♗f2 e6 13 ♘e3 a5 14 ♘c4 ♕c7 15 e5!

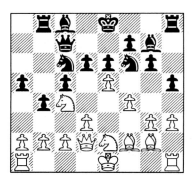

15...dxe5 16 ♗xc5 and White has a clear advantage, A.Ledger-O'Shaughnessy, British League 1998.

d) 9...♘f6!? (this may be the best of Black's alternatives) 10 ♗h6!? (10 h3 0-0 11 f4 ♘d7 12 0-0 a5 13 g4 ♗a6 14 f5 ♘de5 15 ♗h6 ♘d4 16 ♗xg7 ♔xg7 17 ♘f4 a4 18 ♘e3 a3 was unclear in Kosten-Georgiev, Toulon 1999) 10...0-0 11 ♗xg7 ♔xg7 12 ♘e3 ♗b7 13 0-0 ♘d4 14 f4 e6 15 g4 ♘xe2+ 16 ♕xe2 ♘d7 17 g5 and I prefer White, De Jager-Hoeksema, Dutch League 2000.

10 0-0 ♘ge7

Black continues to develop sensibly. 10...h5 should once again be answered by 11 f4 h4 12 f5! and Black already looks to be in trouble.

11 ♗h6 0-0 12 ♗xg7 ♔xg7

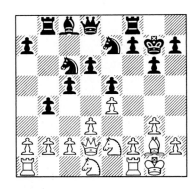

13 a3!?

Alternatively White can play 13 ♘e3 ♘d4 14 f4 f6 15 ♖f2 a5 16 c3 ♘xe2+ 17 ♖xe2 exf4 18 gxf4 f5 19 ♖ae1 with an unclear looking position, Veresagin-Shtyrenkov, Volgograd 1994.

13...a5 14 axb4 axb4 15 c3 ♗e6 16 f4 f6 17 ♘e3 ♘a5 18 ♖ad1

Bricard-Foisor, St Affrique 1999. Black's position is solid enough, but White has still more possibilities, including d3-d4.

C32)
8...♘d4

Occupying the important d4-square.

9 0-0 b4

Black pushes the knight back to d1. Other moves include:

a) 9...e6 10 ♘d1 ♘e7 11 ♘c1! (11 ♘xd4 cxd4 12 ♗h6 0-0 13 ♗xg7 ♔xg7 14 f4 f6 was equal in Spassky-Portisch, Mexico {3rd matchgame} 1980) 11...0-0 (11...b4 transposes to the main line) 12 c3 ♘dc6 13 ♗h6 d5 14 ♗xg7 ♔xg7 15 exd5 ♘xd5 16 ♘e3 ♘ce7 17 ♘b3 ♕d6 18 d4 ♘xe3 19 fxe3 cxd4 20 exd4 and White's central structure promises a small edge, Markarov-Inarkiev, Moscow 1998.

b) 9...h5!? is very ambitious! With this move Black rules out ♗h6 for a long time and prepares to make use of the h8-rook on its home square. The downside of the advance 9...h5 is that it's another non-developing move.

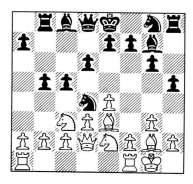

a) 10 h3? ♗xh3! (beware of this trick!) 11 ♗xd4 cxd4 12 ♗xh3 dxc3 13 ♘xc3 ♘f6 14 f4 b4 15 ♘d1 ♕a5 and Black was a little bit better in Castelein-Rogers, Ostend 1992.

b) 10 b4!? (White tries to exploit Black's lack of development in an extreme way) 10...a5!? (10...♘xe2+ 11 ♘xe2 ♗xa1 12 ♖xa1 gives White obvious compensation for the exchange; one amusing continuation would be 12...cxb4 13 ♗xa7 ♖a8 14 ♕xb4! ♖xa7? 15 ♕d4! and we have the unusual situation of the white queen forking two black rooks) 11 bxc5 dxc5 12 ♖ab1 ♗d7! (12...b4 13 ♘a4 ♕c7 14 c3 ♘xe2+ 15 ♕xe2 bxc3 16 ♗xc5 and Black's lag in development begins to tell) 13 e5! (White must continue energetically) 13...♗xe5 14 ♘e4 ♗g4 (Ivanchuk gives the line 14...♗c6 15 c3! ♘xe2+ 16 ♕xe2 ♗xe4 17 dxe4 ♕b6 18 ♖fc1 ♗d6 19 a4 b4 20 cxb4 axb4 21 e5 and Black is in trouble) 15 f3 ♗f5 16 f4 ♗g7 17 ♘xc5, Adams-Ivanchuk, Linares 1999. Black has survived the early onslaught and has a reasonable position, but I still prefer White's activity.

c) 10 h4 (the safest choice) 10...b4 11 ♘d1 e5 12 c3 bxc3 13 bxc3 ♘xe2+ 14 ♕xe2 ♘e7 15 f4 ♗g4 16 ♕d2 ♕a5 17 ♖c1 ♕a3!? (17...0-0 18 f5 gxf5 19 ♗h6 f6 20 ♗xg7 ♔xg7 21 ♘e3 fxe4 22 ♘xg4 hxg4 23 ♕e2 was unclear in Adams-Illescas, Madrid 1998)

18 ♘f2 ♗e6 19 ♖c2 ♗d7 20 ♕e2 with a roughly level position in J.Houska-Nicoara, Saint Vincent 1999. The rest of the game is an illustration of White's continuing attacking chances in this line: 20...♖b6 21 ♘d1 ♗g4 22 ♕f2 ♗xd1 23 fxe5! ♗xc2 24 ♕xf7+ ♔d8 25 ♕xg7 ♖e8 26 ♗g5 dxe5 27 ♗xe7+ ♖xe7 28 ♖f8+ ♖e8 29 ♖f7 ♕a4 30 ♗h3 ♖be6 31 ♗xe6 ♖xe6 32 ♖b7 ♖b6 33 ♕c7+ 1-0.

10 ♘d1

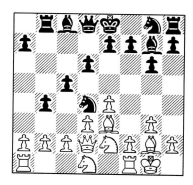

10...e6

At the present time this logical move, preparing ...♘e7, is Black's most popular choice, but there are some other enticing alternatives:

a) 10...a5!? (continuing the policy of no commitment on the kingside) 11 c3 (11 ♘c1!?) ♘xe2+ 12 ♕xe2 ♗a6 and now:

a1) 13 ♖e1?! (this move looks out of place) 13...a4!? 14 ♕d2 a3! and Black has good counterplay – Gelfand.

a2) 13 f4! (it's time to start the launch on the kingside) 13...a4 14 ♖c1! is a promising suggestion from Gelfand. White removes the rook from the long diagonal and takes some sting out of Black's queenside play. In particular 14...a3 can now be answered by 15 b3, keeping the queenside relatively closed. At some point Black must try and catch up in development, while White can continue to push on the kingside.

b) 10...e5!? (once more clamping down on the d4-square – this is a very sensible approach) 11 c3 (11 ♘c1!? ♘e7 12 c3 bxc3 13 bxc3 ♘e6 14 ♗h6 0-0 15 ♗xg7 ♔xg7 16 ♘e3 f5 was equal in A.Ledger-Donaldson, Isle of Man 1997) 11...bxc3 12 bxc3 ♘xe2+ 13 ♕xe2 ♘e7 and now White has two choices:

b1) 14 f4 exf4 15 ♗xf4 0-0! (15...♗e6 16 ♕d2 ♘c6 17 ♗h6 0-0 18 ♗xg7 ♔xg7 19 ♘e3 looks a bit better for White, A.Ledger-Cherniaev, Hastings 2000) 16 ♕d2 ♘c6 17 ♗h6 (17 ♔h1?! ♘e5 was at least okay for Black in Uritzky-Tsesarsky, Tel Aviv 1997) 17...♗a6 18 ♗xg7 ♔xg7 19 ♘f2 ♘e5 20 ♖fe1 with a roughly level position

b2) 14 ♕d2!? (going back to Plan A with ♗h6) 14...0-0 15 ♗h6 and White will follow up with ♗xg7, ♘e3 and either d3-d4 or f2-f4.

c) 10...♘xe2+!? (Black doesn't wait for c2-c3 and prevents White from playing ♘c1) 11 ♕xe2 ♘f6 12 a3 a5 13 axb4 cxb4?! (13...axb4 14 e5! ♘g4 15 exd6 ♕xd6 16 ♗f4 e5 17 ♗d2 0-0 18 h3 ♘f6 19 ♘e3 gives White an edge) and now Adams-Anand, Dortmund 1998, continued 14 ♗d2? ♘d7 and Black was better. However, Klaus Bischoff's suggestion of 14 e5! looks good, for example 14...dxe5 15 ♗a7 ♖b7 16 ♗xb7 ♗xb7 17 ♕xe5 0-0 18 ♕xa5 ♕d7 19 ♘e3 and White has a clear advantage.

11 ♘c1!

At first sight this makes a strange impression, as now White has two knights nestling on the back rank. However, White's whole idea is to evict the d4-knight with c2-c3, swap bishops with ♗h6 (at some point Black must complete development on the kingside) and then advance his knights back into the game. This plan can be very effective.

11...♕a5!?

This suggestion from the American GM Joel Benjamin has caught on over the last few years; at the present time it's the most popular move at Black's disposal.

The main alternative is the developing 11...♘e7, which looks very sensible, although

it does allow White to carry out his plan. After 12 c3 bxc3 13 bxc3 ♘dc6 14 ♗h6 0-0 15 ♗xg7 ♔xg7 16 ♘e3 Black has a few options:

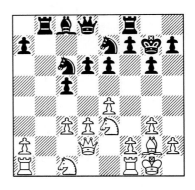

a) 16...♗b7 17 ♘b3 a5 18 a4 ♗a6 19 ♖fb1 ♕b6 20 h4 ♘e5 21 d4 ♘c4 22 ♕e1 cxd4 23 cxd4 ♘xe3 24 ♕xe3 ♖fc8 25 ♔h2 ♘c6 26 ♘c5 ♕a7 27 ♖xb8 ♖xb8 28 ♘xa6 ♘xa6 29 h5 and White has a pleasant initiative, Ljubojevic-Tringov, Lucerne 1982.

b) 16...d5 17 ♘b3 ♕d6 18 ♖ad1 ♗a6 19 exd5 ♘xd5 20 ♘xd5 exd5 21 ♖fe1 ♖fd8 22 d4! and Black's slightly vulnerable d5-pawn gives White the faintest of edges, A.Ledger-Mah, British League 1998.

c) 16...e5 17 ♘e2 ♗a6 18 f4 f6 19 ♖ac1 ♕a5 20 ♖c2 ♖b7 21 ♗h3! ♖fb8 22 ♗e6 ♖b1 23 ♘c1 ♕b6 24 ♕f2 ♖f8 25 h4 ♕d8 26 f5 and White's attack is beginning to unfold, Short-Hossain, Dhaka 1999.

12 a3!?

This move, counterattacking on the queenside, is the latest word on this line. Previously the main line was 12 c3 bxc3 13 bxc3 ♘c6!. Now ♘b3 isn't possible due to ...♖xb3 – one of the points of 11...♕a5. In contrast 13...♘b3? loses to 14 ♕b2! and 13...♘b5 14 ♘b3 ♕c7 15 d4 is good for White. White has a few options after 13...♘c6, but Black seems to be okay, for example 14 ♗f4 e5 15 ♗e3 ♘ge7 16 ♘b2 ♗e6 17 ♘c4 ♕c7 18 ♘e2 0-0 19 ♖ab1 with an equal position, J.Houska-Calzetta, Saint

Vincent 1999.

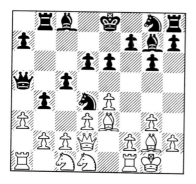

After 12 a3!? Black has some fresh problems to solve. It's not clear what his best continuation is.

a) 12...♘e7? (natural, but not good) 13 ♗xd4! (this anti-positional move works well here) 13...cxd4 14 ♘b3 ♕b6 15 axb4 and White is simply a pawn up.

b) 12...♕a4 13 ♗xd4! (once again White gives up the dark-squared bishop) 13...cxd4 (13...♗xd4 14 ♘b3 is good for White) 14 b3 ♕a6 15 ♘b2 ♘e7 16 ♘c4 0-0 17 ♘e2 and Black has some problems on the queenside, A.Ledger-Shaw, Port Erin 1998.

c) 12...♘c6 13 ♘b3 ♕b6 14 axb4 ♕xb4 15 e5!? ♘xe5 16 ♕xb4! (16 ♖xa7 ♘f6 17 d4 cxd4 18 ♗xd4 ♘ed7 was okay for Black in Mason-Abayasekera, British League 1997) 16...♖xb4 17 ♖xa7 and now S.Lalic-Dishman, British League 2001 continued 17...♘xd3?! 18 cxd3 (the immediate 18 ♗c6+ ♔f8 19 ♖a8 ♘e7 20 ♗d7 may be even stronger) 18...♖xb3 19 ♗c6+ ♔f8 (or 19 ..♔d8 20 ♗d2! and there is no good defence to ♗a5+) 20 ♖a8 ♘e7 21 ♗d7 ♗f6 22 ♗h6+ ♗g7 23 ♗xc8 ♗xh6 24 ♗xe6+ and White eventually converted her advantage. In his notes in *Chess*, Richard Palliser gives 17...♘f6! as an improvement for Black, but concludes that White is still better after 18 d4 cxd4 19 ♗xd4 0-0 20 ♘e3.

d) 12...♕a6 looks like a sensible move. In comparison to line 'b', after 13 ♗xd4!? cxd4

White does not gain a tempo on the queen with 14 b3. Perhaps White should play 14 ♘b3 instead, but this line could certainly do with a practical test.

C4)
6...e6

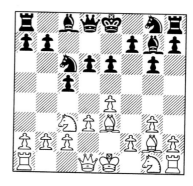

This is perhaps Black's most flexible move. You can see its attractions immediately: Black keeps the long h8-a1 diagonal open and prepares ...♘ge7, once again not blocking the bishop. Black's position is very fluid and can be enhanced by such moves as ...♘d4 and perhaps ...♘ec6 and/or ...♖b8 with ...b7-b5-b4.

7 ♕d2!

Preparing to meet ...♘ge7 with ♗h6. Now Black has a choice:

C41: 7...♘d4
C42: 7...♖b8
C43: 7...♕a5
C44: 7...♘ge7

C41)
7...♘d4

This advance looks premature, as the knight is soon kicked away. As a very general rule in the Closed Sicilian, Black should wait for both ♗e3 and ♘f3/e2 before playing ...♘d4. Then ♘xd4 is often impossible as it allows ...cxd4 forking c3 and e3, while after ♘d1 and c2-c3 Black has the option of exchanging knights on e2 or f3.

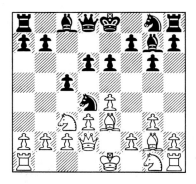

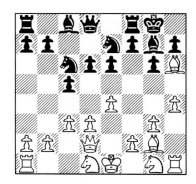

8 ♘d1!

Preparing to kick the knight away with c2-c3, after which White will be ready to play ♗h6 (once the g8 knight moves).

8...♘e7

Or:

a) 8...f5 looks a bit too weakening. After 9 c3 ♘c6 10 ♘e2 ♘f6 11 exf5 exf5 12 0-0 0-0 13 h3 ♗d7 14 c4 ♕b6 15 ♘dc3 ♖ae8 16 ♖fe1 White had an advantage in Spassky-B.Ivanovic, Niksic 1983 (Black has a slightly weaker king and White has good control over d5).

b) 8...♘f6 doesn't really fit in well with ...e7-e6. Svetushkin-Bologan, Linares 1999, continued 9 c3 ♘c6 10 h3 b6 11 f4 ♗a6 12 ♘e2 d5 13 e5 ♘d7 14 0-0 f6 15 c4 ♘e7 16 f5!? ♘xe5 17 ♘f4 exf5 18 ♘e6 ♕d7 19 ♘xg7+ ♔f7 20 ♘xf5 gxf5 21 ♗f4 and White was better. Instead of entering these complications, White could also simply opt for 10 ♗h6, which looks good enough for an edge. 8...e5 9 c3 ♘c6 10 ♘e2 ♘ge7 11 ♗h6 0-0 12 ♗xg7 ♔xg7 13 ♘e3 ♗e6 14 h4 d5 (Blatny prefers 14...f5) 15 exd5 ♘xd5 16 h5 and White has a dangerous kingside initiative, Hjartarson-Novikov, Tilburg 1992.

9 c3 ♘dc6 10 ♗h6!

Naturally.

10...0-0 11 h4

White was also better after 11 ♗xg7 ♔xg7 12 f4 e5 13 ♘e3 exf4 14 gxf4 f5 15 ♘e2, Zaichik-Hazai, Kecskemet 1983.

11...f6 12 ♗xg7 ♔xg7 13 ♘e3 e5 14 ♘e2 ♗e6 15 h5 g5 16 d4

White has a comfortable positional advantage, Ljubojevic-Small, Thessaloniki Olympiad 1984.

C42)
7...♖b8

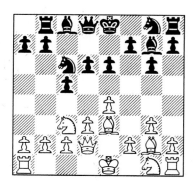

8 ♘f3!?

A tricky move, which is an interesting attempt to exploit Black's move order. If White is not happy with this, then 8 ♘ge2 should transpose to earlier lines, for example:

a) 8...b5 and now:

a1) 9 0-0 b4 10 ♘d1 transposes to Variation C31.

a2) 9 d4!? b4 10 ♘d1 cxd4 11 ♘xd4 ♘ge7 (11...e5 12 ♕e2 ♕a5 13 ♘b3 ♕a4 14 ♗d4 ♘e7 15 f4 ♗a6 16 ♕d2 ♘c4 17 ♕f2 ♗xd4 18 ♕xd4 0-0 19 0-0 was better for White in Westerinen-Hjorth, Gausdal 1999) 12 ♘xc6 ♘xc6 13 0-0 ♕c7 14 ♗h6 0-0 15 ♗xg7 ♔xg7 16 ♘e3 ♗a6 17 ♖fd1 and White's pressure on the vulnerable d6-pawn ensured an edge in Klinger-Schumi, Zurich 1993.

b) 8...♘d4 9 0-0 (9 ♗xd4 cxd4 10 ♘b5 ♕b6 11 ♕b4 ♗e7 12 ♕b3 ♗d7 is okay for Black) 9...b5 10 ♘d1 b4 11 ♘c1 transposes to Variation C32.

8...b5

8...♘d4?! looks natural enough, but in fact it's bad in this situation. White can play 9 ♗xd4! cxd4 10 ♘b5 ♕b6 (or 10...♘e7 11 ♘bxd4 and White has simply won a pawn) 11 ♕b4 ♔d7

(11...♔e7 12 e5 is good for White) 12 e5! dxe5 13 ♘d2! and White has a strong attack, for example 13...a5 (13...a6 14 ♘c4 ♕xb5 loses to 15 ♕d6+ ♔e8 16 ♕xb8) 14 ♕a4 ♘e7 (14...♔d8 15 ♘c4 ♕a6 16 ♕a3 ♗d7 17 ♘bd6 ♗f8 18 ♘xb7+ ♔c7 19 ♕xa5+ ♕xa5+ 20 ♘bxa5 ♗b4+ 21 ♔d1 ♗a4 22 ♘b3 and White was a clear pawn up in Kovalevskaya-Arakhamia, Elista Olympiad 1998) 15 ♘c4 ♕a6 16 ♘cd6 ♘d5 17 ♘xf7 ♖f8 18 ♘fd6 ♔d8 19 ♕c4 ♕c6 20 0-0 ♗d7 21 a4 ♔e7 22 ♕b3 ♕c5 23 c3 dxc3 24 bxc3 ♗xb5 25 ♘e4 ♗xa4 26 ♖xa4 ♕b6 27 ♕a2 ♕c6 28 ♖xa5 ♖fd8 29 ♕a3+ ♔e8 30 c4 and White won, Kovalevskaya-Hernandez, Elista Olympiad 1998.

8...e5!? loses a tempo over the immediate

...e7-e5, but on the other hand, now d3-d4 has been ruled out and White's knight is committed to f3: 9 0-0 ♘ge7 10 ♗h6 0-0 11 ♗xg7 ♔xg7 12 ♘h4 ♘d4 13 ♖ae1 f5 14 exf5 ♘dxf5 15 ♘xf5+ ♗xf5 16 f4 was slightly better for White in Narciso Dublan-Catalan Escale, Barcelona 1996.

9 0-0!?

9 d4!? looks logical, but after 9...b4 10 ♘e2 ♘a5 11 b3 ♘f6 the attack on the e4-pawn is rather awkward (this is no problem when White's knight is on e2). 12 e5 ♘e4 (12...dxe5 13 dxe5 ♕xd2+ 14 ♘xd2 ♘d7 15 f4 is pleasant for White) 13 ♕d3 d5 looks unclear, for example 14 dxc5 ♕c7 15 0-0 ♘xc5 16 ♕d4? (A.Ledger-Collier, British League 1998) and now 16...♘c6! is good, as 17 ♕xc5 loses to 17...♗f8.

9...b4 10 ♘d1 ♘d4 11 ♘e1!?

11 c3 ♘xf3+ 12 ♗xf3 ♘e7 13 ♗h6 0-0 14 ♗xg7 ♔xg7 15 d4 looks roughly level. After 11 ♘e1!? we've reached a position similar to Variation C32, except that the knight is on e1, rather than c1.

11...♘e7 12 ♗h6 0-0 13 ♗xg7 ♔xg7 14 c3

Also interesting is 14 f4!? e5 15 c3 ♘dc6 16 ♘e3.

14...bxc3 15 bxc3 ♘dc6

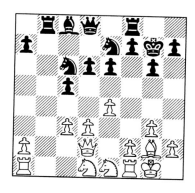

White now has to decide where to put his knights:

a) 16 ♘e3 d5 17 exd5 (17 ♘g4?! f5 18 exf5 exf5 19 ♕h6+ ♔h8 20 ♘e3 d4 was slightly better for Black, S.Lalic-G.Jones, British League 2001) 17...exd5 18 ♘1c2 d4 19 cxd4 ♘xd4 20 ♘xd4 ♕xd4 21 ♘c2 is equal.

b) 16 ♘c2!? may be stronger, for example 16...d5 17 exd5 exd5 (17...♘xd5 18 ♘de3) 18 d4 cxd4 19 ♘xd4 ♕b6 20 ♘e3 and White has an edge due to Black's isolated d-pawn.

C43)
7...♕a5

Recommended by Joe Gallagher in *Beating the Anti-Sicilians*. Black delays developing the g8-knight, pins the knight on c3 to the white queen and supports ...b7-b5.

8 f4!?

A slight departure from our normal lines. White's idea is to play as in the f4 lines where Black's queen is already committed to the a5-square.

White can also continue with 8 ♘ge2, for example 8...♘d4 9 0-0 ♘e7 10 ♘c1!? 0-0 11 ♘b3 and now:

a) 11...♕d8 12 ♘d1 b6 13 c3 ♘xb3 14 axb3 ♗b7 15 ♗h6 e5 16 ♗xg7 ♔xg7 17 f4 f6 18 ♘e3 with an edge for White in Rohde-Rechlis, Beersheba 1987.

b) 11...♕b6 12 ♘d1 0-0 13 ♘c1 a5 14 c3 ♘dc6 15 ♗h6 e5 16 ♗xg7 ♔xg7 17 ♘e3 f5 18 f4 exf4 19 gxf4 ♗e6 20 ♘e2 c4 21 d4 fxe4 22 ♗xe4 d5 was unclear in Spraggett-Vaisser, Oropesa del Mar 1996.

8...♘ge7 9 ♘f3 ♘d4

If Black delays this move, then White can contemplate advancing with d3-d4, for example 9...0-0 10 0-0 ♖b8 11 d4! cxd4 12 ♘xd4 ♘xd4 13 ♗xd4 and White has a pleasant game.

10 0-0 ♘ec6!?

Adding extra support to d4. Black has two significant alternatives:

a) 10...0-0 11 ♘d5 (11 e5?! ♘ef5! is fine for Black) 11...♕d8 (11...♘xf3+ 12 ♗xf3 ♕d8 13 ♘xe7+ ♕xe7 14 d4 was slightly better for White in Jurkovic-Bakalarz, Ceske Budejovice 1995) 12 ♘xe7+ ♕xe7 13 c3 ♘c6

(J.Houska-Ioseliani, Bundesliga 1999) and here I like the simple 14 d4.

b) 10...♗d7 and now:

b1) 11 ♘xd4!? cxd4 12 ♘e2 ♕xd2 (12...♕c5 13 ♗f2 0-0 14 c3 ♘c6 15 ♖ab1 ♖fc8 is better for White) 13 ♗xd2 ♖c8 14 c3 dxc3 15 ♗xc3 is equal according to Donev.

b2) 11 ♕f2!? ♘xf3+ (after 11...♘ec6 Donev gives 12 e5!, which looks good for White, for example 12...dxe5 13 ♘xe5 ♘xe5 14 fxe5 0-0 15 ♘e4!) 12 ♗xf3 with a further split:

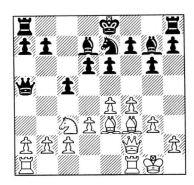

b21) 12...♗xc3!? 13 bxc3 ♕xc3 14 e5! and the absence of Black's dark-squared bishop gives White excellent compensation for the pawn.

b22) After 12...0-0 both 13 d4 and 13 e5!? look promising.

b23) 12...♘c6 13 e5! (Donev) 13...dxe5 14 ♗xc6 ♗xc6 15 fxe5 ♕c7 16 ♗xc5 ♗xe5 17 ♖ae1 ♗g7 18 d4 and White has a strong attack.

11 e5!?

This pawn break is typical for the f4 lines of the Closed Sicilian, although it's quite rare in this actual position. If White wants a quieter life he could consider either 11 a3 or 11 ♕f2.

11...dxe5

Taking the pawn is too risky: 11...♘xf3+ 12 ♗xf3 dxe5?! (Short suggests 12...d5!?) 13 ♗xc6+ bxc6 14 fxe5 ♗xe5 15 ♕f2 and White hits both f7 and c5.

12 ♘xe5 0-0!

Or 12...♘xe5 13 fxe5 ♗xe5 14 ♕f2! and now:

a) 14...f5 15 ♘e4! ♕c7 16 ♘xc5 ♕xc5 17 c3 and White regains the piece with an advantage.

b) 14...0-0 15 ♘e4 ♘f5 (15...f5 16 c3! ♗d7 17 ♘xc5! is good for White) 16 ♗xc5 b6 (or 16...♗xb2 17 g4! ♗xa1 18 ♖xa1) 17 ♗xf8! ♗d4 18 ♕xd4 ♘xd4 19 ♗d6 f5 (19...♘f5 20 b4 ♕a4 21 ♘f6+ ♔g7 22 ♗e5 ♕xc2 23 ♗xa8 was clearly better for White in Dudek-Schmenger, Germany 2000) 20 ♘f6+ (20 ♘f2!?) 20...♔g7 21 ♘e8+ ♔f7 22 ♗xa8 ♔xe8 23 c3 ♘c2 24 ♖ac1 ♘e3 25 ♖fe1 and White's two rooks and two bishops should outweigh the queen, knight and bishop, Rohacek-Kottnauer, Bratislava 1948.

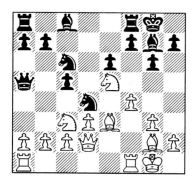

An important position for the assessment for 8 f4. White has several possibilities:

a) 13 ♗xc6?! ♘xc6 14 ♘c4 ♕a6 15 ♗xc5 ♖d8 with good compensation for the pawn. Black will follow up with ...b7-b6 and ...♗b7.

b) 13 ♖ae1!? and now:

b1) 13...f5?! 14 ♗xc6 ♘xc6 15 ♘xc6.bxc6 16 ♘d1! ♕xa2 7 ♗xc5 ♖d8 18 b3 ♖b8 19 ♖f2 and White's better pawn structure gave him an advantage in Short-Kasparov, Wijk aan Zee 2000.

b2) Black should be brave and grab a pawn with 13...♘xe5! 14 fxe5 ♗xe5 15 ♗h6 ♗g7 16 ♗xg7 ♔xg7 17 ♕f2 and now Short gives 17...f5 18 ♘e4 ♘xc2 19 ♖c1 ♘d4 20

♘xc5 with good compensation for the pawn. This seems right, especially as 20...e5 21 ♖fe1 ♖e8 22 ♖xe5! ♖xe5 23 ♕xd4 wins for White. However, Donev's suggestion of 17...f6!? is a very tough nut to crack. After 18 ♘e4 e5! Black hangs on, as 19 ♘xf6? fails to 19...♕d8.

c) In view of the above variation White may want to consider deviating with 13 ♘xc6!?. I prefer White after both 13...bxc6 14 ♕f2 and 13...♘xc6 14 ♕f2.

C44)
7...♘ge7

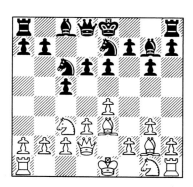

A consistent follow-up to 6...e6, but this allows White to carry out one of his main plans.

8 ♗h6!

Of course!

8...0-0

After 8...♗xh6 9 ♕xh6 ♘d4 10 0-0-0 ♘ec6 11 ♘ge2 White is better simply because Black cannot castle for the moment. Hort-Hodgson, Wijk aan Zee 1986, continued 11...♗d7 12 ♘xd4 cxd4 13 ♘e2 ♕a5 14 ♔b1 ♕a4 15 c3 dxc3 16 ♘xc3 ♕b4 17 d4 ♖c8 18 ♕g7 ♖f8 19 ♖he1 ♘a5 20 ♘d5 ♕a4 21 ♕f6 ♘c6 and now 22 ♕h4! would have been very strong.

9 h4

Or 9 ♗xg7 ♔xg7 10 h4 h6 11 f4 f6 and now 12 g4 ♘d4 13 ♘h3 ♘ec6 14 0-0 f5 was unclear in Smyslov-Brinck Claussen, Copenhagen 1986, but maybe the quieter 12 ♘f3 gives White an advantage.

9...♗xh6

Black has to be very careful, for example 9...♘d4 10 0-0-0 f5 11 h5 ♖f7 12 ♘h3 ♗xh6 13 ♕xh6 ♖g7 14 ♘g5 fxe4 15 hxg6 ♘df5 16 gxh7+ ♔h8 17 ♕f6 ♕e8 18 g4 ♕g6 19 ♕f8+ and Black resigned, Dworakowska-Madejska, Brzeg Dolny 1995.

10 ♕xh6 f6!

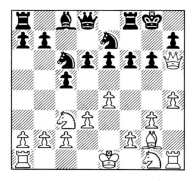

At first sight this move only seems to weaken Black's position further, but in fact this clever move is directly aimed against the idea of h4-h5.

11 ♕d2!

Now it's White's turn to be careful. 11 f4? fails to 11...♘d4! 12 0-0-0 ♘df5!, while 11 h5? runs into 11...g5, and Black will trap White's queen with ...♔h8 and ...♘g8.

After 11 ♕d2 Black may be doing okay theoretically, but White's position is easier to play and in practice White has scored quite heavily from this position.

11...e5

Freeing the c8-bishop. Black now sensibly opts to put his pawns on dark squares.

12 f4

Or 12 h5 g5 13 h6! (13 f4 h6 and Black's position is rock-solid) 13...♘g6 14 ♘d5 ♘ce7 15 ♘e3 ♗e6 16 ♘e2 d5 17 exd5 ♘xd5 18 ♘c3 ♘ge7 19 0-0-0 ♘xe3 20 ♕xe3 ♕d4 21 ♘e4 ♕xe3+ 22 fxe3 ♗d5 23 ♖d2 b6 24 c4 ♗xe4 25 ♗xe4 ♖ad8 26 g4

and White's bishop is superior to Black's knight, Golubovic-Boyd, Cannes 1996.

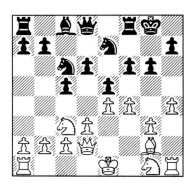

Most players would prefer White in this position. Here are three practical examples:

a) 12...exf4 13 gxf4 ♗g4 14 ♗f3 ♕d7 15 ♗xg4 ♕xg4 16 ♘ge2 d5 17 exd5 ♘d4 18 0-0-0 ♘xe2+ 19 ♘xe2 ♘xd5 20 h5 and White has a strong attack, Shaw-Berry, Marymass 1999.

b) 12...♗g4 13 ♘h3 ♕d7 14 h5!? gxh5 15 f5 ♖f7 16 ♗xg4 hxg4 17 ♖h4 ♖g7 18 ♘d1 d5 19 ♘f2 ♔h8 20 ♘xg4 ♘g8 21 0-0-0 with an edge to White in A.Ledger-Novikov, Port Erin 1996. The rest of the game is interesting: 21...♖d8 22 ♘e2!? dxe4 23 dxe4 ♕f7 24 ♕xd8! ♘xd8 25 ♖xd8 ♕xa2 26 ♘c3 ♕a5 27 ♖f8 ♕a1+ 28 ♔d2 ♕a6 29 ♘d5 ♕d6 30 ♖e8 ♖f7 31 ♖xg8+ ♔xg8 32 ♘h6+ ♔g7 33 ♘xf7 ♔xf7 34 ♖xh7+ ♔g8 35 ♖xb7 ♕a6 36 ♖c7 ♕a5+ 37 c3 ♔f8 38 ♖c6 ♕b5 39 ♖xf6+ ♔g7 40 ♖g6+ ♔f7 41 ♖f6+ ♔g7 42 ♖g6+ ½-½.

c) 12...h5 13 ♘f3 ♗g7 14 0-0 ♘d4 15 ♖f2 ♗e6 16 ♖af1 ♕d7 17 ♘h2 ♖ad8 18 ♘d1 exf4 19 ♖xf4 d5 20 ♘c3 and White has good pressure on the kingside, Hamdouchi-Bezold, France 1999.

Points to Remember

1) The plan of ♗e3, ♕d2 and then ♗h6 is often positionally desirable, especially if Black has moved his e-pawn. The exchange of the dark-squared bishops leaves the black king

without his most powerful defender and weakens the dark squares on the kingside (f6 and h6).

2) More often than not, Black plays his g8-knight to the e7-square. If he plays it to f6 instead, then a good long-term plan for White is a kingside pawn storm, involving h2-h3, g3-g4(-g5) and f4-f5. White gains time by attacking the knight along the way.

3) One of Black' normal ideas is to occupy the d4-square with a knight, and to gain space on the queenside with ...b7-b5-b4, chasing the White knight away from c3. White often reacts to this plan by playing ♘d1, before preparing to eject the knight from d4 with c2-c3. Often this is done in conjunction with removing the king's knight from either f3 or e2, so as not to allow Black a simplifying exchange after c2-c3 (see Variation C32, for example).

4) Black must be careful not to play ...♘d4 too early, as this can sometimes be punished (see Variation A).

5) If Black refrains from playing ...♘d4 White is sometimes in a position to play an advantageous d3-d4.

Main Line 2:
Black plays ...e6 and ...d5

1 e4 c5 2 ♘c3 e6

Black plans to play an early ...d7-d5. This is nowhere near as popular as the ...g6 lines,

but it's certainly a solid continuation that should be respected; Garry Kasparov, amongst others, has used this move order before.

3 g3

White fianchettoes as normal.

3...d5

Black still has a chance to transpose into earlier lines with 3...♘c6 4 ♗g2 g6.

4 exd5 exd5

Now I'm going to give two quite different suggestions:

A: 5 d4!?
B: 5 ♗g2

A)
5 d4!?

White immediately strikes back in the centre. Black's d-pawn will become isolated and White hopes to benefit from this. Unusually for the Closed Sicilian, play becomes very sharp at an early stage.

Black's main choice are:

A1: 5...♘f6!?
A2: 5...cxd4

Another interesting option here is 5...♘c6!? 6 dxc5 (6 ♗g2!?) 6...d4 7 ♘e4 ♗xc5 and now 8 ♘xc5 ♕a5+ 9 ♗d2 ♕xc5 10 ♗g2 has been given as advantageous to White in some texts, but I think the matter is far from clear after the accurate counter 10...♗f5!.

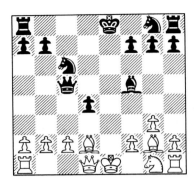

Black's speedy development and the attack on the c2-pawn are awkward for White, for example 11 ♖c1 ♘b4! or 11 c3 0-0-0, while 11 ♕e2+? ♔d7! 12 ♕f3 ♘f6 13 ♕b3 ♖ae8+ 14 ♘e2 ♔c8 gave Black a strong attack in Bauerndistel-Langhein, correspondence 1982.

For this reason I prefer the less committal 8 ♗g2!, for example 8...♗f5 9 ♘e2 ♕e7 10 ♘xc5 ♕xc5 11 c3, after which 11...dxc3 12 ♘xc3 ♖d8 13 ♕e2+ ♘ge7 14 ♗e3 ♕a5 15 ♖d1 gives White an edge due to having the bishop pair in an open position, while after 11...d3!? 12 ♘f4 ♖d8 13 0-0 it's not clear whether Black's passed pawn on d3 is a strength or a weakness.

A1)
5...♘f6!? 6 ♘ge2!?

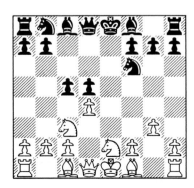

This is a clever move order designed not to expose White's queen too early. Alternatively, White has 6 ♗g2 cxd4 and now:

a) 7 ♘ce2 ♘c6 8 ♘xd4 ♗c5 9 ♘ge2 0-0 10 0-0 ♗g4 and Black has a very comfortable game. Schubert-Kerek, Budapest 2000, continued 11 ♘b3 ♖e8 12 ♖e1? ♗xf2+! 13 ♔xf2 ♕b6+ 14 ♔f1 ♘e4 and White was in big trouble (15 ♗xe4 ♖xe4 16 ♔g2 ♖ae8 win for Black).

b) 7 ♕xd4 ♘c6 8 ♕a4 d4 9 ♘ce2 ♗d7 and Black is not worse here – White's queen is awkwardly placed.

6...♘c6

6...♗g4!? 7 ♗g2 cxd4 forces White to recapture with 8 ♕xd4, but the big difference with the previous note is that the black bishop is already committed to g4, so after 8...♘c6 9 ♕a4 the white queen is now well placed (there are tactical possibilities against the light-squared bishop).

a) 9...♗b4 10 0-0 0-0 11 ♗g5 and the pressure on the d5-pawn gives Black some problems.

b) 9...♗c5!? 10 ♘xd5!? (10 0-0 0-0 11 ♗g5 d4 12 ♗xf6 ♕xf6 13 ♘e4 ♕e7 14 ♖fe1 is a safe way to play) 10...♗xe2 11 ♗g5! (11 ♘xf6+? ♕xf6 12 ♕e4+ ♔f8! 13 ♕xe2 ♖e8 14 ♗e3 ♗xe3 15 fxe3 ♘d4 16 ♕c4 ♖xe3+ and White's king was in trouble in Tseshkovsky-Gorelov, Aktjubinsk 1985) 11...0-0 12 ♗xf6 ♕e8 13 ♔d2 with a very unclear position. White's a pawn up, but his king is wandering around in the centre. However, it's not clear if Black can take advantage of this.

7 ♗g2 cxd4 8 ♘xd4 ♗b4
Or:

a) 8...♗e7 9 0-0 0-0 10 ♖e1 ♗g4 11 ♕d3! ♘b4 12 ♕d2! (White's queen is awkwardly placed at the moment but Black is in no position to exploit this and his pieces will soon be pushed back) 12...♖e8 13 h3 ♗c8 14 ♕d1 ♗c5 15 ♖xe8+ ♕xe8 16 ♗e3 ♗b6 17 ♔h2 ♗d7 18 ♕d2 ♖c8 19 ♖e1 ♕d8 20 a3 ♘c6 21 ♘xd5 ♘xd5 22 ♗xd5 and White went on to win in Kupreichik-Lau, Meisdorf 1996.

b) 8...♗g4 9 ♕d3 ♗e7 10 h3 ♗e6 11 ♘xe6 fxe6 12 0-0 0-0 13 ♗g5 h6 14 ♗d2 ♕d7 15 ♖ae1 and White's two bishops plus the weakness on e6 promises White a clear plus, Fischer-Bertok, Rovinj/Zagreb 1970.

9 0-0 0-0 10 ♗g5 ♗xc3 11 bxc3 h6 12 ♗xf6

12 ♗f4 ♗g4 13 ♕d3 ♕d7 14 ♖fe1 ♖fe8 looked okay for Black in Spassky-Garcia Gonzales, Linares 1981.

12...♕xf6

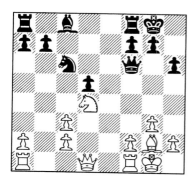

Both sides have pawn weaknesses here, but White is slightly more active. Now White must make a choice between grabbing on d5 or increasing the pressure on the queenside.

a) 13 ♗xd5!? ♖d8 (13...♗h3 14 ♗g2 ♗xg2 15 ♔xg2 ♖ad8 16 ♕f3 ♘xd4 17 ♕xf6 gxf6 18 cxd4 ♖xd4 19 ♖ad1 gave White a tiny edge in Maslik-Babayev, Bratislava 1993, while Black had no compensation for the pawn after 13...♘xd4? 14 ♕xd4 ♕xd4 15 cxd4 ♖d8 16 c4, Vershinin-Yurkov, Briansk 1995) 14 ♗xc6 bxc6 15 ♕f3 ♕xf3 16 ♘xf3 c5 with an unclear position; Black has sufficient compensation for the pawn in the form of light square control and White's doubled c-pawns.

b) 13 ♖b1 (I think this causes Black more problems) 13...♖d8 14 ♖e1 ♖b8 (14...♘xd4 15 ♕xd4 ♕xd4 16 cxd4 b6 17 c4 ♗e6 18 ♖e5 won a pawn in Parkanyi-Orso, Budapest 2000) 15 ♖b5 ♗e6 16 f4 ♘xd4 17 cxd4 b6 18 ♖e5 ♖bc8 19 ♖b3 ♕g6 20 c3 occurred in

Morovic Fernandez-Illescas, Leon 1993. White can claim an edge here; his pieces are still more active – White's bishop is superior to its counterpart.

A2)
5...cxd4

Black's main answer to 5 d4. White's queen is forced out into the open.

6 ♕xd4 ♘f6 7 ♗g5

We've now reached a position similar to the Goring Gambit Declined (with colour reversed), which arises after 1 e4 e5 2 ♘f3 ♘c6 3 d4 exd4 4 c3 d5 5 exd5 ♕xd5 6 cxd4 ♗g4. This line of the Goring is considered at least equal for Black and possibly more. In the Closed Sicilian the extra move for White is g2-g3, which in some lines is probably a slight hindrance.

7...♗e7

7...♘c6 8 ♗b5 ♗e7 transposes in the main line. White should take this path, as 8 ♗xf6 ♘xd4 9 ♗xd8 ♘xc2+ 10 ♔d2 ♘xa1 11 ♗g5 d4 12 ♘d5 ♗d6 13 ♗b5+ ♗d7 14 ♗xd7+ ♔xd7 15 ♘e2 ♖ac8! 16 ♖xa1 ♖c5 looks good for Black. In this line g2-g3 is definitely a hindrance.

8 ♗b5+ ♘c6 9 ♗xf6 ♗xf6 10 ♕c5 ♗xc3+

Also possible for Black is 10...♕b6!? 11 ♕xb6 axb6 12 ♘ge2 (or 12 ♘xd5 ♗xb2 13 ♘c7+ ♔d8 14 ♘xa8 ♗xa1 15 ♘xb6 ♗f5 and Black has some compensation for the pawn) 12...0-0 13 a3 ♖a5, which looks roughly level.

11 bxc3 ♕e7+ 12 ♕xe7+ ♔xe7 13 0-0-0 ♗e6 14 ♘e2 ♔d6!

I believe Black best way to equalise is to activate his king, which should find a pleasant home on c5. Gdanski-Wojtkiewicz, Warsaw 1993, continued 14...♖hd8 15 ♖he1 ♖d6 and now King's suggestion of 16 ♘f4 keeps an advantage for White – the d5-pawn is more vulnerable than the c3-pawn.

15 ♖he1

Lane-Nunn, Stroud 1980 now continued 15...♔c5! 16 c4!? (16 ♗a4 is equal) 16...dxc4 (16...♖ad8!?) 17 ♗xc6 bxc6?! 18 ♘f4 ♗g4 19 ♖e5+ ♔b4? 20 ♖d4! and White had a winning attack. However, Black's king was far too adventurous here. 19...♔b6 would have been stronger, while Lane points out that earlier 17...♔xc6 18 ♘d4+ ♔c7 19 ♘xe6+ fxe6 20 ♖xe6 ♖he8 leads to a level rook ending.

B)
5 ♗g2

see following diagram

This is White's most logical move. Black is forced to do something about his threatened d-pawn. Black can choose between the two replies:

B1: 5...d4
B2: 5...♘f6

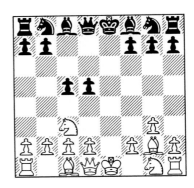

B1)
5...d4

Theoretically speaking, this move is meant to be inferior to 5...♘f6, but in my opinion things are not so clear.

6 ♕e2+!

This move interferes with Black's development plans. Notice that 6 ♘e4? f5 leaves the knight with nowhere to go. However, 6 ♘d5 is playable, for example 6...♗d6 (6...♘f6? 7 ♕e2+!) 7 d3 ♘c6 8 ♘e2 ♘ge7 9 ♘xe7 ♘xe7 10 ♗f4 0-0 11 0-0 ♗g4 12 ♗xd6 ♕xd6 with an equal position, Klinger-Rovid, Budapest 1993.

6...♗e7

6...♗e6? 7 ♗xb7 is obviously bad, while 6...♕e7? 7 ♘d5 ♕xe2+ 8 ♘xe2 gives White a big lead in development – 8...♗d6 can be answered very effectively by 9 b4!. The line 6...♘e7 7 ♘d5 ♘bc6 8 d3 is also good for White – Black is rather tied up.

7 ♘d5 ♘c6 8 d3 ♗e6 9 ♘f4!

9 ♘xe7 gains the bishop pair, but allows Black to complete his development with ease. Following 9...♘gxe7 10 ♘f3 0-0 11 0-0 ♖e8 12 ♘g5 ♗d5 Black has equalised comfortably.

9...♗d7

9...♗d7?! 10 ♘xe6 ♕xe6 11 ♕xe6 fxe6 12 ♘f3 is clearly better for White: the backward pawn on e6 is a real weakness.

10 g4!?

This energetic move, played by the German FM Rene Borngässer, may well be White's best chance for an advantage. Two other moves come into consideration. 10 ♘d5 ♗e6 11 ♘f4 ♗d7 12 ♘d5 is good for a draw if that's what White wants (this was actually how Davies-Beim, Tel Aviv 1992 ended). The other try is simple development with 10 ♘f3 ♘f6 11 0-0 0-0, although this looks reasonably comfortable for Black. For example 12 ♘e5 ♘xe5 13 ♕xe5 ♖e8! 14 ♘h5 (14 ♗xb7? ♗f8 15 ♕g5 h6 16 ♕h4 ♖b8 and ...g5 is coming) 14...♕b6 and Black was better in Westerinen-Ihonen, Kuopio 1992.

10...♘f6

This allows White to gain a large space advantage on the kingside, but it's not easy to suggest worthwhile alternatives. 10...♘h6 11 ♘h5! 0-0 (11...♗xg4? 12 ♘xg7+ ♔f8 13 ♗xh6 wins for White, while 11...♘xg4 12 h3 ♘ge5 13 ♘xg7+ ♔f8 14 ♗h6 is promising) 12 ♗xh6 gxh6 13 0-0-0 looks good for White – Black's kingside is a bit of a mess. The move 10...h6!? prevents the immediate g4-g5, but White could consider following up with 11 h4!?.

11 g5 ♘g4 12 ♘d5 ♘ge5 13 ♗f4

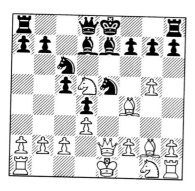

Borngässer-Mozny, Prague 1990, continued 13...♘g6 14 ♗c7 ♕c8 15 h4 ♗e6 (15...♗g4!?) 16 ♗g3 ♗d8 17 h5 ♘ge7 18 h6 ♘xd5 19 hxg7 ♖g8 20 ♗xd5 ♖xg7 21 ♘f3 ♕d7 and now King suggests that both 22 ♗b3 and 22 ♗e4 keep a white advantage.

This seems right, as the h7-pawn is weak and White has some pressure down the half-open h-file.

B2)
5...♘f6

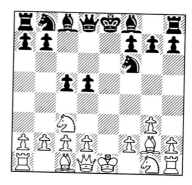

This sensible move, protecting the d5-pawn, is Black's most popular choice. We will now consider two different approaches for White.

B21: 6 ♘ge2
B22: 6 d3

B21)

6 ♘ge2 d4 7 ♘e4 ♘xe4 8 ♗xe4 ♘d7!

Preparing to attack the bishop with ...♘f6 is Black's most solid response to White's play. After 8...♗e7 9 0-0 ♘c6 10 d3 0-0 11 ♘f4 White has an advantage – the bishop is well centralised on e4 and it's hard for Black to challenge it.

9 0-0 ♘f6 10 ♗g2 ♗d6 11 c3!

Challenging the centre gives Black something to think about and the chance to go wrong. 11 d3 0-0 12 ♗f4 ♗g4 13 ♗xd6 ♕xd6 14 h3 ♗d7! 15 ♘f4 ♖fe8 16 ♕d2 ♗c6 is very comfortable for Black.

11...d3!?

Black has two alternatives to this ambitious move:

a) 11...dxc3?! 12 dxc3! reveals one of the points of White's move order. 12...0-0 13 ♕c2 is very uncomfortable for Black – the g2-bishop pressurises b7 and Black will have some problems after ♖d1.

b) 11...0-0 (this is Black's safest response) 12 cxd4 cxd4 13 d3 ♖e8 14 ♘f4 (14 ♘xd4 ♗xg3 15 hxg3 ♕xd4 and Black is very active – King) 14...♕b6 15 ♕b3 ♕a5 16 ♕c2 ♗f5 17 ♗d2 (17 ♗xb7 ♖ab8 18 ♗g2 ♖bc8 gives Black too much compensation for the pawn) 17...♗b4 18 ♗xb4 ♕xb4 19 a3 ♕b5 and the position looks equal, Hug-Ribli, Lucerne 1982 – both d-pawns are weak.

12 ♘f4 0-0

12...♗xf4?! 13 ♕a4+! ♗d7 14 ♖e1+ ♔f8 15 ♕xf4 is very good for White; the bishop can develop with b2-b3 and both the d3- and b7-pawns are vulnerable.

13 ♘xd3

White must get rid of this troublesome pawn, otherwise it would be very difficult to finish developing.

13...♗xg3

Regaining the pawn with this discovered attack.

14 fxg3 ♕xd3 15 ♕f3!

White must challenge Black's dominating queen.

15...♕xf3

Against 15...♖d8 King gives 16 ♕xd3 ♖xd3 17 ♖e1, with the idea of ♗f1.

16 ♗xf3 ♗h3

Or 16...♖d8 17 b3 ♗h3 (17...♖b8 18 d4! cxd4 19 ♗f4 ♖a8 20 ♖fd1 d3 21 ♖d2, followed by ♖ad1, is good for White) 18 ♗xb7 ♖ab8 19 ♗g2 ♗xg2 20 ♔xg2 ♘e4 21 ♖e1! ♘xd2 22 ♖e2 and the black knight is trapped as in the game Dudek-Kern, Bundesliga 1997.

17 ♗xb7!

17 ♖d1 ♗g4!, exchanging off one of the bishops, eases Black's task.

17...♖ae8

After 17...♗xf1 18 ♗xa8 ♗d3 19 ♗f3 ♖e8 20 b3 White is slowly untangling, leaving Black with little compensation for the pawn deficit.

18 ♗g2

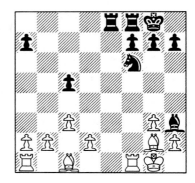

In this position White remains a pawn to the good, but Black's activity and White's undeveloped queenside balances the scales.

a) 18...♗g4? loses the initiative. After 19 b3 ♖e2 20 ♗a3 ♖c8 21 ♖f2 White was clearly better in Thimognier-Muneret, correspondence 1991.

b) 18...♗xg2 19 ♔xg2 ♖e2+ 20 ♖f2 ♖fe8 21 b3 ♖xf2+ 22 ♔xf2 ♘g4+ 23 ♔g2 f5 24 h3 ♘e5 25 d4 cxd4 26 cxd4 ♘d3 27 ♗g5 h6 28 ♖d1 hxg5 29 ♖xd3 ♖e2+ 30 ♔f3 ♖xa2 31 d5 ♔f7 32 d6 ♔e8 (in the stem game Spassky-Kasparov, Bugojno 1982, the players agreed a draw here) 33 g4 g6 34 gxf5 gxf5 35 ♖d5 g4+ 36 hxg4 fxg4+ 37 ♔xg4 ♔d7 38 ♔f5 ♖e2 39 ♖a5 ♔xd6 40 ♖xa7 ½-½ J.Claesen-Chuchelov, Belgian League 1998. In the final position White's extra pawn is meaningless – the position is drawn.

B22)
6 d3!?

In most people's view this is more combative than 6 ♘ge2, the reason being that after Black plays ...d5-d4 and White replies with ♘e4, White can answer ...♘xe4 by recapturing with the pawn, thus creating an asymmetrical pawn structure and a more unbalanced position.

6...d4

Black may also refrain from this central advance, for example 6...♗e7 7 ♘ge2 0-0 8 0-0 ♘c6 9 ♗g5 d4 10 ♗xf6 ♗xf6 11 ♘e4

♗e7 12 ♘f4 ♗f5 (12...♖e8 13 ♖e1 ♗f8, as in Panbukchian-Poluljahov, Anapa 1991, is also possible) 13 ♖e1 ♖c8 14 ♘d5 ♗e6 15 ♘xe7+ ♘xe7 16 ♕h5!.

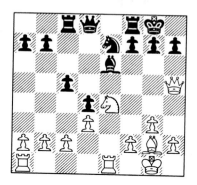

Larsen-Suetin, Copenhagen 1965, continued 16...♗f5 17 ♖e2 ♕d7 18 ♖ae1 ♘d5 19 ♘d6! ♕xd6 20 ♕xf5 ♘f6 21 ♗xb7 ♖b8 22 ♖e7 and White was a pawn to the good.

7 ♘e4 ♘xe4 8 dxe4 ♘c6

Or 8...♗d6 9 ♘e2 ♘c6 10 0-0 0-0 11 a3!? (the immediate 11 f4 looks reasonable) 11...a5 12 f4 f5 13 c3 ♔h8?! (13...fxe4 looks stronger) 14 cxd4 ♘xd4 15 e5 ♗c7 16 ♗e3 ♘e6 17 ♕c2 ♖b8 18 ♖fd1 ♕e7 19 ♘c3 and White had a very pleasant position in A.Ledger-Stephenson, British Championship 1998 – White's minor pieces have much more scope than their counterparts.

9 ♘e2 ♗e7

9...♗e6!?, with ideas of ...♗c4, is another option for Black. Now 10 ♘f4 ♗c4 11 ♘d3 ♗d6 12 0-0 0-0 13 f4 f6 14 b3 was unbalanced in Lagvilava-Skripchenko, FIDE Women's World Championship, New Delhi 2000, while after 10 0-0 ♗d6 11 ♘f4 ♗xf4 12 ♗xf4 0-0 13 ♕h5 f5 14 ♖fe1, Kovalevskaya-Skripchenko, Belgrade 2000, I slightly prefer White, as the two bishops may become very useful when the position opens up.

10 0-0 0-0 11 ♘f4 ♖e8

Black can also try to exchange a pair of minor pieces with 11...♗g5, for example 12

c3 (12 ♖e1 ♖e8 13 ♘d5!? or 12 ♘d5 look interesting) 12...♗xf4 13 ♗xf4 ♗e6 and now the game Short-Topalov, Sarajevo 1999 finished abruptly after 14 ♕h5 b6 15 e5 ♗d5 16 ♗g5 ♕d7 17 ♗f6 ♗h8 18 ♗h3 ♗e6 19 ♗xg7+ ♔xg7 20 ♕g5+ and it's perpetual check.

12 ♘d5

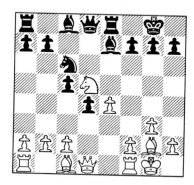

I very much like White's well centralised knight here. Donev-Felsberger, Austrian Team Championship 1995, continued 12...♗d6 13 c4 dxc3 (13...♘e7 14 ♗g5 ♕d7 15 ♗xe7 ♗xe7 16 f4 b6 17 ♕d3 ♗b7 18 ♖ae1 is better for White according to Donev) 14 bxc3 ♖b8 15 ♕c2 ♗e6 16 ♖d1 f6 17 ♗f4 ♗xf4 18 ♘xf4 ♕e7 and now White kept an edge with 19 ♘xe6 ♕xe6 20 ♖d5, but it is also possible to play more aggressively with 19 e5!? (threatening ♘xe6) 19...♗c4 20 e6, followed by the move 21 ♗e4.

Important Points

1) Line A is very tricky and could lead to success, even against experienced players. Theoretically speaking, however, Black should be fine.

2) Line B is more of a serious try for the advantage, 5...d4 is not as bad as some people have made out, while lines with d2-d3 (B22) are probably White best chance for an advantage or, at the very least, a complex position.

Other Variations:
Black plays typical Sicilian moves

Playing the Closed Sicilian, you are bound to face many lines with ...♘c6 and ...g7-g6, or ...e7-e6 and ...d7-d5. Some opponents, however, will carry playing typical Sicilian moves, regardless of how you carry on. This may include a classical set-up with ...d6, ...e6, ...♘c6 and ...♘f6, or an early queenside expansion with ...a6 and ...b5. We will take a brief look a these lines here.

1 e4 c5 2 ♘c3

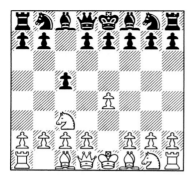

2...♘c6

Alternatively:

a) 2...d6 is a move order often chosen by Najdorf players. The reason is that after 2...♘c6 3 ♘f3 or 3 ♘ge2 White has the possibility of playing for an Open Sicilian where Black has committed his knight to c6 and thus cannot play the Najdorf. With 2...d6 3 ♘ge2 (or 3 ♘f3) 3...♘f6 4 d4 cxd4 5 ♘xd4 a6 Black has his beloved set-up.

This doesn't really affect the Closed Sicilian player. Following 3 g3 ♘c6 4 ♗g2 g6 5 d3 ♗g7 we have transposed directly to ...g6 lines. Otherwise 4...♘f6 transposes to the text.

b) 2...e6 3 g3 d6 4 ♗g2 ♘f6 5 d3 ♗e7 6 f4 0-0 (Black can miss out ...♘c6 altogether, but this shouldn't concern White – normal development and expansion on the kingside is still the key) 7 ♘f3 ♘bd7 8 0-0 a6 9 h3 b5

10 g4 and White develops an attack on the kingside as normal.

c) 2...a6 (Black pays for an early queenside expansion) 3 g3 b5 4 ♗g2 ♗b7 5 d3 e6 (5...g6 6 ♗e3 d6 7 ♕d2 ♗g7 8 ♘ge2 ♘c6 9 0-0 h5 10 h3 ♘d4 was played in Shaw-MacKay, Scottish Championship 1993; now I like the usual plan of 11 ♘d1 e6 12 ♘c1 ♘e7 13 c3 ♘dc6 14 ♘e2 0-0 15 ♗h6) 6 f4 d6 (after 6...d5 White can play 7 e5) 7 ♘f3 ♘d7 8 0-0 b4 9 ♘e2 ♘gf6 (Spraggett-Gelfand, Moscow Olympiad 1994), and now I like 10 b3!?, preventing ...c5-c4.

3 g3 ♘f6 4 ♗g2 d6

Black can also play for a delayed ...d7-d5; 4...e5 5 f4!? (or 5 d3 d5 – see the 2...e6 and 3...d5 line) 5...d5 6 e5 ♘d7 7 ♘f3 ♗e7 8 0-0 0-0 9 d3 ♖b8 10 ♔h1 b5 11 ♘e2 b4 12 g4 f6 13 exf6 ♘xf6 14 h3 and White will follow up with ♘g3, Lukin-Sveshnikov, St Petersburg 1994.

5 d3 e6

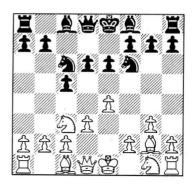

It's not too late for a fianchetto; for 5...g6 6 h3 ♗g7 7 ♗e3 brings us back into ...g6 lines.

6 f4!

With Black avoiding a fianchetto, it makes much more sense to play f2-f4, followed, in time, by a kingside pawn storm.

6...♗e7 7 ♘f3 0-0

7...a6 is a normal Open Sicilian move but it has less point here, although it does prepare ...b7-b5. Spraggett-Vilalta, Manresa

1995, continued 8 0-0 0-0 9 h3 ♕c7 10 g4! (starting the usual expansion) 10...♖e8 11 g5 ♘d7 12 ♘e2 b5 13 ♘g3 ♗b7 14 ♘h2 ♖ad8 15 ♘g4 ♘b6 16 ♘h5 d5 17 ♕e1 ♘d4 18 ♕f2 dxe4 19 dxe4 b4 20 ♔h1 ♘c4 21 c3 bxc3 22 bxc3 ♘b5 23 a4 ♘bd6 24 ♕e2 ♘a5 25 ♖b1 ♘dc4 26 f5 exf5 27 ♖xf5 ♘d6 28 ♖f1 ♗c8 29 ♗f4 ♗e6 30 ♖g1 ♗c4 31 ♕f3 ♕d7

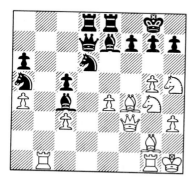

32 ♗e5! ♗xg5 33 ♗xg7 ♘xe4 34 ♕xe4 1-0 (after 34...♖xe4 35 ♗xe4 there is no good defence to ♘gf6+).

8 0-0 ♖b8

Black has many possible ways to develop, but White's reaction is normally the same, for example 8...♗d7 9 h3 ♘d4 (9...♖b8 10 g4 b5 11 f5 b4 12 ♘e2 ♘e8 13 ♕e1 ♘e5 14 ♘xe5 dxe5 15 ♗e3 was better for White in Pinto-Panken, Parsippany 2001) 10 ♗e3 ♘xf3+ 11 ♕xf3 ♗c6 12 ♕e2 ♕c7 13 ♗f2 ♖fe8 14 g4

♘d7 and White is better, Hickl-Martens, Groningen 1988 – Black is passive and has no obvious plan.

9 h3 d5 10 g4

Naturally 10 ♕e1 is also possible, but White has no need to fear an exchange of queens here.

10...dxe4 11 dxe4 ♕c7

Black correctly declines the exchange. After 11...♕xd1 12 ♖xd1 White's advantage holds in the endgame – he will gain more space with e4-e5 and ♘e4.

12 e5 ♖d8 13 ♕e1 ♘e8 14 ♗e3

White has more space and an active position. Spraggett-Lesiege, Vancouver 1998, continued 14...♘d4 15 ♕f2 b5 16 ♔h2 b4 17 ♘e4 ♗a6 18 ♖fc1 ♕b6 19 ♘fd2 f6 20 exf6 gxf6 21 ♘b3 ♗b7 22 ♖g1 ♘g7 23 ♖ad1 e5 24 f5 and White converted his undoubted advantage on the kingside into the full point.

CHAPTER TWO

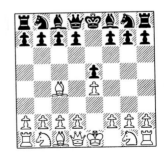

Attacking 1...e5:
The Bishop's Opening

1 e4 e5 2 ♗c4

The Bishop's Opening is probably the most straightforward line to play against 1...e5; White is playing a 'system', and there is relatively little theory to learn. That said, there's still a bit of theory in this chapter – you can't get away with knowing nothing!

The Danish legend Bent Larsen had quite a bit to do with the popularisation of the Bishop's Opening. Before him it was used very rarely at the highest levels, but Larsen used it to beat many grandmasters in the 70s and 80s and showed it could be used as a good weapon. In more recent times players such as Gary Kasparov, Vishy Anand, Vladimir Kramnik and Michael Adams have used it, especially when they've fancied having a day off from heavy theoretical battles.

One of its major appeals is that it cuts out many of Black's popular defences in the Open Games (1 e4 e5). For example, White completely bypasses the super-solid Petroff Defence (1 e4 e5 2 ♘f3 ♘f6), plus all of Black's infinite number of defences against the Ruy Lopez (no need to learn crazy Schliemann lines – 1 e4 e5 2 ♘f3 ♘c6 3 ♗b5 f5!? – or to be bored to death by Kramnik's 'Berlin Wall' – 1 e4 e5 2 ♘f3 ♘c6 3 ♗b5 ♘f6). Black only really has one main defence in 2...♘f6 (other second moves of-

ten transpose to this anyway), so this is a major time-saver on the learning front.

The system that I'm advocating is an aggressive one where White plays ♗c4, d2-d3, ♘c3 and then, if possible, the pawn-break f2-f4!. This is followed by ♘f3 and (again if possible) 0-0.

This can be played against various black set-ups, but White must also be prepared to be flexible; Some black systems are aimed at countering this plan, and on those occasions it's better for White to play without f2-f4.

Main Line:
Black plays 2...♘f6

1 e4 e5 2 ♗c4 ♘f6

This is by far the most popular choice for Black at move two. Black develops his king's knight, prepares to castle and attacks the e4-pawn.

3 d3

With this move we are choosing to play a 'Bishops Opening Proper', rather than transposing into the Vienna Game with 3 ♘c3. Often the Bishop's Opening transposes in to the Vienna in any case (for example, 3 ♘c3 ♘c6 4 d3 gives us another route to Variation B). Choosing the 3 d3 move order, though, cuts out some of Black's options, although I should say it also gives Black some extra ones. For example, after 3 ♘c3 White has to be concerned with 3...♗b4 and 3...♘xe4, both of which are perfectly playable moves. With 3 d3 we avoid these lines; the other side of the coin is that White has to prepare for 3...d5 (this is not such a problem) and the very popular 3...c6.

Now we will a take a look at these black possibilities:

A: 3...c6
B: 3...♘c6
C: 3...♗c5
D: 3...d5
E: 3...♗e7

3...d6 is a passive move, which is seen from time to time. White should continue with the plan of f2-f4, for example 4 ♘c3 ♗e6 5 ♗b3!? ♘c6 6 f4 ♗e7 7 ♘f3 0-0 8 0-0

and White stands better.

A)
3...c6

This line, attributed to Louis Paulsen, is perhaps the critical test of the Bishop's Opening. Black immediately tries to take the initiative in the centre by preparing the logical ...d7-d5 advance. White must now abandon any fanciful ideas of launching his f-pawn (4 f4 is effectively met by the simple 4...d5). Instead White must prepare to do battle in the centre.

4 ♘f3

The most logical move, attacking the pawn on e5 and trying to take advantage of the fact that Black no longer has the c6-square for his knight.

Black can react in the following ways:

A1: 4...d5
A2: 4...♗e7

Or:

a) 4...d6 is likely to transpose to Variation A2 after 5 0-0 ♗e7.

b) 4...♕c7 also transposes to Variation A2 after 5 0-0 ♗e7.

A1)
4...d5 5 ♗b3!

With this move White keeps the pressure on the black centre, without releasing any of the tension. 5 exd5 exd5 6 ♗b5+ ♗d7! is

comfortable for Black, while 6 ♗b3 allows
Black to develop with 6...♘c6.

Now Black must deal with the threat to
his e5-pawn. His choice are:
A11) 5...♗d6
A12) 5...a5!?

Alternatively:
a) 5...d4? runs into 6 ♘g5.
b) 5...dxe4 6 ♘g5 and now:
b1) 6...♗c5!? 7 ♘xf7 ♕b6 8 0-0! (but not
8 ♘xh8?? ♗xf2+ 9 ♔f1 ♗g4 10 ♕d2 e3 and
Black wins!) 8...♗g4 (8...♖f8 9 ♘xe5 leaves
White a clear pawn up) 9 ♘xh8 and I don't
see any real compensation for Black.
b2) 6...♗e6 7 ♗xe6 fxe6 8 ♘xe4 ♘xe4 9
dxe4 ♕xd1+ 10 ♔xd1 and Black's doubled e-
pawns are a permanent liability in the ending,
Honfi-Lukacs, Hungary 1975.
c) 5...♗b4+!? (the point of this mover is to
provoke c2-c3, so that White no longer has
this square for his knight) 6 c3 (or 6 ♗d2
♗xd2+ 7 ♘bxd2 dxe4 8 ♘xe5 0-0 9 dxe4
♘xe4 10 ♘df3 ♘d7 11 0-0 ♘xe5 12 ♘xe5
♕f6 13 ♕d4 and White's pressure on f7
gives him an edge, Larsen-Nunn, London
1986) 6...♗d6 7 ♗g5 ♗e6 8 ♘bd2 ♘bd7 9
d4 exd4 10 exd5 ♗xd5 11 ♗xd5 cxd5 12
♘xd4 ♕e7+ 13 ♗e3 0-0 14 ♘f5 ♕e5 15
♘xd6 ♕xd6 16 0-0 and White was better in
the game Yudasin-Alterman, Tel Aviv 1994 –
the d5-pawn is a permanent weakness for
White to target.

A11)
5...♗d6
The most logical move. Black develops a
bishop, defends the e-pawn and prepares to
castle.
I'll now give two ways forward for White:
A111: 6 ♘c3
A112: 6 exd5!?

A111)
6 ♘c3

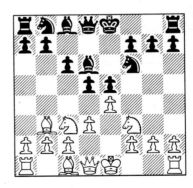

Until recently this was virtually the only
choice, but Black's equalising prospects in
Variation A1112 have forced White to look
elsewhere for an advantage.
Now we will look at the following lines:
A1111: 6...♗e6
A1112: 6...dxe4

Or 6...d4 7 ♘e2 c5 (7...♘a6?! 8 c3 dxc3 9

bxc3 0-0 10 0-0 ♘c5 11 ♗c2 ♗g4 12 ♘g3 ♘h5 13 h3 ♘xg3 14 fxg3 ♗h5 15 g4 ♗g6 16 h4 was clearly better for White, Nunn-Korchnoi, Johannesburg 1981) 8 ♘g3 ♘c6 9 0-0 h6 10 ♘d2 g6 11 ♘c4 ♗c7 12 a4 ♔f8 13 f4 ♔g7 14 f5 and White has a useful space advantage on the kingside, Hendriks-Kroeze, Enschede 1998.

A1111)
6...♗e6

With this move Black tries to keep his centre intact, but practice has shown this to be a difficult task.

7 ♗g5!

Stepping up the pressure on d5.

7...♕a5

Or:

a) 7...♘bd7 8 exd5 cxd5 9 ♗xd5 wins a pawn.

b) 7...d4 8 ♘e2 ♘bd7 (8...♗xb3 9 axb3 and White can continue with ♘g3-f5) 9 ♗xe6 fxe6 10 c3 dxc3 11 bxc3 h6 12 ♗xf6 ♕xf6 13 0-0 0-0 14 ♘g3 was better for White in Nun-Tichy, Czech Team Championship 1999.

8 0-0 ♘bd7 9 ♖e1 0-0-0

A major alternative for Black is 9...0-0 and now:

a) 10 ♘h4, with idea of ♕f3 and ♘f5 gives White an edge – Nunn.

b) 10 ♗d2 ♕c7 11 exd5 ♘xd5 12 ♘e4 ♗e7 (Traut-Kappes, correspondence 1987)

13 d4! and I prefer White.

c) 10 exd5!? and now there's another split:

c1) 10...♘xd5 11 ♘e4 ♗b8 (Sikora-Karch, correspondence 1989) 12 ♗d2! ♕c7 13 ♘fg5, annoying the bishop on e6.

c2) 10...cxd5 11 ♕d2 b6?! (11...d4 is more resilient) 12 ♗xf6 ♘xf6 13 ♘xe5 d4 14 ♘b1 ♗b4 15 c3 ♗xb3 16 cxb4 ♕a6 17 b5 ♕a4 18 ♘a3 and White is a clear pawn up, Nunn-Murey, Lucerne Olympiad 1982.

10 exd5 cxd5 11 ♕d2

Black now has many possible moves, but none seems to reach equality:

a) 11...♕c5 12 d4 exd4 13 ♘xd4 with pressure on e6, Packroff-Kohn, correspondence 1984.

b) 11...♗b4 12 a3 ♗xc3 13 ♕xc3+ ♕xc3 14 bxc3 h6 15 ♗h4 g5 16 ♗g3 e4 17 ♘d4 and White has an excellent pair of bishops, Koch-Mohaupt, correspondence 1965.

c) 11...♗c7 12 ♗xf6 gxf6 13 ♗xd5 ♗xd5 14 b4! ♕xb4 15 ♘xd5 is better for White, Honfi-Radulov, correspondence 1982.

d) 11...h6 12 ♗xf6 ♘xf6 13 ♘xe5 d4 14 ♗xe6+ fxe6 15 ♘b1 and White is a pawn up.

e) 11...d4 12 ♗xe6 fxe6 13 ♘e4!.

f) 11...♖de8 12 d4! exd4 (12...e4 13 ♘xe4!) 13 ♘xd4 ♗b4 14 ♗f4 ♗xc3 15 bxc3 ♘e4 16 ♕d3 ♕xc3 17 ♘b5 ♕f6 18 ♘xa7+ ♔d8 19 ♗e3 ♘e5 20 ♕b5 ♘d6 21 ♕a5+ 1-0 Bodisko-Mitchell, correspondence 1985.

g) 11...♔b8 12 ♗xf6 (12 ♘h4!?) 12...♘xf6 13 ♘xe5 d4 14 ♘b1 ♕c7 15 f4.

A1112)
6...dxe4!?

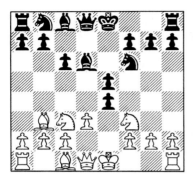

Until recently this move has been mysteriously overlooked, or at least underestimated. Kramnik, however, has shown that Black has good equalising chances with it.

7 ②g5

White can't really hope for much after the quiet 7 ②xe4 ②xe4 8 dxe4, but Black must still be a little careful, for example 8...♕e7?! (8...♗b4+ is safer) 9 ②g5! 0-0 10 ②xh7!! ♔xh7 11 ♕h5+ ♔g8 12 ♗g5 ♕c7 13 ♖d1 ②d7 14 ♖d3 ②c5 15 ♖g3 ♗e7 16 ♗h6 ♗f6 17 ♕g6 ♕a5+ 18 c3 ♕d8 19 ♗xg7 ②xb3 20 ♕h6 ♕d2+ 21 ♕xd2 ②xd2 22 ♗xf6+ ♔h7 23 ♔xd2 and White went on to win in Mitkov-Gabriel, Pula 2000.

7...0-0 8 ②cxe4 ②xe4 9 ②xe4 ♗f5

This is stronger than 9...②a6?! 10 ♕h5! ♕c7 11 ②g5! h6 12 ②e4 ♗e7

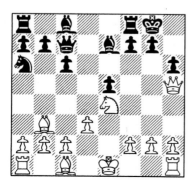

13 ♗xh6 gxh6 14 ♕g6+ ♔h8 15 ♕xh6+ ♔g8 16 h4 and White has a very strong attack, Tischbierek-Beliavsky, Novi Sad Olympiad 1990.

10 ♕f3

10 0-0 ②a6 11 ②xd6 ♕xd6 12 ♕f3 ♗e6 was equal in Anand-Kramnik, Frankfurt (rapid) 1998.

10...♗xe4

Or 10...♗g6 11 h4 ♗xe4 12 dxe4 ②d7 13 c3 ②c5 14 ♗c2 ♕e7 15 ♗g5! f6 16 ♗d2 and White has a tiny edge due to the bishop pair, as in Ki.Georgiev-Alterman, Recklinghausen 1998.

11 dxe4 ②d7 12 c3 a5 13 a4

13 0-0 allows Black to gain space with 13...a4 14 ♗c2 ②c5.

13...②c5 14 ♗c2 b5 15 0-0

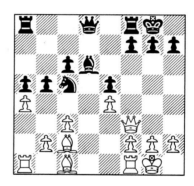

Adams-Kramnik, Tilburg 1998, continued 15...♕c7 16 ♖d1 ♖ab8 17 axb5 cxb5 18 g3 b4 19 cxb4 ♖xb4 20 ♗d2 ♖xb2, and in this level position the players agreed a draw.

A112)
6 exd5!?

This move looks quite promising.

6...②xd5

After 6...cxd5 White can play:

a) 7 0-0 ♗e6 (or 7...0-0 8 ♗g5 ♗e6 9 ②c3 and Black's centre is under pressure) 8 ♗g5 ②bd7 9 ②c3 ♕a5 10 ♖e1 0-0 11 ♕d2 and we have transposed to note 'c2' to Black's ninth move in Variation A1111.

b) 7 ♗g5!? d4 8 ♘bd2 0-0 9 0-0 ♘c6 10 ♖e1 a6 11 h3 h6 12 ♗h4 ♖e8 13 ♘c4 and White was a bit better, Benjamin-Nielsen, FIDE World Championship, Las Vegas 1999.

7 0-0 0-0

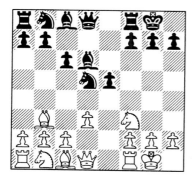

8 ♖e1

White also kept initiative in Malisov-Birnboim, Israeli Championship 1996, after 8 ♘bd2 ♗c7 9 ♖e1 ♘d7 10 ♘e4 h6 11 h3 ♘7f6 12 ♘g3 ♖e8 13 ♗d2 a5 14 a3 a4 15 ♗a2 c5 16 ♘h2 ♗e6 17 ♕f3 ♕d7 18 ♘g4 ♘xg4 19 hxg4 ♘f4 20 ♗xe6 ♘xe6 21 ♘e4 ♘d4 22 ♕d1 ♕c6 23 ♗e3 ♖ad8 24 ♗xd4 exd4 25 ♕f3 ♖e6 26 g3 ♖de8 27 ♔g2.

8...♘d7

Or 8...♖e8 9 ♘bd2 ♗c7 10 ♘e4 ♗g4 11 h3 ♗h5 12 ♘g3 ♗g6 13 ♗g5 ♕d7 14 ♘h4 ♘a6 15 ♘xg6 hxg6 16 d4 exd4 17 ♕xd4 and White has the advantage of the bishop pair in an open position, Tseshkovsky-Agzamov, Yerevan 1982.

9 ♘bd2 ♖e8 10 ♘e4 ♗c7 11 ♗g5 f6 12 ♗d2 ♔h8 13 h3

I quite like the idea of the immediate 13 d4!? as well.

13...♘f8

---
see following diagram

We are following the game Bosboom-Raetsky, Hafnarfjordur 1998. White now keeps a small plus by opening the centre with 14 d4 exd4 15 ♘xd4.

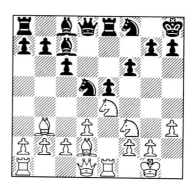

A12)
5...a5!?

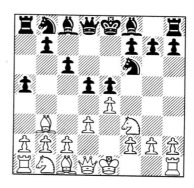

Black gains space on the queenside by threatening to trap White's light-squared bishop. This move came into fashion after the Russian GM Evgeny Bareev utilised it against world number one Garry Kasparov.

6 ♘c3

This was Kasparov's choice, but 6 a3!? is also interesting:

a) 6...a4 7 ♗a2 ♗d6 8 ♘c3 dxe4 9 ♘g5 0-0 10 ♘gxe4 ♘xe4 11 ♘xe4 ♗e7?! (11...♗f5!) 12 ♕h5! ♘d7 13 0-0 ♕e8 14 f4 and White has a very strong attack, Lane-Henris, Brussels 1995.

b) 6...♗d6 7 ♘c3 and now:

b1) 7...♗e6 8 exd5 ♗xd5 (8...cxd5!?) 9 ♘xd5 ♘xd5 10 0-0 0-0 11 ♖e1 ♘d7 12 d4 ♖e8 13 ♗g5 and White is better, Zhelnin-Raetsky, Smolensk 2000.

b2) 7...dxe4 8 ♘g5 0-0 9 ♘cxe4 ♘xe4 10 ♘xe4 ♗f5 11 ♕f3 ♗xe4 12 dxe4 ♘a6 13 0-0 ♘c7 14 ♖d1 and the bishop pair gives White the tiniest of edges, Atlas-Rabiega, Austrian League 2000.

6...♗b4

Kasparov's idea after 6...d4 is 7 ♘xe5! dxc3 8 ♘xf7.

7 a3 ♗xc3+ 8 bxc3 ♘bd7

Alternatively:

a) 8...♗g4?! 9 exd5 ♘xd5 10 h3 ♘xc3 11 ♗xf7+! – Kasparov.

b) 8...a4 9 ♗a2 ♘bd7 10 exd5 cxd5 (or 10...♘xd5 11 ♗d2 0-0 12 0-0 ♖e8 13 ♖e1 h6 14 c4 ♘5f6 15 ♗c3 e4 16 ♘d2 and the position will open up for White's bishop pair, Dam-Bosboom, Leeuwarden 1993) 11 0-0 0-0 12 ♗g5 ♕c7 13 ♕d2 b6 14 ♖ae1 ♖e8 15 ♘h4 ♕c6 16 ♘f5 ♕e6 17 f4!

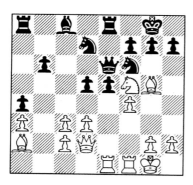

and Black's centre is crumbling, Berkvens-Jonkman, Essent 2000.

c) 8...♕c7!? is an untried suggestion from Kasparov.

9 exd5 ♘xd5!?

Keeping the centre intact with 9...cxd5 looks more natural, although this would undoubtedly come under attack from the white pieces. After 10 0-0 0-0 11 ♖e1 we have:

a) Both 11...e4 12 ♘d4 ♘c5 13 ♗g5 ♗e6 14 ♗a2 h6 15 ♗h4 and 11...a4 12 ♗a2 ♖e8 13 ♗g5 are given by Kasparov; in each line White appears to be more comfortable.

b) 11...♕c7 (Kasparov gives this a ques-

tion mark, but is it really so clear?) 12 ♘xe5 Kasparov (12 ♗b2!? is less committal) 12...♘xe5 13 ♗f4 (Kasparov stops here) 13...♖e8! 14 d4 ♗g4 15 f3 ♘xf3+ 16 ♕xf3 ♕d7 and this looks unclear to me.

10 0-0 0-0

10...a4? 11 ♗xd5 cxd5 12 ♘xe5 is good for White.

11 ♖e1! ♖e8

Kasparov has some impressive analysis refuting 11...♘xc3. The main line runs 12 ♕d2 ♘b5 13 ♗b2 ♘c5 14 ♗a2 e4 15 ♘g5! exd3 16 ♖e5! ♘e6 17 ♘xh7! ♖e8! (17...♔xh7 18 ♖h5+ ♔g8 19 ♗xe6 fxe6 20 ♖h8+! ♔f7 21 ♕f4+ ♔e7 22 ♕g5+ ♔d7 23 ♕xg7+) 18 ♘g5! dxc2 19 ♕xc2 ♘xg5 20 ♖d1 ♗d7 21 ♖xe8+ ♕xe8 22 ♕g6 and White's attack is decisive.

12 c4! ♘e7

Kasparov also gives the lines 12...♘c7? 13 ♗b2 f6 14 c5+ ♔h8 15 d4 and 12...a4!? cxd5 axb3 14 dxc6 bxc2 15 ♕xc2 bxc6 16 ♗b2!.

13 ♘g5! h6 14 ♘e4

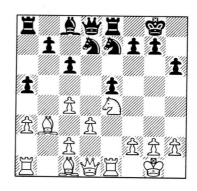

Once again the potential of the bishop pair promises White an advantage. Kasparov-Bareev, Linares 1993, continued 14...a4 15 ♗a2 c5 16 ♘d6 ♖f8 17 c3! ♘g6 18 ♗b1! ♘f6 19 ♘xc8 ♕xc8 20 ♕f3 and White was better.

A2)
4...♗e7

With this move, Black shows he is quite

content to develop before making plans in the centre. More often than not, Black will simply play ...d7-d6, rather than ...d7-d5.

5 0-0

5 ♘xe5?? ♛a5+ has caught out more than one person. Another move, though, is 5 ♘c3 (see Variation E).

5...d6

Alternatively:

a) 5...b5!?, trying to claim space on the queenside, is an interesting strategy. Emms-I.Sokolov, Hastings 2000, continued 6 ♗b3 d6 7 c3 a5 8 ♘bd2 (8 a4!?, preventing Black's expansion on the queenside, is a suggestion of the Hungarian GM Peter Lukacs; he gives 8...b4 9 ♖e1 0-0 10 d4 ♘bd7 11 ♘bd2 with a slight advantage to White) 8...a4 9 ♗c2 0-0 10 d4 ♘bd7 11 ♖e1 ♖e8 12 ♘f1 ♗f8 13 ♘g3 ♛c7 (13...♗b7!?) 14 h3 g6 15 ♗e3 ♗g7 16 ♛d2 ♘f8 17 ♗d3 ♘e6 18 ♖ac1 ♗d7 and now, instead of 19 c4?! exd4 20 ♘xd4 bxc4 21 ♘xe6 ♗xe6 22 ♗xc4, I should have kept an edge with 19 ♗b1 c5 20 d5 ♘d8.

b) 5...♛c7!? (keeping options open with the d-pawn) 6 ♖e1 0-0 and now:

b1) 7 ♘bd2!? d5 8 ♗b3 ♘bd7 9 exd5 (9 d4!? dxe4 10 ♘xe4 exd4 11 ♛xd4 looks interesting) 9...cxd5 10 c4 d4 11 ♘xd4 ♘c5 12 ♘b5 ♛d8 13 ♖xe5 ♘xd3 14 ♖e2 (Larsen-Yusupov, Linares 1983), and here Larsen gives the equalising 14...♗c5! 15 ♘f3 ♘g4 16 ♗e3 ♘xe3 17 fxe3 ♘f4 18 ♖e1 ♘d3.

b2) 7 ♗b3 d6 (7...♘a6 8 d4! d6 9 c3 is

good for White) 8 c3 ♘bd7 9 d4 b5 10 ♘bd2 (10 a4!?) 10...a5 11 ♘f1 a4 12 ♗c2 ♖e8 13 ♘g3 ♘b6 and the position was level, Mainka-Mikhalcisin, Dortmund 1998.

b3) 7 h3!? d5 8 exd5 cxd5 9 ♗b3 ♘c6 10 ♘c3 and Black centre is under some pressure. Note that the natural 10...♗e6? is met by 11 ♘xe5! ♘xe5 12 ♗f4 ♘fd7 13 d4, and White wins material.

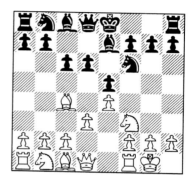

6 ♖e1

White has two other possibilities here:

a) 6 ♗b3 0-0 7 c3 ♗g4!? (7...♘bd7 8 ♖e1 ♘c5 9 ♗c2 ♗g4 10 h3 ♗h5 11 ♘bd2 ♘e6 reaches the same position after eleven moves) 8 ♘bd2 ♘bd7 9 h3 ♗h5 10 ♖e1 ♘c5 11 ♗c2 ♘e6 12 ♘f1 ♘d7! (12...♘e8 13 ♘1h2 ♗g5 14 d4 gave White a pull in Psakhis-Tseshkovsky, Vilnius 1980) 13 ♘g3 ♗xf3 14 ♛xf3 g6 15 ♗e3 ♗g5 and Black has equalised, Gelfand-Yusupov, Munich 1994.

b) 6 h3!? (preventing black ideas involving ...♗g4) 6...0-0 7 ♖e1 ♘bd7 8 a4!? a5 (8...d5 9 exd5 cxd5 10 ♗a2 e4 11 dxe4 dxe4 12 ♘g5 ♗c5 13 ♘c3 was clearly better for White in Vogt-Magerramov, Baku 1980) 9 ♘c3!? h6 (9...♘c5!? 10 d4 exd4 11 ♘xd4 ♖e8 12 ♛f3 gave White an edge in Lau-Treppner, German Bundesliga 1982, while 9...♛c7 is a suggestion from *ECO*) 10 ♗a2 ♖e8 11 d4 ♗f8 12 ♗e3 ♛c7 13 ♘h4 b6 14 dxe5 dxe5 15 ♛f3 ♗c5 16 ♘f5 and White has a very powerful bishop on a2, Vogt-Chekhov, Halle

1981.

6...0-0 7 ♘bd2 ♘bd7 8 a3 ♘c5

8...h6?! is a bit slow: White is better after 9 ♗a2 ♖e8 10 ♘f1 ♘f8 11 ♘g3 ♗e6 12 ♗xe6 ♘xe6 13 d4 (Larsen-Torre, Brussels 1987). White also keeps a typical edge after 8...♕c7 9 ♗a2 b5 10 ♘f1 a5 11 ♘g3 ♘c5 12 c3 ♗e6 13 d4 ♗xa2 14 ♖xa2 ♘e6 15 b3 ♖fe8 16 ♖d2 ♗f8 17 ♗b2 ♖ad8, as in the game Anand-I.Sokolov, London (rapid) 1995.

9 ♗a2

9 ♘f1 d5 10 exd5 cxd5 11 ♗a2 e4 12 dxe4 ♘cxe4 13 ♗e3 a6 14 c4 dxc4 led to an early handshake in Nunn-Rozentalis, Hastings 1997/8, although there is still much to play for in the final position.

9...♖e8 10 ♘f1 ♗f8 11 ♘g3 g6

Lukacs suggests 11...♗e6!? as an improvement.

12 h3 ♗g7 13 c3 d5 14 exd5

14 b4 ♘cd7 15 ♗g5 also looks better for White.

14...♘xd5 15 ♗g5 f6 16 ♗e3

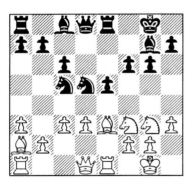

We have been following the game Kornev-Balashov, Samara 2000. After 16...♘e6 Lukacs suggests 17 ♕d2 ♕d6 18 ♗h6 as a way to keep a white advantage.

B)

3...♘c6

Along with 3...c6, this is a very popular move. Black simply develops another piece (knights before bishops!), and keeps his options open over the placement of his dark-squared bishop.

4 ♘c3

This is the move which keeps White's options open regarding the f2-f4 thrust. 4 ♘f3 would simply transpose into the Two Knights Defence, which lies outside the repertoire.

We've now reached a very important crossroads. Black must choose between:

B1: 4...♗c5
B2: 4...♘a5
B3: 4...♗b4

Other moves are less important:

a) 4...♗e7 (this passive move is seen from time to time) 5 f4! d6 6 ♘f3 0-0 (or 6...exf4 7 ♗xf4 ♘a5 8 ♗b3 ♘xb3 9 axb3 0-0 10 0-0 and White has the better structure and more active pieces, Mirumian-Ho Cheng Fai, Yerevan Olympiad 1996; note that 6...♗g4 7 0-0 ♘d4?! 8 fxe5 dxe5? fails to 9 ♗xf7+!) 7 0-0 ♗g4 (or 7...♘d4 8 fxe5 ♘xf3+ 9 ♕xf3 dxe5 10 ♕g3 and White has an automatic kingside attack, Mirumian-Hala, Czech League 1998) 8 h3 (8 ♕e1!? is also interesting; G.Mohr-Rozakis, Ikaria 1993 led to a quick conclusion after 8...♕d7 9 f5 ♗xf3 10 ♖xf3 ♘d4 11 ♖h3! ♘xc2 12 ♕h4 ♘xa1 13 ♗g5 c6 14 ♗xf6 h6 15 ♖g3 ♗xf6 16 ♕xf6 g5 17 ♕g6+ 1-0) 8...♗xf3 9 ♕xf3 ♘d4 10 ♕f2 c6 11 a4 and I prefer White. Isaacson-Assar, Munich 1958, continued 11...♕c7 12 ♗e3 c5 13 f5 a6

14 a5 ♘c6 15 g4 h6 16 ♘d5 ♘xd5 17 ♗xd5 and now 17...♘xa5 is answered by 18 ♕d2 ♘c6 19 ♗xh6!.

b) 4...d6 5 f4 ♘a5 (5...♗e7 transposes into the previous note) 6 f5! ♘xc4 7 dxc4 g6 8 g4 gxf5 (8...h5? 9 g5 ♘h7 10 f6 incarcerates Black's kingside pieces) 9 gxf5 ♗d7 10 ♕f3 ♗c6 11 ♘h3! ♖g8 12 ♘f2 a6 13 ♗e3 b5 14 0-0-0 bxc4 15 ♕e2 ♕b8 16 ♕xc4 ♕b7 17 ♖hg1 ♖xg1 18 ♖xg1 and White has a strong initiative, Morovic Fernandez-Yurtaev, Yerevan Olympiad 1996.

B1)
4...♗c5

With this natural move Black develops his dark-squared bishop onto its most active square.

5 f4!

The most aggressive move. White aims to reach a position that can also arise from the King's Gambit Declined.

5...d6

Black has two noteworthy alternatives
a) 5...0-0!? 6 ♘f3 (6 f5!?) and now:

a1) 6...♘g4!? 7 ♖f1!? (7 ♘g5?! d5! 8 exd5 exf4 9 dxc6? ♕xg5! was awful for White in A.Ledger-Yeo, British League 1998, but 7 ♕e2!? also looks fine) 7...♘xh2 8 ♖h1 ♘xf3+ 9 ♕xf3 and White has the use of a very nice half-open h-file.

a2) 6...exf4 7 ♗xf4 ♘a5 8 ♗g5 ♘xc4 9 dxc4 ♗e7 10 ♕d4 d6 11 0-0-0 ♗e6 12 e5

♘e8 13 ♗xe7 ♕xe7 14 ♖he1 and White has some pressure in the centre, Skytte-De Vreugt, Yerevan 2000.

b) 5...d5!? 6 ♘xd5 ♘xd5 7 ♗xd5 ♗xg1!? 8 ♖xg1 ♘e7 9 ♗b3 exf4 10 ♗xf4 ♕d4; Here Korneev believes that Black has some compensation for the pawn, but after 11 ♖f1 I don't see it.

6 ♘f3

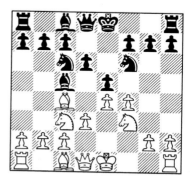

With this move we transpose into a variation of the King's Gambit Declined, which arises after 1 e4 e5 2 f4 ♗c5 3 ♘f3 d6 4 ♘c3 ♘f6 5 ♗c4 ♘c6 6 d3. Theoretically speaking, Black hasn't found a clear route to equality from here, and from a practical viewpoint White has scored quite reasonably from this position (57% on my database; the average for White is 55%).

Black now has three main moves:
B11: 6...♗g4
B12: 6...0-0
B13: 6...a6

a) After 6...♘g4 White has no need to venture into the complications of 7 ♘g5 (they may well be good for White), because 7 ♕e2 leads to a safe and substantial advantage, for example 7...♗f2+ 8 ♔f1 ♘d4 9 ♘xd4 ♗xd4 10 f5 ♕h4 11 g3 ♕h3+ 12 ♕g2 ♕xg2+ 13 ♔xg2 c6 14 ♔f3 ♘f6 15 ♗g5 and Black is very cramped, Kopal-Kalivoda, Czech Team Championship 1995.

b) 6...♘a5!? (this move is underrated) 7

$\&$b3! (7 f5?! allows 7...$\lozenge$xc4 8 dxc4 $\&$b4! 9 $\&$d3 $\&$xc3+ 10 bxc3, after which White is left with the so-called 'Irish Pawn Centre' – not a recommendation!) 7...$\lozenge$xb3 8 axb3 a6 9 $\&$e2 (preparing $\&$e3) and now:

b1) 9...$\&$e7 10 $\&$e3 $\&$xe3 11 $\&$xe3 0-0 (11...$\&$d7?! 12 fxe5 $\lozenge$g4 13 $\&$d2 $\lozenge$xe5 14 $\lozenge$d5 gave White the initiative in Mitkov-Rocha, Porto 2000) 12 0-0 and White has a slight advantage.

b2) 9...$\&$g4 10 fxe5 (10 f5 h6 11 $\&$e3 $\&$d4 12 0-0 0-0 13 h3 $\&$xf3 14 $\&$xf3 Ξe8 was equal in Tischbierek-Smagin, Dresden 1985) 10...dxe5 11 $\&$e3 and White will continue with 0-0.

c) 6...$\&$e6 7 $\&$b5! a6 (7...$\&$d7 8 $\lozenge$a4 $\lozenge$d4 9 $\&$xd7+ $\lozenge$xd7 10 $\lozenge$xc5 dxc5 11 0-0 $\lozenge$xf3+ 12 $\&$xf3 0-0 13 $\&$g3 gives White good attacking chances on the kingside, Emms-Anand, Oakham 1986) 8 $\&$xc6+ bxc6 9 f5!? (9 fxe5 dxe5 10 $\&$e2 and 11 $\&$e3 also promises an advantage – Black has no real compensation for his split pawns on the queenside) 9...$\&$c8 (or 9...$\&$d7 10 $\&$e2 $\&$b8 11 $\lozenge$d1 $\&$b5 12 c3 a5 13 $\&$e3 $\&$c8 14 0-0 $\&$a6 15 c4 $\&$b6 16 $\&$h1 $\&$xe3 17 $\lozenge$xe3 $\lozenge$d7 18 g4 f6 19 g5 with a clear advantage, Fedorov-Norri, European Team Championship, Pula 1997) 10 h3 $\&$e7 11 g4

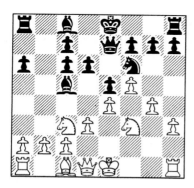

11...$\&$b7 12 $\&$e2 d5 13 $\&$d2 $\lozenge$d7 14 0-0-0 d4 15 $\lozenge$a4 $\&$d6 16 g5 and White has the initiative on the kingside, W.Adams-Yerhoff, Pittsburgh 1946.

6...$\&$g4

Pinning the knight. This is Black's most logical move and also the most popular.
7 $\lozenge$a4!

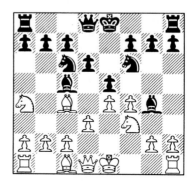

White gets ready to exchange this knight for the bishop on c5. With this done, White will be able to castle kingside.

Black now has two main tries:
B111: 6...$\&$xf3
B112: 6...$\&$b6

Alternatively:

a) 7...$\lozenge$h5 8 $\lozenge$xc5 dxc5 9 f5 $\lozenge$f6 10 $\&$e3 $\&$d6 11 h3 $\&$xf3 12 $\&$xf3 $\lozenge$a5 13 $\&$b5+ c6 14 $\&$a4 b5 15 $\&$d2! $\lozenge$b7 16 $\&$b3 and White was better, J.Kristiansen-Nielsen, Danish Championship 1992.

b) 7...$\lozenge$d4 8 $\lozenge$xc5 dxc5 9 c3! $\lozenge$xf3+ 10 gxf3

10...♗h5 (10...♘xe4? 11 0-0! wins material) 11 ♕e2 (but now 11 fxe5?! is answered by 11...♘xe4!) 11...♕d6 (or 11...♕e7 12 0-0 0-0-0 13 ♕f2 ♘d7 14 ♕g3 and I like White, Pantaleoni-Molzahn, correspondence 1993) 12 ♖g1 g6 13 fxe5 ♕xe5 14 ♗e3 and White's two bishops and pawn centre give him a clear advantage.

B111)
7...♗xf3 8 ♕xf3 ♘d4 9 ♕d1!

For the record, 9 ♕g3!? is also promising, albeit in a more complicated way.
9...b5 10 ♗xf7+!

This sacrifice is much stronger than 10 ♘xc5 bxc4! 11 fxe5 dxc5 12 exf6 ♕xf6, which looks at least equal for Black.
10...♔xf7 11 ♘xc5 dxc5

Black should accept the material. 11...exf4?! 12 ♘b3 ♘e6 (or 12...♘xb3 13 axb3 g5 14 0-0, followed by g2-g3) 13 0-0 g5 14 g3! fxg3 15 ♗xg5 gxh2+ 16 ♔h1 ♘xg5 17 ♕h5+ ♔e7 18 ♕xg5 left Black in big trouble in the game Lane-S.Jackson, British Championship 1989.
12 fxe5 ♘d7 13 c3

It was the Russian grandmaster Yuri Balashov who came up with this move, which is more accurate than 13 0-0-0 ♔g8 14 c3 ♘xe5!. As Tim Harding wrote in *Bishop's Opening*, 'Balashov's improvement appears to guarantee White a slight initiative at worst, and a winning attack if Black tries to hold his

extra material. This is remarkable since White is undeveloped!' Nothing much has happened in the past 28 years to alter this assessment.
13...♘e6
If Black tries to return the piece immediately with 13...♘xe5, White has the very strong reply 14 ♕h5+! and now

a) 14...♔g8 15 ♕xe5 ♕h4+ (15...♘c2+ loses after 16 ♔d2 ♘xa1 17 ♕e6+ ♔f8 18 ♖f1+) 16 g3 ♘f3+ 17 ♔e2 ♘xe5 18 gxh4 and White is a clear pawn ahead. Note that 18...♖d8 19 ♗g5 ♖xd3 loses material after 20 ♗f4.

b) 14...g6? 15 ♕xe5 ♘c2+ 16 ♔d2 ♘xa1 17 ♖f1+ ♔g8 18 ♕e6+ ♔g7 19 ♖f7+ ♔h6 20 ♕h3+ ♔g5 21 ♔d1 mate.

c) 14...♘g6 15 ♖f1+ ♔e8 16 ♗g5 ♕d7 17 cxd4 ♕xd4 18 0-0-0 and White has a clear plus – Black's king is stuck in the centre.

d) 14...♔e6 15 ♕h3+! (15 cxd4 ♕xd4 16 ♕f5+ ♔d6 17 ♗f4 ♖ad8 is unclear – Harding) 15...♔f7 (or 15...♔d6 16 cxd4 cxd4 17 ♗f4 and Black's king is on a dizzy walk) 16 0-0+ ♔g8 17 cxd4 ♕xd4+ 18 ♗e3 ♕d6 19 ♖ad1 and again Black is in big trouble, for example 19...♕e7 20 ♗xc5! ♕xc5+ 21 d4 ♕b6 22 ♕h5!.
14 0-0+ ♔e8
Also possible is 14...♔g8 15 d4 cxd4 16 cxd4 ♘xe5!? (Korchnoi's idea; 16...h6 17 ♕b3 ♔e8 18 ♗e3 leaves White with excellent compensation for the piece) 17 dxe5 ♕xd1 18 ♖xd1 ♔f7 and White has an endgame advantage, Rahman-Lodhi, Dhaka 1995.
15 d4 cxd4 16 cxd4

see following diagram

The stem game Balashov-Matanovic, Skopje 1970 concluded 16...♕e7? 17 ♗e3 ♖f8 18 d5 ♖xf1+ 19 ♕xf1 ♘d8 20 e6 ♘f6 21 ♖c1! ♘xe4 22 ♕xb5+ c6 23 ♖xc6! ♔f8 24 ♖c1 ♔g8 25 ♖c7! ♕d6 26 ♕e8+ ♕f8 27 ♖xg7+! 1-0. Instead of 16...♕e7, Black should restrict White's advantage by giving back the piece with 16...♘xe5! 17 dxe5 ♕xd1 18 ♖xd1 ♔e7.

B112)
7...♗b6

This move doesn't look too threatening, but in fact White must play carefully if he wants to keep the advantage.

8 ♘xb6

This move is made automatically, but there is some point to delaying it and playing 8 c3!? instead. The main point is seen in the variation 8...exf4 9 ♗xf4 ♘h5 10 ♗g5! ♕xg5 (10...♗xf3 11 ♗xf7+!) 11 ♗xf7+! ♔e7 12 ♘xg5 ♗xd1 13 ♖xd1! (with an exchange on b6, the a-pawn would now be hanging) 13...♘f4 14 ♘xb6 axb6 15 0-0 h6 16 ♖xf4 hxg5 17 ♖ff1 and White went on to win in Jonkman-Ellenbroek, Leeuwarden 1995. Compare this to 9...exf4 below.

8...axb6 9 c3

Alternatively:

a) 9 0-0 is the developing move White would like to play. Unfortunately Black can equalise with 9...♗xf3! (but not 9...♘d4? 10 fxe5 dxe5 11 ♗xf7+!, as in Mitkov-Mikhalevski, Mamaia 1991) 10 ♖xf3 (10 gxf3 is answered by 10...♘a5, and 10 ♕xf3 by 10...♘d4 11 ♕d1 b5) 10...♘d4 11 ♖g3!? b5 12 c3 bxc4 13 cxd4 cxd3 14 ♕xd3 0-0.

b) 9 a3!? has the same motive as 9 c3 – to retain the c4-bishop, However, White has problems as the d4-sqaure isn't covered. After 9...exf4!? 10 ♗xf4 ♘h5!? (10...d5!? 11 exd5 ♘xd5 12 ♕e2+ ♔f8! was unclear in Finkel-Mikhalevski, Israel 1999) 11 ♗e3 (11 ♗g5 ♗xf3 12 ♕xf3 ♕xg5 13 ♗xf7+ ♔d8 14 ♕xh5 ♕xg2 is probably a bit better for Black) 11...♘e5 12 ♗b3 ♕f6 Black has sufficient counterplay.

9...0-0

9...d5 10 exd5 ♘xd5 11 h3! ♗xf3 12 ♕xf3 ♘f4 13 0-0 0-0 14 ♗xf4 exf4 15 ♕xf4 ♕d7 16 d4 was better for White in Todorovic-Blagojevic, Herceg Novi 2001; he has a strong centre and a superior minor piece.

Interesting, however, is the immediate 9...exf4!? 10 ♗xf4

Now after 10...d5 11 exd5 ♘xd5 12 ♕e2+! ♔f8 13 ♗g3 White has a clear advantage. Stronger, however, is 10...♘h5!? and now:

a) 11 ♗g5!? with a further split:

a1) 11...♗xf3? 12 ♗xf7+! ♔f8 (12...♔xf7

loses to 13 ♕b3+!) 13 ♕xf3 ♕xg5 14 ♗xh5+ and White is a pawn ahead.

a2) 11...f6 12 ♗e3 ♘e5 13 ♗b3 sees the point of inducing ...f7-f6: Black queen has no route to the kingside.

a3) 11...♕xg5! 12 ♗xf7+ ♔e7 13 ♘xg5 ♗xd1 14 ♔xd1 (14 ♖xd1 h6 15 ♗xh5 hxg5 16 ♗e2 ♖xa2 looks equal) 14...♘f4 15 ♗c4 ♘e5 and Black will regain his pawn.

b) 11 ♗e3 ♘e5 12 ♗b3! (12 0-0?! ♘xc4 13 dxc4 ♕e7 was fine for Black in Zukertort-Anderssen, Leipzig 1877, while 12 ♗b5+ c6 13 d4 ♗xf3 14 gxf3 cxb5 15 dxe5 dxe5 16 ♕xd8+ ♖xd8 17 ♗xb6 ♖d3 looks equal) 12...♗xf3 13 gxf3. Now after 13...♕h4+ 14 ♔d2 Keres assessed the position as better for White. Instead Black should play 13...♕f6! and now:

b1) 14 0-0 ♘f4 15 ♗xf4 ♕xf4 16 d4 ♘g6 17 ♕c1 was equal in De Vilder-Kroeze, Bussum 1995.

b2) 14 d4!? ♕xf3 (14...♘xf3+ 15 ♔e2 g5 16 ♗d5 c6 17 e5!) 15 ♕xf3 ♘xf3+ 16 ♔e2 ♘h4 17 ♖af1 and the two bishops and open lines gives White reasonable compensation for the pawn.

10 0-0 exf4

10...d5 11 exd5 ♘xd5 12 h3 ♗xf3 13 ♕xf3 ♘xf4 14 ♗xf4 exf4 15 ♕xf4 is better for White, as discussed in the note to Black's 9th move.

After 10...♘a5 White can keep the bishop with 11 ♗b5, for example 11...♕e7 12 b4 ♘c6 13 f5 d5 14 ♕e1 ♘a7!? 15 ♗a4 dxe4 16 dxe4 ♘c8 17 ♗b3 and White kept the advantage in Tait-Hawkins, correspondence 1993.

11 ♗xf4 ♘h5

After 11...♘e5 12 ♗xe5 dxe5 13 h3 ♗xf3 14 ♕xf3 ♕e7 15 ♖f2! White will follow up with ♖af1 and perhaps g2-g4-g5, increasing the pressure on f7.

12 ♗e3

Also possible is 12 ♕d2!? ♘xf4 13 ♕xf4 and now:

a) 13...♗xf3 14 ♖xf3 ♘e5 15 ♖g3! ♔h8

(15...♘xc4? loses to 16 ♕h6 g6 17 ♖h3!) 16 ♗b3 and White is better, Kuijf-Leventic, Mitropa Cup 1995.

b) 13...♗e6! 14 ♗xe6 fxe6 15 ♕g4 ♖f6 16 d4 ♕e7 and Black has equalised, Torres-Pergericht, Novi Sad Olympiad 1990.

12...♘e5!?

After 13 ♗b3 ♔h8 (Arizmendi Martinez-Jonkman, Reykjavik 2000) Black has promising counterplay with ...f7-f5.

The queen sacrifice with 13 ♘xe5!? looks more critical. Play continues with 13...♗xd1 14 ♘xf7 ♕e7 (14...♖xf7 15 ♖xf7 is good for White) 15 ♘xd6+ ♔h8 16 ♘f7+ ♔g8 17 ♖axd1 (naturally White can take a draw via a perpetual, but why not play for more?) 17...♘f6 18 e5 b5 19 ♗b3 c5 (19...♖xf7 20 ♗d4!) and now, instead of 20 ♖de1 c4!, which was unclear in Mitkov-Sharif, Lyon 1993, White should play 20 ♗xc5!! (Fritz) 20...♕xc5+ 21 d4, when White has the advantage despite having only a minor piece for the queen. For example 21...♕b6 22 exf6 gxf6 23 ♘e5+ ♔g7 24 ♘d7, 21...♕a7 22 exf6, gxf6 23 ♖d3!, or 21...♕c7 22 exf6 gxf6 23 ♖d3! ♖xf7 24 ♖xf6.

B12)

6...0-0

A sensible looking move, but in some ways Black is just 'castling into it'.

7 f5

Establishing the impressive pawn wedge,

which is the basis of a quick kingside attack. White can also play for an advantage, as against 6...♗g4, with the move 7 ♘a4, for example 7...♗b6 8 ♘xb6 axb6 9 fxe5 (9 0-0 ♘a5! is annoying, while after 9 a3!? exf4 10 ♗xf4 d5 11 exd5 ♖e8+ 12 ♔f1 ♘xd5 13 ♗xd5 ♕xd5 14 ♗xc7 ♗g4 Black has compensation for the pawn) 9...♘xe5 10 ♘xe5 dxe5 11 ♗g5 (11 0-0?! ♕d4+ 12 ♔h1 ♘xe4!; 11 ♕f3!?) 11...♕d6 12 ♕f3 ♗g4 13 ♕g3 ♗h5 14 ♕h4 and White has an edge, Ochsner-A.Christiansen, Aarhus 1983.

7...h6

Black takes steps to prevent the annoying pin with ♗g5. Alternatives include:

a) 7...♘a5 8 ♗g5 c6 9 a3 b5 (9...♘xc4 10 dxc4 h6 11 ♗h4 a5 12 ♕d2 a4 13 g4 gave White a strong attack in Nun-Lehner, Oberwart 1992) 10 ♗a2 ♘b7 11 g4 and White's initiative is very threatening, Becker-Lejlic, Berlin 1997.

b) 7...♘d4 8 ♗g5 c6 9 a3 h6 10 ♗h4 b5 11 ♗a2 a5 12 g4 g5 13 fxg6 ♗xg4 14 ♗xf7+ ♔g7 15 ♘xd4 ♗xd4 (Fischer-Puto, Cicero simultaneous 1964) and now the great man could have won with 16 ♗xf6+ ♕xf6 17 ♕xg4 ♕f2+ 18 ♔d1.

8 ♘d5

8 ♕e2?! is dubious on account of 8...♘d4 9 ♘xd4 exd4! 10 ♘d5 (or 10 ♘a4 ♗xf5!) 10...♘xd5 11 ♗xd5 c6 12 ♗b3 ♗xf5!.

8 a3!?, giving the bishop an escape square on a2, is playable though. The game Jakubowski-Lopusiewicz, Koszalin 1998, continued 8...♘d4 9 ♘xd4 exd4 10 ♘d5 ♘xd5 11 ♗xd5 c6 12 ♗b3 ♕h4+ 13 g3 ♕h3 14 ♕f3 ♖e8 15 ♖f1 d5 16 ♗d2 ♗d6 17 ♖f2 ♗d7 18 0-0-0 dxe4 19 dxe4 c5 20 ♗c4 h5 21 ♕b3! ♖e7 22 ♗g5 and White went on to win the game.

8...♘d4

Black should consider 8...♘a5!?, although after 9 ♘xf6+ ♕xf6 10 g4! ♘xc4 11 dxc4 White still has a powerful attack.

9 ♘xf6+ ♕xf6 10 ♘xd4 ♗xd4 11 c3 ♗b6 12 ♕h5!

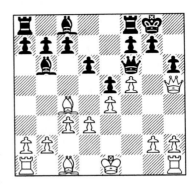

In the game Hebden-Martinovsky, London 1986, Black played 12...c6, and now Gary Lane's suggestion of 13 g4 gives White an awesome attack.

B13)
6...a6

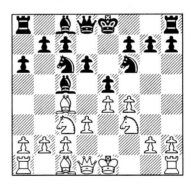

With this move Black expends a tempo in order to nullify the threat of ♘a4 and thus he preserves his dark-squared bishop. White has quite a few ways to proceed now, but I will just be concentrating on two suggestions:
B131: 7 f5
B132: 7 ♘d5

B131)
7 f5 h6

Once again Black takes steps to prevent ♗g5.

The other possibility is here is to attack

the bishop with 7...♘a5, for example 8 a3!? (8 ♗g5 b5! 9 ♗b3 c6 10 ♕d2 ♕b6 looks unclear) 8...♘xc4 9 dxc4 h6 (or 9...c6 10 ♗g5 b5 11 ♕d3 bxc4 12 ♕xc4 a5 13 ♗xf6 gxf6 14 ♘a4 ♗a6 15 ♕c3 ♗a7 16 ♕xc6+ ♔e7 17 0-0-0 with a clear advantage, Schlechter-Janowski, Budapest 1896). After 9...h6 White can proceed in two ways:

a) 10 ♕d3 0-0 11 ♗e3 gives White an edge according to *ECO* (but not 11 h3? ♗xf5!, as in Nikolaev-Faibisovich, USSR 1975).

b) 10 ♕e2!? also looks reasonable, for example 10...♗d7 11 ♗e3 ♗xe3 12 ♕xe3 b5 13 c5 0-0? (13...♕b8 is stronger) 14 0-0-0 ♕b8 15 g4! ♘xg4 16 ♕d2! ♔h8 17 ♖hg1 ♘f6

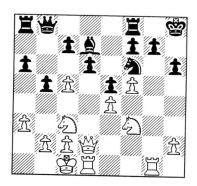

18 ♖xg7! ♔xg7 19 ♖g1+ ♔h7 20 ♘g5+! ♔h8 (20...hxg5 21 ♕xg5 wins) 21 ♘e6! ♘h7 22 ♕xh6 ♖g8 23 ♖g7! ♖xg7 24 ♕xg7 mate, Hartston-Richardson, London 1983.

8 ♘d5

It's also possible to keep the light-squared bishop with 8 a3!? and now:

a) 8...♘g4 9 ♕e2 ♗f2+ 10 ♔f1 ♗a7 11 h3 ♘f6 12 g4 and again Black is cramped on the kingside, Buchanan-Robertson, Scottish Championship 1996

b) 8...g6!? 9 fxg6 fxg6 10 ♘d5 ♘xd5 11 ♗xd5 ♕e7 (Perez-Garcia Bueno, Mondariz 2000) 12 ♕e2! ♗e6 13 ♗xc6+ bxc6 14 ♗e3 ♗xe3 15 ♕xe3 and I prefer White: it's not clear what Black should do with his king.

c) 8...♘e7 9 ♕e2 g6 10 fxg6 ♘xg6 11 ♗d2 ♘h5 12 g3 ♘g7 13 ♖f1 ♗e6 14 ♗xe6 ♘xe6 15 0-0-0 c6 16 ♗e3 ♕e7 17 ♗xc5 dxc5 18 ♕f2 0-0-0 19 ♘d2 with an edge, Schiffers-Von Bardeleben, Frankfurt 1887

d) 8...♕e7?! 9 ♘d5 ♘xd5 10 ♗xd5 ♗d7 11 c3 0-0-0 12 ♕e2 g6 13 b4 ♗b6 14 fxg6 fxg6 15 ♗e3! ♗xe3 16 ♕xe3 ♘b8 17 0-0 ♖df8 18 a4 and White's pawn attack on the queenside is virtually decisive, Emms-Olesen, Hillerod 1995

e) 8...♘d4!? (a suggestion of the Scottish grandmaster Paul Motwani) 9 ♘xd4 ♗xd4 10 ♘d5 (10 ♕f3!?) 10...♘xd5 11 ♗xd5 c6 12 ♗b3 g6!? with an unclear position.

8...♘a5

Given the chance, Black should whip the bishop off. Instead 8...♘d4?! 9 c3 ♘xf3+ 10 ♕xf3 c6 11 ♘xf6+ ♕xf6 12 g4 b5 13 ♗b3 ♗b7 14 h4 0-0-0 15 g5 ♕e7 16 f6 gxf6 17 gxh6 gave Black many problems in Tomescu-Bracaglia, Padova 1999.

9 b4!?

9 ♕e2 b5 10 ♗b3 ♘xb3 11 ♘xf6+ ♕xf6 12 axb3 ♗b7 13 ♗e3, as in Gallagher-Davidovic, Szolnok 1987, is probably enough for a small advantage.

9...♘xd5

English GM Stuart Conquest gives the line 9...♘xc4 10 ♘xf6+ ♕xf6 11 bxc5 ♘a5 12 ♗b2, assessing the position as slightly better for White.

10 bxc5

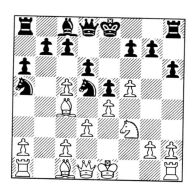

The game Conquest-Smejkal, German Bundesliga 1996, continued 10...♘f6 11 ♗b3 dxc5 12 ♘xe5 ♘xb3 13 axb3 ♕d4!? (13...♗xf5 14 ♗b2 ♗e6 15 0-0 gives White good play on the dark squares) 14 ♗f4 ♘xe4 15 dxe4 ♕xe4+ 16 ♕e2 ♕xe2+ 17 ♔xe2 ♗xf5 18 ♔d2! and White's knight was worth slightly more than Black's three extra pawns. In his notes to the game Conquest suggests 10...♘xc4, giving the unclear continuation 11 exd5 ♘a5 12 ♗d2 b6 13 c6 (13 cxb6 cxb6 14 ♗xa5 bxa5 15 0-0 ♗xf5 16 ♘xe5 dxe5 17 ♖xf5 ♕xd5 18 d4 ♕xd4+ 19 ♕xd4 exd4 20 ♖e1 looks equal) 13...♗xf5 14 0-0 0-0 15 ♕e1.

B132)
7 ♘d5

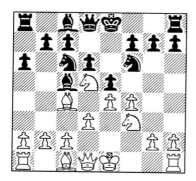

This move has been played by the young Belarussian grandmaster Alexei Fedorov. It certainly makes more sense to move this knight to d5, now that ♘a4 is no longer effective.

7...♗g4

Alternatives include:

a) 7...♗e6?! 8 ♘xf6+ ♕xf6?? 9 f5 ♗xc4 10 ♗g5 and White wins. This trick is well worth remembering.

b) 7...b5? 8 ♘xf6+ ♕xf6 9 ♗d5 ♗b7 10 fxe5 dxe5 11 ♖f1 0-0? 12 ♘g5 1-0 Delanoy-Carrasco, Paris 1994.

c) 7...♘xd5 8 ♗xd5 0-0 (after 8...♕e7 9 c3 ♗g4 10 h3 ♗xf3 11 ♕xf3 White will con-

tinue with ♗d2 and 0-0-0, while after 8...♗e6 9 ♗xc6+ bxc6 10 fxe5 dxe5 White plays 11 ♕e2 and ♗e3) 9 f5 (here comes the attack!) 9...♘d4 10 c3 (10 ♘xd4 ♗xd4 11 ♕h5 c6 12 ♗b3 d5 13 c3 ♗a7 14 ♕f3 dxe4 15 dxe4 ♕b6 16 ♗d2 c5 17 0-0-0 was also good for White, Hresc-Wiechert, Kirchheim 1990) 10...♘xf3+ 11 ♕xf3 c6 12 ♗b3 b5 13 h4 ♔h8 14 g4 ♖a7 15 ♗g5 f6 (or 15...♕b6 16 f6! g6 17 ♗h6) 16 ♗d2 d5 17 0-0-0 and White's attack is stronger, Al.Sokolov-Karpatchev, Nizhnij Novgorod 1998.

d) 7...♗g4!? 8 ♕e2 ♗f2+ 9 ♔f1 (this looks stronger than 9 ♔d1, which was played in Rahman-Booth, Los Angeles 1991) 9...♘d4 10 ♘xd4 ♗xd4 11 c3 ♗a7 12 h3 (12 f5!?) 12...♘f6 13 fxe5 dxe5 14 ♗g5 ♗e6 15 ♕f3 ♗xd5 16 ♗xd5 c6 17 ♗b3 and White can follow up with ♔e2 and ♖hf1.

8 c3

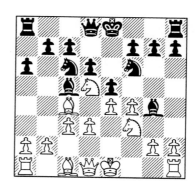

8...0-0

Again Black has a few alternatives:

a) 8...h6!? (preparing ...♗e6) 9 f5 (9 h3 ♗e6!) 9...g6 10 fxg6 fxg6 11 b4 ♗a7 12 ♕e2 and White will play ♗e3.

b) 8...♘xd5 9 ♗xd5 0-0 (9...exf4 10 ♗xf4 0-0 11 d4 ♗b6 12 0-0 was good for White in Sonnet-Poupinel, correspondence – Black's bishop on b6 is out of the game) 10 h3 (10 f5!?) 10...♗e6 11 ♗xc6 bxc6 12 f5 ♗c8 (Jackson-Bisguier, Ventura 1971) and here I like 13 ♕e2, planning ♗e3.

c) 8...♘h5 9 f5! h6 (9...♘e7 10 ♗g5 f6 11

♘e3 is good for White – Bangiev) 10 b4!
♗a7 11 ♗e3 ♘e7 (after 11...♗xe3 12 ♘xe3
♗xf3 13 ♕xf3 ♘f6 14 0-0 0-0 White will
continue with 15 ♔h1 and g4-g5) 12 ♗xa7
♘xd5 13 ♗xd5 ♖xa7 14 0-0 ♘f4 15 ♗b3 h5
16 d4 ♕e7 17 ♕d2 h4 18 ♖ae1 and White
was better, Fedorov-Fyllingen, Aars 1999.

After 8...0-0 White has a few promising
tries:

a) 9 h3 ♗xf3 (but not 9...♗e6?! 10 ♘xf6+
♕xf6? 11 f5 ♗xc4 12 ♗g5!) 10 ♕xf3 ♘a5
11 b4 ♘xc4 12 ♘xf6+ ♕xf6 13 bxc5 ♘a5 14
cxd6 cxd6 15 0-0.

b) 9 b4 ♗a7 10 h3 ♗xf3 11 ♕xf3 ♘xd5
12 ♗xd5 exf4 13 ♗xf4 ♕f6 14 ♖c1 and I
like White's bishop pair, Sebestyen-
Hermann, Sopot 1951.

c) 9 f5 ♘b8!? 10 h3 (10 ♗g5!?) 10...♗xf3
11 ♕xf3 ♘xd5 12 ♗xd5 c6 13 ♗b3 a5 14
♕g4 ♔h8 15 ♗g5 f6 16 ♗d2 a4 17 ♗e6 and
again White is a little better, Laird-Sharif,
Jakarta 1978.

B2)
4...♘a5

Despite Black breaking the 'golden rule' of
moving the same piece twice in the opening,
4...♘a5 should not be underestimated. We've
already seen how effective it can be to exchange this knight for the light-squared
bishop, so expending a couple of tempi to do
this is by no means an extravagance. Indeed,
many white players see this as a spoiler's

move, as the positions that arise are not as
sharp as the ones arising after 4...♗b4 or
4...♗c5 5 f4!.

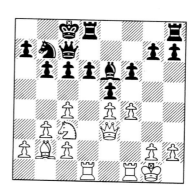

5 ♕f3!?

A speciality of the Australian grandmaster
Ian Rogers, this move has also recently
found support elsewhere. The thinking behind this is that the queen is well placed on
f3, so White moves it there before playing
♘ge2.

The older line is 5 ♘ge2 ♘xc4 (5...c6 is
also possible) 6 dxc4 ♗c5 7 0-0 (but not 7
♗g5? ♗xf2+) 7...d6 8 ♕d3 and now:

a) 8...c6 9 b3!? (9 ♘a4!?) 9...♗e6 10 ♘a4!
♘d7 (10...♗b6? 11 ♗a3 ♗c7 12 ♖ad1 puts
lots of pressure on d6) 11 ♘xc5 ♘xc5 12
♕e3 b6! (12...♕e7 13 ♗a3 b6 14 ♗xc5 dxc5
15 f4 gives White an bigger advantage) 13 f4
f6 14 ♗a3 ♘b7! 15 ♘c3 (15 f5!?) 15...♕c7
16 ♖ad1 0-0-0 17 ♗b2

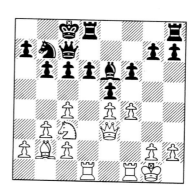

and White is more comfortable, Short-Karpov, Tilburg 1991.

b) 8...♗e6 (this seems more reliable than 8...c6) 9 b3 0-0 10 ♗e3 ♗xe3 11 ♕xe3 ♔h8 12 ♖ad1 (12 f4!?) 12...b6 13 h3 ♘d7 14 ♘g3 with an equal position, Tischbierek-Kuzmin, Biel 1993.

5...♘xc4 6 dxc4 d6

6...♗b4!? is interesting. Rogers-Tunasly, Singapore 1997, continued 7 ♘ge2 d6 8 h3 ♗e6 9 b3 ♘d7 10 0-0 0-0 11 ♘g3 ♕f6 12 ♕xf6 ♘xf6 13 ♗b2 and a roughly equal ending was reached.

7 ♘ge2

If White wants to avoid any ...♗g4 ideas, then playing 7 h3 now looks like a good idea.

7...♗e6

Or 7...♗g4 8 ♕g3 ♗xe2 9 ♔xe2 (White can get away with 'castling by hand' as the centre is fairly closed) 9...♗e7 10 ♖d1 0-0 11 ♔f1 ♕d7 12 ♔g1 ♕e6 13 b3 c6 14 a4 ♗d8 15 a5 a6 16 h3 ♗c7 with a level position, Rogers-Beliavsky, Polanica Zdroj 1996.

8 b3 ♗e7

After 8...c6 9 ♗e3 ♗e7 10 h3 0-0 11 g4 ♕a5 12 ♗d2 ♕c7 13 ♖g1!? White can play for a kingside attack.

9 h3 0-0 10 0-0 c6

Gaining some control over d5 but, at the same time, weakening the d6-pawn. A.Ledger-Spanton, Port Erin 1998 went instead 10...♘d7 11 ♘g3 ♗g5 12 ♘d5 ♗xc1 13 ♖axc1 ♗xd5 14 cxd5 g6 15 c4 a5 16 ♖fe1 ♕g5 17 ♕g4 ♕xg4 18 hxg4 and White held an endgame advantage. The rest of the game is quite instructive: 18...b6 19 f3 ♔g7 20 ♔f2 ♘f6 21 a3 ♘d7 22 ♖c3 ♖h8 23 ♖h1 h6 24 ♔e3 ♖he8 25 ♘e2 ♖a7 26 ♖cc1 ♘c5 27 ♖b1 ♖c8 28 ♘c3 ♘d7 29 ♘b5 ♖aa8 30 ♖h2 ♘f6 31 ♖bh1 h5 32 g5 ♘d7 33 g4 hxg4 34 ♘xc7! ♖ab8 35 ♘e6+! 1-0.

11 ♖d1 ♕c7 12 ♘g3 ♖fd8 13 a4 a5 14 ♗a3

see following diagram

White's position is slightly more comfort-

able; Black must always be aware of pressure on his vulnerable d6-pawn. The game Rogers-Sinclair, New Zealand Championship, continued 14...♖d7 15 ♖d2 ♖ad8 16 ♘d5! cxd5 17 cxd5 ♖c8 18 c4 ♗xd5 19 exd5 ♕b6 20 ♖e1 ♗f8 21 ♖de2 ♖a8 22 ♘f5 ♖c7 23 ♕e3 ♕xe3 24 ♖xe3 ♖d8 25 ♖f3 ♘e8 26 g4 g6 27 ♘g3 and Rogers eventually converted his advantage.

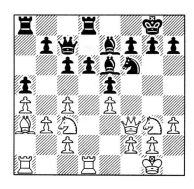

B3)
4...♗b4

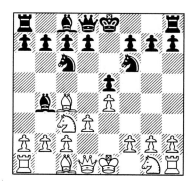

This move is considered by many leading players to be Black's safest response at move four. I also gave this as my recommendation for Black in *Play the Open Games as Black*. By pinning the knight Black prepares the freeing advance ...d7-d5, which in turn makes White very wary of opening up too quickly with f2-f4. For example, the immediate 5 f4?! d5 6 exd5 ♘xd5 7 ♘ge2 ♗g4 gives Black very active play.

5 ♘e2

Protecting the knight on c3 and keeping the option open of playing f2-f4. 5 ♘e2 is sharper than the alternatives 5 ♗g5 and 5 ♘f3.

5...d5

The most consistent reply. Against other moves White can castle and then play for f2-f4. For example, 5...0-0 6 ♗g5 h6 7 ♗xf6 ♕xf6 8 0-0 d6 9 ♘d5 ♕d8 10 c3 ♗a5 11 b4 ♗b6 12 a4 a6 13 ♘xb6 cxb6 14 f4 and White was better, Malivanek-Kulhanek, Czech Team Championship 1998.

6 exd5 ♘xd5 7 0-0

7...♗e6

Protecting the knight is the most popular choice, but Black does have two major alternatives:

a) 7...♗xc3 8 ♘xc3 ♘xc3 9 bxc3 0-0 10 f4! ♘a5 11 ♗b3 exf4 12 ♗xf4 ♘xb3 13 axb3 ♕d5 (or 13...f6 14 ♕h5 ♗e6 15 ♖fe1 ♖e8 16 ♕c5! and White won a pawn in Mirumian-Biolek, Czech Team Championship 1998) 14 ♕e1 f6 15 ♕g3 c5 16 c4! (White has a nice diamond shaped pawn structure!) 16...♕c6 17 c3 b6 18 d4 cxd4 19 cxd4 b5 20 d5 ♕c5+ 21 ♔h1 ♖d8 22 ♗e3 ♕e7 23 ♗d4 and White's passed pawns are very threatening, Lengyel-Von Buelow, Vienna 1996.

b) 7...♘xc3 8 bxc3 and now:

b1) 8...♗d6!? 9 f4 (or 9 ♘g3 0-0 10

♕h5!?) 9...0-0 10 f5 ♕h4?! (10...♘a5 looks stronger) 11 ♗d5 ♘e7 12 ♗e4 ♕h5 13 ♕e1 f6 14 ♗e3 ♔h8 15 ♖f3 and White has the makings of a strong kingside attack, Levitsky-Nikolaev, Kiev 1903.

b2) 8...♗e7 9 ♘g3 (9 f4!?) 9...♘a5 10 ♗b3 0-0 11 ♕h5 ♘xb3 12 axb3 ♖e8 13 ♖e1 ♗e6 14 ♗b2 (there doesn't seem too much wrong with grabbing a pawn by 14 ♖xe5) 14...f6 15 d4 ♗d6 16 ♘e4 ♗f7 17 ♕f3 exd4 18 cxd4 ♗b4 19 c3 ♗f8 20 c4 and White was more active, A.Ledger-Mestel, British Championship 1997.

b3) 8...♗c5 9 d4!? (9 ♘g3 0-0 10 ♖e1 ♕h4 11 ♖e4 ♕f6 12 ♕e2 ♗d7 13 ♖b1 b6 was equal in D.Ledger-Kennaugh, British Championship 1998, but White could try 10 ♕h5!?).

After 9 d4 it's very risky for Black to accept the pawn sacrifice:

b31) 9...exd4 10 cxd4 ♘xd4 11 ♘xd4 ♕xd4 (after 11...♗xd4 12 ♗a3! looks strong – 12...♗xa1 loses after 13 ♕e2+ ♗e6 14 ♗xe6 ♗f6 15 ♗b3+ ♔e7 16 ♖e1) 12 ♕e2+ ♔f8 13 ♗e3 ♕e5 14 ♗xc5+ ♕xc5 15 ♖ad1 and White has more than enough compensation for the pawn.

b32) 9...♗d6 10 a4!? 0-0 11 a5 a6 12 ♘g3 was interesting in Richards-Ford, British League 1999. Note that it's too risky for Black to try and win a pawn with 12...exd4 13 cxd4 ♗xg3, as after 14 fxg3! ♕xd4+ 15 ♕xd4 ♘xd4 16 ♗a3 White keeps the advantage.

After 7...♗e6 I'm giving two possibilities for White.

B31: 8 ♗xd5
B32: 8 ♘e4!?

B31)
8 ♗xd5

Traditionally this has been White's most popular choice. The knight is removed from d5 in preparation for f2-f4.

8...♗xd5 9 f4

9...0-0

Preparing to castle queenside with 9...♕d7 is probably too slow. White can immediately gain a tempo with 10 ♘xd5, and after 10...♕xd5 11 fxe5 0-0-0 12 c3 ♗e7 13 d4 ♘xe5 14 ♘f4 ♕d7 15 ♕b3 White is in control.

10 f5

The point of White's previous play. Instead of meekly exchanging on e5, the f-pawn moves further forward and acts as a spearhead for a white attack on the kingside.

10...♗xc3

A difficult decision to have to make. With this move Black gives up the bishop pair and cedes the d4-square as a possible outpost. On the other hand, White's queenside pawn structure is compromised, and, if kept, the dark-squared bishop could actually prove to be a liability. The other main option is 10...f6 and now:

a) 11 ♘g3 ♗f7 12 ♘ce4 (12 ♗e3 ♗a5 13 ♔h1 ♗b6 14 ♗d2 a5 15 a3 ♘d4 16 ♖c1 ♕e7 17 ♘ce4 c5 18 ♕g4 ♖fd8 19 ♗e3 a4 20 ♖f2 ♖a6 was unclear in Mitkov-Motwani, Yerevan Olympiad 1996) 12...♔h8 13 a3 ♗a5 14 ♔h1 ♘d4 15 ♗e3 with a tense position, Mitkov-Norri, European Team Championship, Pula 1997

b) 11 ♘xd5 (it seems logical to eliminate Black's light-squared bishop) 11...♕xd5 12 ♘g3 and now:

b1) 12...♗c5+ 13 ♔h1 ♖ad8 14 ♘e4 ♗b6 15 ♗d2 and here Black should offer the exchange of bishops with 15...♗a5!. Instead Emms-Eames, London 1997, continued 15...♘d4?, which lost material after 16 c4! ♕c6 17 c5 ♗xc5 18 ♖c1 b6 19 b4.

b2) 12...♖f7 13 ♘e4 ♗f8 14 ♗e3 b6 15 ♕h5 was better for White in Kosteniuk-Shchekachev, Moscow 2000 – White can follow up with ♖f3-h3.

11 bxc3 f6 12 ♘g3

12 c4?! is inaccurate: Emms-Parker, Cambridge 1996, continued 12...♗f7 13 ♖b1 ♗h5! 14 ♕e1 ♗xe2 15 ♕xe2 b6 16 ♗e3 and now instead of 16...♘d4, Black should play 16...♕d6 17 ♖f3 ♘d4 18 ♗xd4 ♕xd4+ 19 ♕f2 ♖fd8, when if anything Black is better due to White's inferior pawn structure.

12...♖e8

12...♘e7 13 c4 ♗c6 14 ♗a3 ♕d7 15 ♕g4 looks promising for White.

13 ♕g4 ♔h8

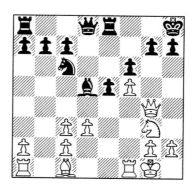

We are following the game A.Ledger-Twyble, British League 1999. After 14 a4 ♕d7 15 ♗a3 ♖ad8 16 ♖ae1 e4!? a very unclear position arose.

B32)
8 ♘e4

This move has been played with some success by the young Romanian player Vigen Mirumian. I think I underestimated the strength of this move when studying it for *Play the Open Games as Black*. Objectively speaking, Black should be okay, but he has to play accurately.

8...♗e7
Alternatively:

a) 8...h6 9 ♘2g3 ♕d7?! 10 ♘h5! 0-0-0 (10...0-0 allows 11 ♗xd5 followed by ♘f6+!) 11 ♘xg7 ♗g4 12 f3 f5 13 fxg4 fxe4 14 dxe4 ♕xg7 15 ♗xd5 ♗c5+ 16 ♔h1 and White went on to win in Mirumian-Brestak, Komarno 1997

b) 8...♕d7 9 ♘g5 0-0-0 10 ♘xe6 ♕xe6 11 a3 ♗c5 12 b4 ♗f8 13 ♘c3 ♘ce7 14 ♕f3 c6 15 ♖e1 and White has strong pressure, Mirumian-Kolar, Czech Team Championship 1998.

c) 8...0-0 9 ♘g5 (9 ♘2g3!? may be stronger) 9...♗g4 10 f3 ♗h5 11 ♘e4 ♔h8 12 ♘4g3 ♗g6 13 ♔h1 ♘ce7 14 f4 exf4 15 ♘xf4 ♘xf4 16 ♗xf4 ♗d6 17 ♕f3 ♗xf4 18 ♕xf4 was equal in Winawer-Alapin, Berlin 1897.

9 ♘2g3!?
9 f4? loses material after 10...exf4 10 ♘xf4 ♘xf4 11 ♗xf4 ♕d4+! 12 ♔h1 ♗xc4, while 9 ♗b3!? 0-0 10 f4 exf4 11 ♘xf4 ♘xf4 12 ♗xf4 ♘d4 was equal in Belkhodja-Hebden, French League 1988.

9...0-0
Or:

a) 9...f5!? 10 ♘g5! ♗xg5 11 ♕h5+ g6 12 ♕xg5 ♕xg5 13 ♗xg5 f4 14 ♘e4 ♔f7 15 f3 (15 ♗h6!? looks stronger) 15...h6 16 ♗xd5 ♗xd5 17 ♗h4 ♗xe4 18 dxe4 g5 19 ♗f2 ♖hd8 20 ♖fd1 with an equal ending, Maidla-Tiilikainen, Tuusula 1997

b) 9...♕d7 10 ♘g5 ♗xg5 11 ♗xg5 f6 12 ♗d2 0-0-0 13 ♘e4 ♕e7 14 ♖b1 ♔b8 15 b4 and White can attack on the queenside, Huber-Wenaas, North Bay 1998.

10 ♕h5!

Now the game Mirumian-Barglowski, Trinec 1998, continued 10...♕d7 11 ♘g5 ♗xg5 12 ♗xg5 f6 13 ♗d2 ♘b6 14 ♗xe6+ ♕xe6 15 f4 exf4 16 ♖xf4 ♕e5 17 ♘f5! and White had a strong attack. 10...♘f4!?, however, looks more resilient. In Dumont-Cipolli, Sao Paulo 1995, Black equalised after 11 ♗xf4 exf4 12 ♘e2 g6 13 ♕f3 ♗xc4 14 dxc4 ♘d4 15 ♘xd4 ♕xd4 16 b3 f5 17 ♘c3 c6 18 ♘e2 (18 ♖ad1!?) 18...♕e4 19 ♘xf4 ♕xc2 20 ♖ae1 ♗b4 21 ♖e2 ♕c3.

C)
3...♗c5

Another natural move. Black develops his dark-squared bishop and prepares to castle.

4 ♘c3

Keeping the option open of f2-f4.

4...d6

Also possible is 4...c6!? and now:

a) 5 f4!? exf4!? (5...d6 see Short-Speelman below) 6 ♗xf4 (6 e5 d5 7 exf6 ♕xf6! looks at least equal for Black) 6...d5 7 exd5 cxd5 8 ♗b5+ ♘c6 9 d4 ♗b6 10 ♘f3 0-0 11 0-0 ♗g4 12 ♘e2 ♘e4 13 c3 f6 14 ♗d3 ♕d7 15 ♕b3 ♖ae8 16 ♖ae1 with a roughly level position, Jaksland-Cooper, Hastings 1995.

b) 5 ♘f3 d6 (5...d5 6 ♗b3 dxe4 7 ♘g5 0-0 8 ♘gxe4 looks nice for White) 6 0-0 0-0 (6...♗b6 7 d4!? ♘bd7 8 ♗e3 ♗c7 9 ♘g5! 0-0 10 ♗xf7+ ♖xf7 11 ♘e6 ♕e7 12 ♘xc7 ♖b8 13 dxe5 ♘xe5 14 ♗xa7 ♕xc7 15 ♗xb8 ♕xb8 16 ♕d4 was better for White in Tischbierek-I.Sokolov, Antwerp 1998) 7 ♘e2 ♕e7 and now White should continue with 8 ♗b3 ♘bd7 9 ♘g3.

5 f4!?

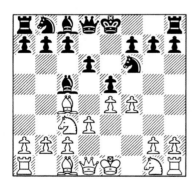

White once again aims to transpose into the King's Gambit Declined, but here Black has extra options:

C1: 5...♘g4
C2: 5...♗e6

Alternatively:

a) 5...♘c6 6 ♘f3 transposes to Variation B1.

b) 5...c6 6 ♘f3 b5 7 ♗b3 ♕e7 8 ♕e2 (8 ♖f1!?) 8...♘bd7 9 ♖f1 ♗b4 (9...♗b6!?, intending ...♘c5, may be stronger) 10 fxe5 dxe5 (Short-Speelman, London {2nd match-game} 1991) and now 11 ♕f2! 11...0-0 12 ♘h4 looks strong for White.

c) 5...♗xg1 (this exchange on g1 is rarely good for Black, as White can always castle long) 6 ♖xg1 ♗g4 7 ♕d2 exf4 8 ♕xf4 ♘bd7 9 h3 ♗h5 10 g4 ♗g6 11 h4 was good for White in Tartakower-Jankowitsch, Hamburg 1910.

C1)

5...♘g4

This looks very enticing for Black, but in fact it's White who has all the fun!

6 f5!

The only move, but a good one.

6...♘f2

Or:

a) 6...h5 7 ♘h3 ♕h4+ 8 ♔f1 ♘e3+ 9 ♗xe3 ♗xe3 10 ♘d5 ♗b6 11 ♕d2 gives White a clear advantage, Honfi-Witkowski, Munich Olympiad 1958.

b) 6...♕h4+ 7 g3 ♕h5 (or 7...♗f2+ 8 ♔f1 ♗xg3 9 hxg3 ♕xh1 10 ♕xg4) 8 h3 ♗xg1 9 ♕xg4 ♕xg4 10 hxg4 ♗b6 11 g5 and White makes use of the half-open h-file.

7 ♕h5

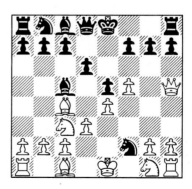

Now Black must deal with the threat of mate.

7...g6

Other defences are:

a) 7...♕d7? 8 ♗e6 ♕e7 9 ♘d5 g6 10 ♕h6 ♕f8 11 ♗xc8 ♘xh1 12 ♗xb7 ♗xg1 13 ♗xa8 ♔d7 14 ♕xf8 ♖xf8 15 ♗h6 and Black resigned, Emms-A.Jackson, Port Erin 1999.

b) 7...0-0 8 ♗g5 ♕e8 9 ♘d5! ♘xh1 (or 9...♘d7 10 ♘xc7) 10 ♘f6+! gxf6 11 ♗xf6 and Black cannot prevent mate.

c) 7...♖f8 (this may be the most resilient) 8 ♗g5 (8 ♘f3!? ♘xh1 9 ♗g5 is also a very dangerous attack) 8...g6 (8...♕d7!? 9 ♗e6 ♕c6 10 ♗xc8 ♘xh1 11 0-0-0 requires further investigation!) 9 ♕h6 f6 10 fxg6 hxg6 11 ♕xg6+ ♔d7 12 ♗h6! ♘xh1 13 ♕g7+ ♕e7 14 ♕xf8 ♕xf8 15 ♗xf8 ♗xg1 16 ♔e2 and White is better.

8 ♕h6! ♘xh1

There's no time to turn back: 8...♘g4 9 ♕g7 ♕f6 10 ♗xf7+! wins for White.

9 ♗g5! f6 10 fxg6!

10 ♕g7 ♖f8 11 ♘d5 ♘d7 is less clear.

10...fxg5

Or 10...hxg6 11 ♕xh8+ ♔d7 12 ♗e6+ ♔e7 13 ♕xf6+ and White wins.

11 g7 ♔d7

After 11...♖g8 White simply captures on g8 and then promotes the g-pawn.

12 ♕e6+ ♔c6 13 ♕d5+! ♔d7

13...♔b6 14 ♘a4+ ♔a5 15 ♘xc5 is winning for White.

14 ♕f7+! ♔c6 15 ♗b5+! ♔b6

16 ♗e8!!

I like this move very much! White uses the motifs of line clearance (the b-file) and inter-

ference (the eighth rank) to come up with a stunning way to win.

16...♕xe8 17 ♕b3+ ♔a6 18 gxh8♕

and White wins (18...♕xh8 19 ♕b5 mate).

C2)
5...♗e6!?

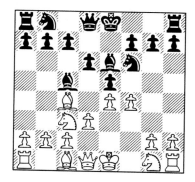

A more sober approach from Black.

6 ♗xe6

6 ♗b3!? ♘c6 7 ♘f3 looks like a playable alternative for White. Following 7...0-0 I like 8 ♘a4.

6...fxe6 7 ♘f3

7 fxe5 dxe5 8 ♕e2 ♘c6 9 ♗e3 ♗xe3 10 ♕xe3 0-0 was equal in Spielmann-Tarrasch, Bad Kissingen 1928.

7...exf4!?

7...0-0 is met by 8 ♘a4. After 7...a6 8 fxe5 dxe5 9 ♘xe5?! ♕d4! 10 ♘g4 ♘xg4 11 ♕xg4 ♕f2+ 12 ♔d1 0-0 Black had an attack in Vasiesiu-Olarasu, Sovata 1998, so White should be content with 9 ♗g5.

8 ♗xf4 0-0 9 ♘a4! ♗b4+

9...♘xe4? loses to 10 dxe4 ♖xf4 11 ♘xc5.

10 c3 ♗a5 11 b4 ♗b6 12 ♘xb6 axb6 13 0-0 ♘c6

Now 13...♘xe4 is met by 14 ♘d4! ♘xc3 15 ♕d2.

14 b5! ♘e7 15 ♕b3 ♕d7 16 ♘d4 d5

We are following the game Short-Speelman, London (4th matchgame) 1991. Here Kavalek suggests 17 ♗g5!, leaving White with an advantage.

D)
3...d5!?

This move is just about playable, but probably a bit too ambitious. Black's e5-pawn comes under tremendous pressure early on. Indeed, in the main line, Black sacrifices the pawn, but practice has shown that he doesn't get enough compensation.

4 exd5 ♘xd5 5 ♘f3 ♘c6

5...♗g4 6 h3 ♗xf3 7 ♕xf3 c6 8 0-0 is obviously nice for White.

6 0-0

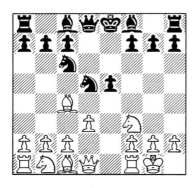

6...♗e7

A major alternative here is 6...♗g4!? 7 ♖e1 and now:

a) 7...♗e7 transposes to the note to Black's seventh move.

b) 7...f6? loses to the trick 8 ♘xe5!.

c) 7...♗c5?! 8 h3 (now 8 ♘xe5? loses to 8...♗xf2+! 9 ♔xf2 ♕h4+) 8...♗h5 9 d4!

♗xd4 10 g4! and White wins material.

d) 7...♕d6 (the best move; I can find nothing devastating against this) 8 h3 ♗h5 9 ♘c3 (9 d4!? ♗xf3! 10 ♕xf3 ♘xd4! 11 ♕xd5 ♕xd5 12 ♗xd5 ♘xc2 is very unclear) 9...♘xc3 10 bxc3 ♗e7 and White is better, but Black's position is quite playable.

7 ♖e1 ♘b6

Or 7...♗g4 8 h3 ♗xf3 (8...♗h5 9 g4 ♗g6 10 ♘xe5 ♘xe5 11 ♖xe5 ♘b6 12 ♗b3 transposes to the text) 9 ♕xf3 ♘d4 (9...♘f6 10 ♗b5 ♕d6 11 ♗xc6+ bxc6 12 ♕g3 is clearly better for White – Larsen) 10 ♕g4! ♘xc2 (after 10...0-0 11 ♖xe5 ♘f6 12 ♕d1 White is just a clear pawn ahead, Larsen-Berger, Amsterdam 1964) 11 ♖xe5 c6 (or 11...♘xa1 12 ♕xg7 ♖f8 13 ♗h6 ♔d7 14 ♖xd5+ ♗d6 15 ♕g4+) 12 ♕xg7 ♖f8 13 ♖xd5! and White wins.

8 ♗b3 ♗g4

With this move Black is ready to sacrifice a pawn. 8...♘f6 9 ♘c3 0-0 10 h3 ♗f5 11 ♘e4 was good for White in Vallejo Pons-Baena, Cala Galdana 1994, but 9 ♗f4 looks even stronger.

9 h3 ♗h5 10 g4 ♗g6 11 ♘xe5 ♘xe5 12 ♖xe5 0-0 13 ♘c3 ♔h8 14 ♗d2

Black has some compensation for the pawn in the shape of White's loose kingside, but White is well developed to cope with this. Play continues with 14...f5 15 ♕f1! ♗d6 16 ♖e2 ♗e8 and now both 17 ♗e6 fxg4 18 hxg4 ♗c6 19 ♘e4 (Dolmatov-Chekhov,

USSR Championship 1980) and 17 gxf5 ♗h5 18 ♗e6!? ♗xe2 19 ♕xe2 ♘d7 20 ♘e4 ♗e7 21 ♗c3 ♗f6 22 ♘xf6 ♘xf6 23 ♔h1 c5 24 ♖g1 (Kuczynski-Breutigam, Germany Bundesliga 1996) led to white victories.

E)
3...♗e7

At first sight this looks like a passive move, but it's actually quite deceptive. Black plans to castle quickly and then strike in the centre with ...d7-d5 (with or without ...c7-c6).
4 ♘c3 0-0

Alternatively:

a) 4...♘c6 5 f4 d6 6 ♘f3 transposes to Variation B, note to Black's fourth moves.

b) 4...c6!? 5 ♘f3 0-0 (5...d6 6 0-0 0-0 transposes) 6 0-0 (6 ♘xe5!? d5 7 ♗b3 d4 8 ♘xf7 ♖xf7 9 ♘e2 looks interesting) 6...d6 7 h3 b5 8 ♗b3 8...♘bd7 9 a3 (9 ♗e3 ♕c7 10 a4 b4 11 ♘e2 d5 12 exd5 cxd5 13 ♖c1 d4 14 ♗d2 ♗b7 15 ♘g3 a5 was unclear in Vogt-Garcia Gonzales, Leningrad 1977) 9...♘c5 10 ♗a2 ♗e6 11 ♗xe6 ♘xe6 12 d4 and White was slightly better in the game Mirumian-Comp P ConNers (a computer), Lippstadt 1999.
5 f4 exf4

5...d6 6 ♘f3 ♘c6 7 0-0 once again transposes to Variation B, note to Black's fourth moves. In general Black is trying to avoid playing the passive ...d7-d6.
6 ♗xf4 c6 7 e5

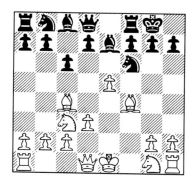

7...♘e8

Black has two interesting alternatives:

a) 7...d5?! 8 exf6 ♗b4 9 ♗b3 ♕xf6 (9...♖e8+ 10 ♔f1 ♕xf6 11 ♕f3 ♗xc3 12 bxc3 ♕xc3 13 ♖b1 and White won, Keogh-De Bruycker, Ostend 1975) 10 ♘ge2 d4 11 0-0 dxc3 12 ♗xb8 ♕e7 13 bxc3 ♗c5+ 14 d4 and White is winning, Pulkkinen-Norri, Finnish Championship 1995.

b) 7...♘d5!? 8 ♗xd5 (8 ♘xd5 cxd5 9 ♗b3 d6 10 ♘f3 dxe5 11 ♘xe5 looks interesting) 8...cxd5 9 ♘xd5 d6 10 ♕f3 ♘c6 11 exd6 ♗xd6 12 ♘e2 ♗xf4 13 ♘dxf4 ♘b4 14 ♔d2 ♗d7 and Black has some compensation for the pawn, Pulkkinen-Pihlajasalo, Finnish Team Championship 1997.
8 ♘f3

Another idea here is 8 d4!?, for example 8...♗g5 (or 8...d5 9 ♗d3) 9 ♕d2 ♗xf4 10 ♕xf4 d6 11 ♘f3 dxe5 12 dxe5 ♗e6 13 ♗d3 f6 14 0-0-0 and White has a good lead in development, Del Rio-Kopp, Hessen 1992.
8....d5 9 exd6 ♘xd6

Or 9...♗xd6!? 10 ♕d2 ♕c7 11 ♗e3 ♗g4 12 ♘e4 ♘d7 13 0-0 ♗xf3 14 gxf3 ♘b6 15 ♗b3 ♘d5 16 f4 ♖d8 17 ♖ae1 ♔h8 18 ♔h1 and White is more active, Larsen-Nikolic, Buenos Aires 1992.
10 ♗b3 ♘d7 11 d4 ♘b6

After 11...♘f6 12 0-0 ♗g4 13 ♕d2 ♘fe4 14 ♘xe4 ♘xe4 15 ♕e3 ♘f6 16 ♖ae1 White has a good attacking position, Pulkkinen-Salimaki, Helsinki 1999. This whole line seems to be something of a Finnish speciality!

12 0-0 ♗g4 13 ♕d3

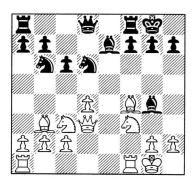

White has a good attacking position, with play on the half-open f-file and a powerful bishop on b3. Kharlov-Kuzmin, Alushta 1992, continued 13...♗f5 14 ♕e2 ♗g4 15 ♖ad1 ♗f6 16 ♕f2 ♗h5 17 d5 ♗xf3 18 ♕xf3 ♗xc3 19 dxc6 ♗b4 20 cxb7 ♖b8 21 ♕c6 ♖xb7 22 ♖xd6 ♗xd6 23 ♕xb7 ♗c5+ 24 ♔h1 and White went on to win.

Other Second Moves for Black

1 e4 e5 2 ♗c4

2...♘f6 is by far Black's most popular choice against the Bishop's Opening. There are, however, quite a few playable alternatives, although sometimes these merely transpose to 2...♘f6 lines. We shall look at

the following lines:
A: 2...♘c6
B: 2...♗c5
C: 2...c6

Or:

a) 2...d6 could well transpose into earlier lines involving ...d7-d6. One independent example is 3 ♘c3 ♗e6!? 4 d3 ♘f6 5 ♘ge2 ♗e7 6 0-0 0-0 7 ♗xe6 fxe6 8 d4 ♘c6 9 d5 exd5 10 exd5 ♘b8 11 ♘g3 ♘bd7 12 f4 and White was better in Vogt-Braun, Strausberg 1971.

b) 2...f5 is the so-called Calabrese Counter Gambit; this looks incredibly risky, but it's not that bad! Here are a couple of interesting tries for White:

b1) 3 d3 ♘f6 and now:

b11) 4 f4!? is given by *ECO* (amongst others), but 4...♘c6! seems an effective reply, for example 5 ♘f3 fxe4 6 dxe4 ♘xe4 7 fxe5 (7 ♗d5!?; 7 ♗d5 ♘f6 8 fxe5 ♘xd5 9 ♕xd5 d6 looks equal) 7...♘xe5!, as in Emms-Lyell, British Championship 1986.

b12) 4 ♘f3 looks more sensible. After 4...♘c6 5 0-0 ♗c5 6 ♘c3 d6 7 ♗g5 it's Black who's playing the King's Gambit Declined with a tempo less. White can try to make use of this extra tempo, for example, 7...♘a5 8 ♗xf6 ♕xf6 9 ♘d5 ♕d8 10 b4! ♘xc4 11 bxc5 fxe4 12 dxc4 exf3 13 ♕xf3 and White is better.

b2) 3 f4!? (why not?) 3...exf4 (or 3...♘f6 4 fxe5 ♘xe4 5 ♘f3, after which Black has trouble castling; 3...♘c6!? look interesting) 4 ♘c3 ♕h4+ (4...d5 5 ♘xd5; 4...♘f6 5 d3 c6 6 ♗xf4 d5 7 exd5 cxd5 8 ♗b3 ♗b4 9 ♕e2+ ♔f7 10 ♘f3 ♖e8 11 ♘e5+ ♔f8 12 d4 was better for White in Westerinen-Kiltti, Jyvaskyla 1994; both this and the next reference came via the move order 1 e4 e5 2 f4 exf4 3 ♗c4 f5!?) 5 ♔f1 ♘f6 (5...fxe4 6 ♘xe4 ♘f6 7 ♘f3 ♕h5 8 ♘xf6+ gxf6 9 d4 looks good for White) 6 ♘f3 ♕h5 7 d3 fxe4 8 dxe4 ♕c5 9 ♕e2 g5 10 e5 and White has a strong attack, Anderssen-Mayet, Berlin 1855.

A)

2...♘c6 3 ♘c3 ♗c5

Or:

a) 3...♘f6 transposes to 2...♘f6 3 ♗c4 ♘c6.

b) 3...d6!? 4 d3 (or, for the more adventurous, 4 f4!? exf4 5 d4 ♕h4+ 6 ♔f1 ♗g4 7 ♕d3) 4...♘a5 5 ♗b3 (5 f4!?) 5...♘xb3 6 axb3 and White follows up with f2-f4.

c) 3...g6 4 d3, followed by f2-f4.

4 ♕g4!?

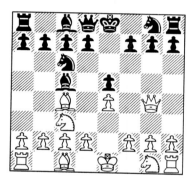

This aggressive move contains a devilish trap and causes Black quite a few problems. For the more sedate minded White can play 4 d3 d6, transposing to Variation B, although Black could also try 4...♘a5!?.

After 4 ♕g4!? Black must decide what to do about the attack on the g7-pawn. He has two main options, both of which result in a weakening of his position:

A1: 4...♕f6
A2: 4...g6

Or 4...♔f8 5 ♕g3 d6 (alternatively, 5...♘f6 6 ♘ge2 d6 7 d3 h6 8 ♘a4 ♗b6 9 ♘xb6 axb6 10 f4 was better for White in the game Rogers-Olarasu, Saint Vincent 2001) 6 ♘ge2 ♘d4 7 ♘xd4 exd4 8 ♘a4 ♗e6 9 ♗xe6 fxe6 10 ♘xc5 dxc5 11 ♕b3 ♕c8 12 ♕f3+ ♔e7 13 ♕g3 ♔f7 14 ♕f4+ ♔g6 15 ♕g4+ ♔f6 16 d3 and Black's king was very uncomfortably placed, Anand-Ravisekhar, New Delhi 1986.

A1)

4...♕f6

A very natural reaction, defending g7 and attacking f2 at the same time, but...

5 ♘d5! ♕xf2+ 6 ♔d1

And suddenly Black is in some trouble. There are threats to both g7 and c7. More importantly, though, Black's queen is lacking retreat squares.

6...♘f6

This looks a bit desperate, but alternatives show how much danger Black is in.

a) 6...g6 7 ♘h3 ♕d4 8 d3 (threatening c2-c3) and now:

a1) 8...d6 9 ♕f3 ♗xh3 10 ♖f1! f5 11 gxh3 ♗b6 12 c3 ♕c5 13 b4 and White won, Ford-Blackburn, Bruges 1999.

a2) 8...♗d6 9 c3 ♕c5 10 b4! wins a piece.

a3) 8...♗f8 9 ♕f3 ♔d8 10 ♘g5 ♘h6 11 ♕f6+ 1-0 Stripunsky-Oparaugo, Passau 1997.

a4) 8...♗b6 9 ♕f3 f6 10 ♖f1 d6 11 c3 ♕c5 12 b4 and again White wins, Emms-Hawksworth, British Championship 1986.

b) 6...♔f8 7 ♘h3 ♕d4 8 d3 d6 9 ♕f3 ♗xh3 10 ♖f1! ♗e6 11 c3 and Black's queen is trapped.

c) 6...♘ge7 7 ♘h3 ♕d4 8 ♕xg7 ♘g6 9 d3 ♗e7 10 ♖f1 ♔d8 11 ♘g5 ♖f8 12 ♕xf8+! 1-0 Leisebein-Tuchtenhagen, correspondence 1990.

7 ♕xg7 ♘xd5 8 exd5!

8 ♕xh8+? is less accurate. The game Moody-Thompson, Trenton 1994, continued

8...♔e7 9 exd5? ♕xg2 10 dxc6 d6! 11 ♗e2 ♗g4 and it was White who had to resign!

8...♗f8 9 ♕xh8 ♕xg2 10 dxc6

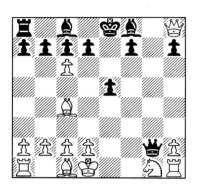

10...d6

Or 10...♕xh1 11 ♕xe5+ ♗e7 12 ♕g3 ♕xc6 13 ♕g8+ 1-0 Leisebein-Andre, correspondence 1990. After 10...d6 the game Leisebein-Fiebig, correspondence, concluded 11 cxb7 ♗g4+ 12 ♔e1 ♕e4+ 13 ♗e2 ♖b8 14 d3 ♕xh1 15 ♗h6 ♔e7 16 ♗g5+ 1-0.

A2)
4...g6

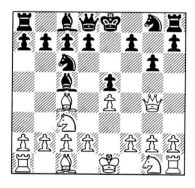

5 ♕f3

5 ♕g3!? also promises White an edge after 5...♘f6 6 d3 d6 7 ♘ge2 and now:

a) 7...♗e6?! 8 ♗g5 ♘h5 (after 8...h6? 9 ♕h4 and 8...♗xc4? 9 ♕h4 White makes use of the pin on the knight) 9 ♕h4 f6?! (better is 9...♕d7 10 ♘d5) 10 ♗xf6! ♕xf6 11 ♕xf6

♘xf6 12 ♗xe6 and White is a pawn up, Bangiev-Steinkohl, Dudweiler 1996.

b) 7...♘h5 8 ♕f3 ♕f6 (8...♗e6 9 ♘d5 ♗xd5 10 exd5 ♘e7 11 ♗b5+ ♔f8 12 c3 h6 13 g4 ♘g7 14 ♘g3 ♗b6 15 h4 gave White a strong attack in Conquest-Kristensen, Espergarde 1992) 9 ♕xf6 ♘xf6 10 ♗g5 ♘h5 11 ♘d5 ♗b6 12 ♘g3 h6 13 ♗d2 ♘g7 14 a4 ♘d4 15 ♔d1 c6 16 ♘xb6 axb6 17 c3 when White's bishop pair and Black's dark-squared weaknesses give White a clear edge, Stripunsky-Tolstikh, Volgograd 1994.

5...♘f6

5...♕f6 6 ♘d5 ♕xf3 7 ♘xf3 ♗b6 8 d3, Capablanca-Gomez, Panama 1933, gives White a pleasant ending – the weakness that ...g7-g6 creates is quite noticeable.

6 ♘ge2 d6 7 d3 ♗g4

Or 7...h6 8 h3 ♕e7 9 g4 (9 ♘a4!?) 9...♘h5 10 g5 ♘g8 11 ♘d5 ♗xd5 12 ♗xd5 ♘d8 13 h4 c6 14 ♗b3 ♘e6 15 gxh6 and White was better in Milutinovic-Savic, correspondence 1972.

8 ♕g3 h6

8...♗e6 transposes to note 'a' to White's fifth move, while 8...♕d7 9 ♕h4! is good for White.

9 f4 ♕e7 10 ♘d5 ♘xd5 11 ♕xg4

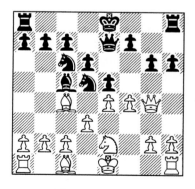

We have been following the game Larsen-Portisch, Santa Monica 1966, which continued 11...♘f6 12 ♕h3 ♘a5?! 13 ♗b5+ c6 14 ♗a4 b5 15 ♗b3 and White was clearly better. Larsen suggests 11...♘e3 as an improvement, but White still holds the advantage after 12 &xe3 &xe3 13 f5.

B)

2...&c5

The Symmetrical Defence. This is most likely to transpose into one of the lines we have already studied.

3 &c3 d6

3...&c6 transposes to Variation A, while 3...&f6 4 d3 transposes to 2...&f6 3 d3 &c5 4 &c3.

4 d3

4 f4 &xg1! 5 &xg1 &h4+ is a bit annoying, but the immediate 4 &a4!? looks playable.

4...&c6

4...&f6 5 f4 transposes to Variation C in the Main Line.

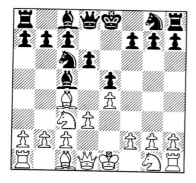

5 &a4!

White will exchange off Black's dark squared bishop, and then he will play for f2-f4.

5...&ge7

Or:

a) 5...&b6 6 a3 (6 &xb6 axb6 7 f4 &a5!) 6...&f6 7 &e2 &e6 8 &xb6 axb6 9 &xe6 fxe6 10 0-0 0-0 11 &g3 &d7 12 &e3 &h4 13 c3 &f6 14 f3 and White's better pawn structure gives him an small edge, Evans-Addison, New York 1969.

b) 5...&f6 6 &xc5 dxc5 7 &e3 b6 8 &d2 &ge7 9 &e2 &e6 10 &b5 &g6 11 f4! &xg2

12 &g1 &xh2 13 0-0-0 0-0-0 14 f5 &d7 15 &h1 &g2 16 &dg1 &f3 17 &f1 &g2 18 &e1 &d4 19 &xd4 cxd4 20 &xd7+ &xd7 21 &d2 g5 22 &fg1 and finally Black's queen is trapped, Mitkov-De Vreugt, Bolzano 1999.

c) 5...&a5!? 6 &xc5 dxc5 (6...&xc4!?) 7 &b3 &xb3 8 axb3 &f6 9 &e2, followed by f2-f4.

6 &xc5 dxc5 7 f4 exf4 8 &xf4 &g6 9 &g3 &ce5 10 &b3 &g4 11 &e2 &g5 12 &c1 &xc1+ 13 &xc1 0-0-0 14 &c3

We are following the game Mitkov-Stojcevski, Skopje 1998. White once again has the advantage of the bishop pair in an open position. White's next move will be to castle kingside.

C)

2...c6

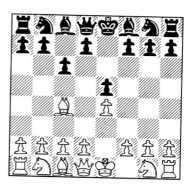

Aiming for a quick counter with ...d7-d5.

3 d4! d5

Or 3...♘f6 4 dxe5 ♛a5+ (4...♘xe4 5 ♛e2 is better for White – Keres) 5 ♘c3 ♘xe4 (5...♛xe5 6 ♘f3 and Black's queen is kicked around) 6 ♛f3 d5 7 exd6 ♘xd6 8 ♗b3 and I prefer White.

4 exd5 cxd5 5 ♗b5+ ♗d7 6 ♗xd7+ ♘xd7 7 ♘c3

Also possible is 7 dxe5 ♘xe5 8 ♛e2 (8 ♘e2 ♘f6 9 0-0 ♗e7 10 ♘bc3 gives White an edge – Lisitsin) 8...♛e7 9 ♘c3 0-0-0 10 ♗f4 ♘g6 11 ♗g3 h5 12 h4 ♘f6 13 0-0-0 ♛c5 14 ♘f3 ♗d6 15 ♗xd6 ♖xd6 16 ♘d4 and White can hope to put pressure on the isolated d-pawn, Zifroni-Boim, Ramat Hasharon 1993.

7...♘gf6 8 dxe5 ♘xe5 9 ♛e2 ♛e7 10 ♗e3 ♘c6 11 0-0-0 0-0-0 12 ♘f3 ♛c7 13 ♘d4 ♛a5 14 ♘b3

White has some awkward pressure on the d5-pawn. Marcelin-Boim, Herzeliya 2000, continued 14...♛b4 15 a3 ♛g4 16 ♛xg4+ ♘xg4 17 ♘xd5 and White was better.

Important Points

Lines with f2-f4:

1) Be aware of the cramping effect on Black's position after a suitable f4-f5.

2) Remember the idea of ♘a4, attempting to trade off the knight for Black's dark-squared bishop. This is normally a positionally desirable exchange and will allow White to castle kingside.

3) Remember also that Black has the same idea of ...♘a5, attacking the bishop on c4. Sometimes it's worth expending a tempo to keep the bishop with a2-a3 or c2-c3.

4) If the idea of ♘a4 is not suitable, White has different approaches: he can consider queenside castling, or neutralising Black's dark-squared bishop with ♛e2 and ♗e3.

5) Watch out for ...♘g4, although usually this move is not as threatening as it looks!

More generally:

1) f2-f4 is not usually a good idea if Black can strike out effectively with ...d7-d5 – see the Main Line, Variation A as an example of this.

2) Often ♘f3 is a good answer to ...c7-c6, as now Black cannot defend the e-pawn with ♘c6.

3) In the Main Line, Variation A1, White has to decide when it's best to keep the tension in the centre and when it's best to play exd5. Likewise, Black has to decide whether to try and keep his centre intact, or to play a simplifying ...dxe4.

CHAPTER THREE

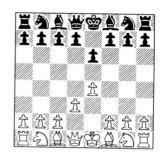

Attacking the French:
The King's Indian Attack

1 e4 e6 2 d3

2 d3 introduces the King's Indian Attack (KIA), a very respectable system, which can actually be played against most defences to 1 e4. For example, White can play 1 e4 c5 2 ♘f3 and 3 d3, 1 e4 c6 2 d3 and even 1 e4 e5 2 ♘f3 ♘c6 3 d3 (the only reasonable defence which avoids the KIA is 1 e4 d5).

However, the King's Indian Attack is probably most effective, and certainly most popular, when it is played against the French Defence. The point is that Black is already committed to the move ...e7-e6, even though in a lot of lines he would prefer his e-pawn to be on either e7 or e5! Indeed, in Main Line 2 we shall be looking at variations where Black loses a tempo early on to play the desirable ...e6-e5, (1 e4 e6 2 d3 ♘c6 3 ♘f3 e5!? being one extreme example).

The King's Indian Attack has been utilised by many world class players. One could list World Champions Mikhail Botvinnik, Vassily Smyslov and Tigran Petrosian, while Bobby Fischer turned to it when he was having trouble proving any advantage in the main lines of the French. More recent advocates include such attacking geniuses as Alexei Shirov and Alexander Morozevich.

White's idea is pretty straightforward and easy to play. To a certain extent White plays the same moves regardless of how Black plays. The set-up involves developing moves such as ♘d2, ♘gf3, g2-g3, ♗g2, 0-0 and ♖e1.

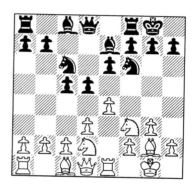

Here's a typical position, White having just played the move ♖e1. A characteristic plan of action would begin with the move e4-e5. This 'pawn wedge' on e5 acts as a catalyst for a kingside attack, as it gives White plenty of space to manoeuvre on the kingside, and it deprives Black the use of the f6-square, the normal position for a defensive knight. White can follow up e4-e5 with such moves as h2-h4, ♘f1, ♗f4, ♘1h2-g4 and perhaps h4-h5-h6. It's easy to see how a potentially lethal attack can arise, especially if Black is not careful. Naturally White will alter his general plan according to which set-up Black chooses, but this plan of a kingside attack crops up many times.

I can't promise a theoretical advantage in all lines of the KIA, but even when Black chooses the best defences, positions arise which are lively and knife-edged; this is why the KIA is a favourite weapon for the attacking player.

Main Line 1:
Black plays ...d7-d5 and ...c7-c5

1 e4 e6 2 d3 d5 3 ♘d2 c5 4 ♘gf3 ♘c6 5 g3

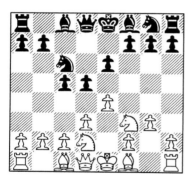

At all levels this is the most popular way of handling the black side of the King's Indian Attack. With the moves ...d7-d5 and ...c7-c5, Black has claimed a fair share of the centre and can develop comfortably. Indeed, as we shall now see, Black has a number of different development methods from which to choose.
A: 5...♘f6
B: 5...g6
C: 5...♗d6

Here are some rare alternatives.

a) 5...♘ge7 6 ♗g2 (6 h4!?, planning to meet 6...g6 with 7 h5, looks worth a try) 6...g6 7 0-0 ♗g7 transposes to Variation B.

b) 5...b6 6 ♗g2 ♗b7 7 0-0 ♘f6 transposes to Variation A.

c) The game Dyce-Mikuev, Elista Olympiad 1998, followed an original course after 5...g5!? (the chances of meeting this move are quite slim; I found only one example on my database!) 6 exd5 exd5 7 ♕e2+ ♗e6 8 ♗h3 ♕e7 9 ♗xe6 fxe6 10 ♘b3 h6 11 h4 g4 12 ♘e5 and White was better.

A)
5...♘f6

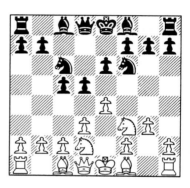

A very popular choice. With this move Black plans to develop classically; he will continue with ...♗e7, and this is followed by ...0-0 or, more ambitiously, by ...b7-b6, ...♕c7 and ...0-0-0.
6 ♗g2 ♗e7

6...♗d6 is generally frowned upon as it doesn't mix well with ...♘f6. In particular Black will generally have to expend a tempo preventing a later e4-e5 by White, which would otherwise fork two pieces. After 7 0-0 0-0 8 ♖e1 the threat of e4-e5 forces Black to act immediately:

a) 8...♗c7 9 c3 d4 (9...e5 10 exd5 ♘xd5 11 ♘c4 puts annoying pressure on the e5-pawn, for example 11...f6 12 d4! cxd4 13 cxd4 b5 14 ♘e3 and Black's position is riddled with weaknesses) 10 cxd4 cxd4 11 e5 ♘d7 12 ♘c4 ♖b8 13 ♗g5 f6 14 exf6 ♘xf6 15 ♘fe5 ♘xe5 16 ♘xe5 h6 17 ♗d2 and White held the advantage in Oratovsky-Gravel, Montreal 1998 – White's pieces are well placed and Black has some problems along the half-open e-file.

b) 8...♛c7 9 ♕e2 (once again threatening e4-e5) 9...dxe4 10 dxe4 e5 11 c3 b6 12 h3 a5 13 a4! ♝a6 14 ♘c4! (this self-pin is easily broken) 14...♘e8 15 ♝f1 ♜c8 16 ♕c2 ♕b7 17 ♘h4 ♝e7 18 ♘f5 ♝xc4 19 ♝xc4 ♘d6 20 ♘xd6 ♝xd6

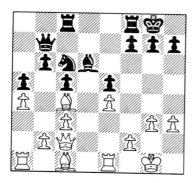

with a clear plus for White in Loginov-Szirti, Budapest 1992 – compare White's bishop on c4 to Black's on d6!

6...b6!?, however, makes some sense. This may just transpose to Variation A1, but Black can also delay playing ...♝e7, in the hope that the bishop may have other options. After 7 0-0 ♝b7 8 ♜e1 ♕c7 we have:

a) 9 c3 0-0-0 10 a3 ♝e7 transposes to Variation A12.

b) 9 e5!? ♘d7 10 c4! (10 ♕e2 g5! or 10...h6 11 h4 g5! is Black's idea: the bishop may develop on g7) 10...♘cxe5!? (for 10...♝e7 see Variation A11) 11 cxd5 ♘xf3+ 12 ♕xf3 e5 13 ♘c4 ♝d6 14 ♕g4 g6 15 ♝h6 f5 16 ♕e2 ♔f7 17 ♜ac1 and White was slightly better in M.Saunders-Milnes, correspondence 1993.

7 0-0

---

see following diagram

Now Black faces a major decision: whether to castle kingside or to develop on the other wing.

A1: 7...b6

A2: 7...0-0

Alternatively:

a) 7...b5?! (beginning early queenside operations, but this is too loose) 8 exd5! exd5 9 c4! bxc4 10 dxc4 0-0 11 b3 ♝f5 12 cxd5 ♘xd5 13 ♝b2 was clearly better for White in Schöneberg-Zinn, Germany 1972: White's pieces are well placed and Black has weak pawns on the queenside.

b) 7...♕c7 (a sneaky move order) 8 ♜e1 h6!? 9 c3 (9 e5?! ♘d7 10 ♕e2 g5! 11 h3 h5! gives Black a quick attack against the e5-pawn; White must always be careful of this when playing an early e4-e5) 9...b6 10 a3 (now 10 e5 gives Black counterplay after 10...♘d7 11 d4 cxd4 12 cxd4 ♘b4, while 10 exd5 ♘xd5 11 ♘c4 ♝b7 12 a4 ♜d8 was equal in Jansa-Marjanovic, Nis 1983) 10...a5!? (10...♝b7 transposes to Variation A12) 11 a4!? (securing the b5-square; 11 e5 ♘d7 12 d4 also looks good as Black no longer has ...♘b4 ideas) 11...♝a6 12 exd5 ♘xd5 13 ♘c4 ♜d8 14 ♕e2 ♝f6 15 ♝d2 ♜d7 16 h4 ♝b7 17 ♘h2 ♔d8 18 ♘g4 ♔c8 19 ♕d1 ♝a6 20 ♕b3 and I prefer White, Seeman-Alzate, Elista Olympiad 1998.

A1)

7...b6

Planning to develop the bishop on a6 or, more normally, b7. This move is also an indication that Black is more likely to castle on the queenside.

8 ♜e1

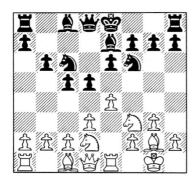

8...♗b7

Alternatively Black can play a cunning move order with 8...♕c7!?, not yet committing the bishop to b7. After 8...♕c7 White can play:

a) After 9 a3 Black should play 9...♗b7, when 10 c3 transposes to Variation A12.

b) 9 c3 ♗a6!? (this is Black's idea: the bishop develops on a6 and hits the d3-pawn) 10 exd5 (10 e5?! ♘d7 11 d4 cxd4 12 cxd4 ♘b4 is very annoying for White) 10...♘xd5 11 ♘c4 0-0 12 a4 ♖ad8 13 ♕b3 ♗f6 14 ♗d2 ♖d7 15 ♖ad1 ♖fd8 with an equal position in Frias-Cifuentes Parada, Wijk aan Zee 1991.

c) 9 e5!? ♘d7 and now:

c1) 10 ♘f1!? ♘dxe5!? (10...♗b7 11 ♗f4 transposes to Variation A11) 11 ♘xe5 ♘xe5 12 ♗f4 ♗d6 (12...f6 13 ♘e3 ♗d7 14 ♘g4 ♗d6 15 ♘xe5 fxe5 16 ♗xe5! gives White a slight edge due to Black's backward pawn on e6 – 16...♗xe5 is answered by 17 ♕h5+!) 13 ♕h5 ♘g6! (13...g6 is answered by 14 ♕xe5!) 14 ♕xd5 ♘xf4 15 ♕c6+ ♔f8 16 ♕xa8 ♘xg2 17 ♕xg2 ♗b7 18 f3 h5 with an unclear position. White is the exchange up but will face some uncomfortable moments on the kingside

c2) 10 ♕e2 with a further split:

c21) 10...♗b7 11 h4! (preventing ...g7-g5) 11...0-0-0 12 ♘f1 h6 13 ♘1h2 ♖dg8 14 ♘g4 ♘f8 (14...g5 15 h5! ♔b8 16 c3 ♖e8 17 ♗d2 f5 18 exf6 ♘xf6 19 ♘fe5 and White has a

firm grip on the e5-square, Bates-Vallin, Witley 1999) 15 ♗f4 g5 16 hxg5 hxg5 17 ♗d2 with a typically complex position, C.Hansen-Kasparov, La Valetta 1980; White's pieces are more actively placed but Black may be able to use the open h-file at some point.

c22) 10...g5!? 11 g4 (11 c4, trying to exploit Black's lack of development, is critical, but after 11...g4 12 cxd5 gxf3 13 ♘xf3 exd5 14 e6 ♘f6 15 ♗f4 ♕b7 16 exf7+ ♔xf7 it's doubtful that White has enough compensation, V.Fedorov-Khait, Yerevan 1969) 11...h5 12 h3 hxg4 13 hxg4 ♗b7 14 ♘f1 0-0-0 with another unclear position. Black will try to follow up with ...♘f8-g6.

c3) 10 c4!? may be White's most testing answer. Now Black has the following choices:

c31) 10...♗b7 transposes to Variation A11.

c32) 10...♘b4 11 cxd5 exd5 12 d4! cxd4 13 ♘xd4 ♘xe5 14 ♘2f3 and White has good compensation for the pawn.

After 8...♗b7 I'm giving the white player a choice of two different lines:

A11: 9 e5
A12: 9 c3

A11)
9 e5

With this move White blocks the centre
9...♘d7

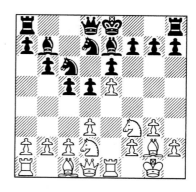

10 c4!?

Striking out at the d5-pawn. If this pawn moves, White will gain possession of the important e4-square.

The more traditional method for White is with 10 ♘f1 and now:

a) 10...g5!? (the normal pawn lunge: Black is hitting back on the kingside and undermining White's support of the e5-pawn) 11 ♘e3! (11 g4 h5! 12 h3 hxg4 13 hxg4 ♕c7 14 ♕e2 0-0-0 15 c3 ♖dg8 has been played a few times and Black has good results; he will continue with ...♘f8-g6) 11...h5 (11...♘dxe5!? 12 ♘xe5 ♘xe5 13 ♘xd5 ♗xd5 14 ♖xe5 ♗xg2 15 ♔xg2 ♗f6 16 ♖e4 is slightly better for White: Black's king has no safe place to hide) 12 c4 d4 13 ♘d5 exd5 (or 13...♖g8!? 14 ♘xe7 ♕xe7 15 a3 g4 16 ♘h4 a5 17 ♕a4 ♖c8 18 ♖b1 ♔d8 19 ♗f4 and White's king is much safer than Black's, Masola-Cristobal, Mar del Plata 1993) 14 cxd5 g4 15 dxc6 ♗xc6 16 e6! fxe6 17 ♘xd4 ♗xg2 18 ♘xe6 ♗f3 19 ♘xd8 ♗xd1 20 ♘c6 ♖h7 21 ♗g5 ♗f3 22 ♘xe7 ♔f7 23 ♗h4 and White is a pawn up as in the game Schlenker-Raicevic, Linz 1980.

b) 10...♕c7 11 ♗f4 0-0-0 12 h4 h6 13 ♕d2 ♖dg8 14 h5! (taking the sting out of ...g7-g5) 14...g5 (or 14...♕d8 15 ♗h3 ♘f8 16 ♘1h2 d4 17 ♘g4 ♘b4 18 ♗g2 ♘d5 19 c4 ♘xf4 20 ♕xf4 f5 21 exf6 gxf6 22 ♘d2 ♗xg2 23 ♔xg2, which was unclear in Kasparov-Sturua, Tbilisi 1976) 15 hxg6 ♖xg6. Now Konstantinopolsky-Banas, correspondence 1985, continued 16 ♘e3 h5 17 ♘xd5!? (this trick occurs quite often in the KIA – see later) 17...exd5 18 e6 ♕d8 19 exd7+ ♕xd7 20 ♖xe7!? ♕xe7? 21 ♗h3+ ♖g4 22 ♖e1 and White went on to win. More resilient, however, is 20...♘xe7! 21 ♘e5 ♕f5, after which the position is still very unclear.

10...d4

This advance looks very natural, but it's actually quite accommodating to White, who now has possession of the important e4-square. Black should consider alternatives.

a) 10...♘b4!? 11 cxd5 ♗xd5 (or 11...exd5 12 ♘f1 0-0 13 a3 ♘c6 14 h4 and White will continue with ♗f4 and ♘1h2) 12 ♘e4 (once again White has the e4-square under control) 12...♘xa2!? 13 ♖xa2 ♗xa2 14 b3! b5 15 ♕c2 ♗xb3 (15...♕a5 16 ♖e2 picks up the bishop) 16 ♕xb3 ♖b8 17 ♘d6+ ♗xd6 18 exd6 0-0 19 ♗g5 ♘f6 20 ♕c3 ♖b6 with a complex position, although I prefer White's attacking chances to Black's queenside pawns, Ree-Vogel, Leeuwarden 1974

b) 10...♕c7 (this could arise from the move order 8...♕c7 9 e5 ♘d7 10 c4 ♗b7 and may well be Black's most promising move) 11 cxd5 (11 ♕e2?! dxc4 12 dxc4 g5! puts White's e5-pawn under early pressure, Hracek-Kveinys, European Team Championship, Debrecen 1992) 11...exd5 12 d4!? (12 e6!?) 12...♘f8 (12...cxd4 13 ♘b3 regains the pawn) 13 ♘f1 ♘e6 14 ♘e3 ♖d8 15 ♘f5 0-0 16 h4 with a complex position, Milanovic-Arsovic, Belgrade 1989.

11 h4!

11 ♘e4!? ♘dxe5 12 ♘xe5 ♘xe5 13 ♘xc5 ♗xg2 14 ♔xg2 bxc5 15 ♖xe5 looks pretty equal, while *ECO* just gives 11 a3 ♕c7 12 ♕e2 g5 (Banas-Novak, Trencianske Teplice 1974) as unclear. 11 h4 looks like an improvement, as counterplay involving ...g7-g5 is suppressed.

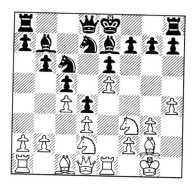

11...♕c7

Or 11...h6 12 h5! (preparing to meet ...g7-g5 by capturing *en passant*) 12...♕c7 13 ♕e2

0-0-0 14 a3 ♖dg8 15 b4! (opening up the queenside) 15...g5 16 hxg6 ♖xg6 17 bxc5 bxc5 18 ♖b1 h5 19 ♘e4 h4 20 ♗f4 hxg3 21 fxg3 ♗a8 22 ♖b5 a6 23 ♖b2 ♕a5 24 ♖eb1 ♔c7 25 ♘d6 ♗xd6 26 exd6+ ♔c8 27 ♘e5 ♘dxe5 28 ♗xe5 ♖hg8 29 ♕f3

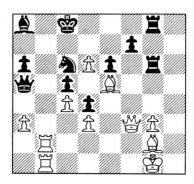

29...♘xe5 (29...f5 loses to 30 ♕xc6+!! ♗xc6 31 ♗xc6 ♖xg3+ 32 ♗xg3 ♖xg3+ 33 ♔f2) 30 ♕xa8+ ♔d7 31 ♕b7+ ♔xd6 32 ♖b6+ ♘c6 33 ♕xc6+ ♔e5 34 ♖f1 1-0 Rogoff-Bellon Lopez, Stockholm 1969.

12 ♘e4!

This pseudo pawn sacrifice is very effective, although White was also better after the quieter 12 ♕e2 0-0-0 13 a3 h6 14 ♘f1 ♖dg8 15 ♘1h2 g5 16 hxg5 hxg5 17 ♘g4 ♖h5 18 ♗d2 ♖gh8 19 b4, as in Hartston-Trikaliotis, Siegen Olympiad 1970.

12...♘cxe5

12...0-0-0 is probably safer. White should reply with 13 ♗f4 h6 14 h5!, followed by a2-a3 and b2-b4!.

13 ♘xe5 ♘xe5

13...♕xe5 14 ♘xc5 ♕xc5 15 ♗xb7 is better for White – he has the bishop pair and can expand on the queenside with a2-a3 and b2-b4.

14 ♗f4

see following diagram

Now Jadoul-Kruszynski, Copenhagen 1988, continued 14...0-0 15 ♕h5 f6 (15...f5? loses to 16 ♗xe5 ♕xe5 17 ♘g5) 16 ♘g5!

fxg5 17 ♗xe5 ♕d7 18 hxg5 ♗xg2 19 ♔xg2 with a large advantage for White. Black has problems down both the e- and h-files. The game concluded 19...♕e8 20 ♕xe8 ♖fxe8 21 f4 ♔f7 22 ♖e2 ♗f8 23 ♔f3 h6 24 gxh6 gxh6 25 a4 ♖ec8 26 ♖h1 a6 27 b3 ♖a7 28 g4 ♔g6 29 ♗d6 ♔g7 30 ♖xe6 ♔f7 31 f5 ♖c6 32 ♗b8 1-0.

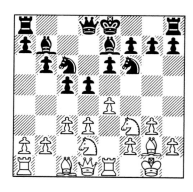

A12)
9 c3

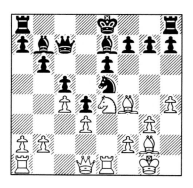

This move is more flexible than 9 e5. White keeps the tension in the centre and begins play on the queenside in anticipation of Black castling long.

9...♕c7 10 a3!?

Preparing b2-b4 in some lines. White could also consider 10 ♕e2!?, which transposes to the text after 10...0-0-0 11 a3, but eliminates some of Black's 10th move alternatives. If Black plays 10...0-0 White plays on the kingside with 11 e5 ♘d7 12 ♘f1 ♖ae8 13 ♗f4.

10...0-0-0

Black has quite a few alternatives:

a) After 10...0-0 White reverts back to Plan A with 11 e5! ♘d7 12 d4 cxd4 13 cxd4 (now a2-a3 has proved useful in preventing ...♘b4) 13...♘a5 14 ♘f1 ♖fc8 (preparing ...♕c2) 15 b4 ♘c4 16 h4 b5!? (16...a5 17 b5!) 17 ♘g5 with the initiative on the kingside, Psakhis-Paunovic, Minsk 1986.

b) 10...a5 and now:

b1) 11 a4!? expends a tempo in order to win the b5 square as an outpost; this is a common theme. Again we have a further split:

b11) 11...0-0-0 12 e5 ♘d7 13 d4 g5 14 ♘b1! (preparing ♘a3-b5) 14...h6 15 ♘a3 ♘db8 (or 15...g4 16 ♘d2 cxd4 17 ♘b5!) 16 ♗e3 ♗a6 17 ♘b5 ♕d7 18 ♖c1

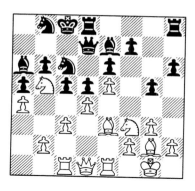

and White had the initiative in Psakhis-Kohlweyer, Vienna 1990.

b12) 11...0-0 12 e5 ♘d7 13 ♕e2 (13 d4 cxd4 14 cxd4 ♘b4 gives Black counterplay) 13...♖ae8!? (13...♖fe8 14 ♘f1 f5 15 exf6 ♗xf6 16 ♘g5 ♘f8 17 h4 ♖e7 18 ♘h2 ♗e5 19 h5 gives White good attacking chances on the kingside, Knezevic-Jovcic, Yugoslavia 1975) 14 ♘f1 f6 15 exf6 ♗xf6 16 ♘g5 ♘de5 with a very messy position, Ostermeyer-Breutigam, German Bundesliga 1988.

b2) 11 ♘f1!? (perhaps White does best to ignore ...a7-a5) 11...0-0-0 12 ♕b3!? ♗a6 13

♗f4 ♕b7 14 e5 ♘d7 15 c4 h6 16 cxd5 exd5 17 h4 c4 18 dxc4 ♗xc4 19 ♕c2 and I prefer White, Hall-B.Sorensen, Danish Team Championship 1999 – Black's king is a bit vulnerable.

c) 10...dxe4 (Black normally avoids this exchange as it gives up the control over the e4-square, but here White's a2-a3 and c2-c3 encourages Black to open things up a little) 11 dxe4 ♖d8 12 ♕e2 0-0 13 e5 ♘d7 14 h4 b5 (14...♕c8!? 15 a4 ♕a8 16 ♗h3 ♘a5, as in Varavin-Vunder, St Petersburg 2000, looks interesting) 15 a4 b4 16 ♘c4 ♘b6 17 ♘xb6 axb6 18 ♗f4 bxc3 19 bxc3 ♘a5 20 h5 h6 21 ♖ab1 with an unclear position, Varavin-Moskalenko, Leningrad 1989.

d) 10...h6 11 ♕e2 (11 b4!?) 11...0-0-0 transposes the main text.

11 ♕e2 h6

Preparing the advance ...g7-g5. The game Mkrtchian-Kovaljov, Tallinn 1997, varied with 11...♗a6 12 e5! ♘d7 13 h4 h6 14 h5! (we already know the idea behind this move) 14...g6 15 hxg6 fxg6 16 ♗h3 ♘f8 17 b4! and White's attack is quicker.

12 b4!

Softening up Black's queenside pawn structure.

12...g5

Alternatively:

a) 12...c4!? 13 exd5 cxd3 (13...♘xd5 14 dxc4 ♘xc3 15 ♕f1 ♗f6 16 ♘b3 ♘a4 17 ♖a2 g5 18 ♖c2 ♔b8 19 c5 bxc5 20 ♘xc5

♘xc5 21 ♖xc5 wasn't a pleasant experience for me in Jansa-Emms, Hillerod 1995 – Black has only one defensive pawn left on the queenside and even that isn't much use) 14 ♕xd3 ♘xd5 15 ♕c2 ♗f6 16 ♗b2 ♔b8 17 c4 ♗xb2 18 ♕xb2 ♘f6 19 c5! and again White's attack is faster, Psakhis-Nikitin, Berlin 1991.

b) 12...♘e5 (a suggestion from Mark Dvoretsky) 13 exd5 ♘xf3+ 14 ♘xf3 ♘xd5 15 ♗b2 ♗f6 16 bxc5 bxc5 17 d4! c4 18 ♘d2 ♘b6 19 ♗xb7+ ♔xb7 20 a4!, followed by ♗a3, promises White the advantage.

13 bxc5!?

Or:

a) *ECO* only gives 13 ♘b3 dxe4 14 dxe4 g4 15 ♘fd2 ♘e5 as unclear in Osmanovic-Martinovic, Sarajevo 1981.

b) 13 h3!? ♖hg8 14 ♘b3 c4 15 exd5 cxd3 16 ♕xd3 ♘xd5 17 ♕c2 ♗f6 18 ♗b2 ♘de7 19 c4 ♗xb2 20 ♕xb2 and once again White looks to have the safer king, Kraschl-Niklasch, Budapest 1993.

13...♗xc5 14 ♘b3 ♗e7 15 exd5 ♘xd5 16 ♗b2

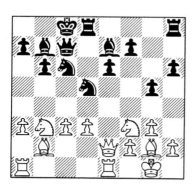

White must now look to advance both the c- and d-pawns in order to prise open the queenside. Fries Nielsen-Cramling, Copenhagen 1982, continued 16...g4 17 ♘fd4 h5 18 c4 ♘f6 19 ♘b5 ♕d7 20 d4! a6 21 d5! axb5 22 cxb5 ♘xd5 23 ♖ac1 ♖he8 and now 24 bxc6! ♗xc6 25 ♕a6+ seems to be winning for White; for example, 25...♔c7 26 ♗e5+

♗d6 27 ♘d4 or 25...♔b8 26 ♘a5! bxa5 (26...♗a8 27 ♗e5+ ♗d6 28 ♗xd5 ♗xd5 29 ♗xd6+ ♕xd6 30 ♖b1) 27 ♗e5+ ♗d6 28 ♗xd6+ ♕xd6 29 ♖xc6.

A2)
7...0-0

This is still Black's most common choice, despite White scoring a healthy 60% from this position on my database. Black gets his king out of danger, at least for the time being, and will concentrate on creating counterplay on the queenside.

8 ♖e1

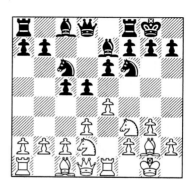

Now Black has a choice of ways forward:
A21: 8...dxe4
A22: 8...♕c7
A23: 8...b6
A24: 8...b5

A21)
8...dxe4

The King's Indian Attack would lose a lot of its sting if Black were able to successfully simplify in the centre like this. Fortunately this exchange almost always helps White more than Black. White now has more presence in the centre than Black, and after e4-e5 White will be able to use the important e4-square.

9 dxe4 b5

Alternatively:

a) 9...b6 10 e5 ♘d7 (10...♘d5 11 ♘e4

♘db4 12 ♘d6 ♗xd6 13 exd6 ♗b7 14 c4 ♕d7 15 a3 ♘a6 16 ♗f4 looks good for White – the passed d-pawn is a real thorn in Black's side) 11 ♘e4 (11 ♘d4! cxd4 12 ♗xc6 ♖b8 13 ♘b3 also looks good for White) 11...♗a6 12 ♗f4 b5 13 c3 and White was better in Petrosian-Kan, Moscow 1955. The game continued 13...♕b6 14 ♕c2 ♖fd8 15 h4! ♘f8 16 h5 ♖ac8?! (16...h6) 17 h6! and White's attack on the kingside was far more effective than Black's on the other wing

b) 9...e5 (a radical move which prevents e4-e5 but at the same time weakens the d5-square) 10 c3 h6 11 ♘c4! ♕xd1 (after 11...♕c7 White should play 12 ♘e3) 12 ♖xd1 ♘xe4 (12...♗g4 13 h3 ♗xf3 14 ♗xf3 ♖fd8 15 ♖xd8+ ♖xd8 16 a4 b6 17 ♔f1 ♗f8 18 ♔e2 was better for White in Tkachiev-Handoko, Jakarta 1996 – White has the bishop pair and the d5-square) 13 ♘fxe5 ♘xe5 14 ♘xe5

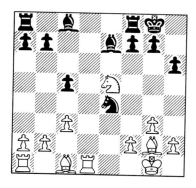

and White had a big endgame plus in the game Badea-Danilov, Bucharest 1998. In particular the bishop on g2 is a very strong piece.

10 e5 ♘d5 11 ♘e4 ♕c7 12 c3 ♗b7

12...♘xe5 13 ♘xe5 ♕xe5 14 c4 bxc4 15 ♘c3 ♕d6 16 ♘xd5 exd5 17 ♗xd5 ♗e6 18 ♗xa8 is winning for White – Shirov.

13 ♗g5 ♗xg5

Safer is 13...h6 14 ♗xe7 ♘cxe7 15 a4 a6, but White still enjoys some advantage after 16 ♘d6.

14 ♘exg5 h6

Now Shirov-Estrada Gonsalez, French League 1995, continued 15 ♕c2! (15 ♘e4 ♕b6 16 ♕e2 is slightly better for White) 15...hxg5 16 ♘xg5 g6 17 ♘xe6 fxe6 18 ♕xg6+ ♔h8 19 ♖e4 and White had a very strong attack.

A22)
8...♕c7

In anticipation of e4-e5, Black develops his queen to put extra pressure on that square. There is a question mark, however, as to whether the queen is well placed here. On the minus side White has tricks involving ♘f1, ♗f4 and then ♘e3xd5. It's surprising how often this theme works for White.

9 e5 ♘d7

9...♘g4 is a little loose. White was clearly better after 10 ♕e2 f6 11 exf6 ♗xf6 12 ♘b3 b6 13 c4! dxc4 14 dxc4 e5 15 h3 ♘h6 16 ♗xh6 gxh6 17 ♘h2 in Savon-Radulov, Sinaia 1965.

10 ♕e2 b5

Black has two major alternatives:

a) 10...b6 (with this move Black's bishop will not be blocked when it goes to a6, but in general Black's counterplay on the queenside is slower) 11 ♘f1 ♗a6 12 h4 and now:

a1) 12...♘d4 (this idea is double-edged; after the exchange Black has play down the half-open c-file, but the pawn on d4 can become vulnerable) 13 ♘xd4 cxd4 14 ♗f4

♖ac8 15 ♖ec1! (the other rook is required to cover b2) 15...♘c5 16 ♘h2 ♔h8? (Black should play 16...♘a4, which is answered by 17 ♖ab1) 17 ♘f3 ♘a4 18 ♘xd4 ♘xb2 19 c4 and White wins material, Berg-Rian, Novi Sad Olympiad 1990.

a2) 12...♖fe8 13 ♗f4 ♘f8 14 h5 h6 15 ♘1h2 ♘h7 16 ♕d2 c4 17 dxc4 ♗xc4 18 ♘g4 ♗f8 19 c3 ♖ad8 20 ♕c2 a5 21 ♖ad1 and White has a pleasant space advantage, Quinteros-Bjelajac, Novi Sad 1982.

b) 10...f6!? 11 exf6 ♘xf6 12 ♘b3 and now:

b1) 12...♗d6 13 c4 (or 13 ♘g5 e5 14 c4!?) 13...♗d7 14 ♗e3 b6 15 ♖ac1 ♖ae8 16 d4! and the tension in the centre favours White, Matera-Nunn, Birmingham 1975

b2) 12...♗d7 13 ♗f4 ♗d6 14 ♗xd6 ♕xd6 15 ♘e5 ♘xe5 16 ♕xe5 ♕xe5 17 ♖xe5 (the weakness on e6 gives White a slight pull) 17...♖ac8 18 d4! b6 19 dxc5 bxc5 20 c4 ♘g4 21 ♖e2 dxc4 22 ♘a5 ♗b5 23 a4 and White went on to win, Reshevsky-De Winter, Siegen Olympiad 1970.

11 ♘f1 b4

Alternatively:

a) 11...♗a6 (it seems strange putting the bishop in front of the a-pawn, but Black plans a quick-fire ...♖fc8 and ...♘d4) 12 h4 ♖fc8 13 ♗f4 ♘d4? (but this is too early; Black should prepare it with 13...♕b6) 14 ♘xd4 cxd4

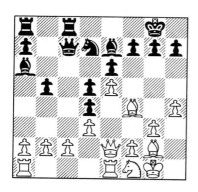

15 ♗xd5! (this standard combination is

often advantageous to White) 15...exd5 (in Votava-Stocek, Turnov 1996, Black simply gave up the pawn with 15...♗b7?!) 16 e6 ♗d6 17 exd7 ♕xd7 18 ♗xd6 ♕xd6 19 ♖ac1 with a clear advantage to White. Black's bishop is looking silly on a6 and White will follow up with ♘h2-f3 and ♕e5, picking up the loose d4-pawn.

b) 11...a5 (this may transpose to the text, but here we will concentrate on lines where Black refrains from playing an early ...b5-b4) 12 h4.

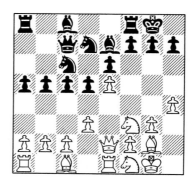

Now Black has a further choice:

b1) 12...♘d4!? 13 ♘xd4 cxd4 14 ♗f4 ♖a6! (planning ...♖c6) 15 ♘h2 (15 ♗xd5?! is ineffective here due to the surprising zwischenzug 15...♗b4! 16 ♖eb1! – 16 ♖ec1? exd5 17 e6 ♖xe6 18 ♕xe6 ♕xf4 19 ♕xd7 loses to 19...♕xc1! – 16...exd5 17 e6 ♕c6 18 exd7 ♗xd7 and Black is okay) 15...♖c6 16 ♖ac1 ♗a6? (Black should play 16...♕b6) 17 ♗xd5! (now this works well) 17...exd5 18 e6 ♕d8 19 exd7 ♖e6 20 ♕g4 f5 21 ♕h5 ♕xd7 22 ♘f3 g6 23 ♕h6 ♗f6 24 ♖xe6 ♕xe6 25 ♗e5! and White had a big advantage in Fischer-Geller, Netanya 1968. This game concluded 25...♖xe5 26 ♖e1 f4 27 ♖xe5 ♕d7 28 h5 fxg3 29 hxg6 gxf2+ 30 ♔xf2 hxg6 31 ♕xg6+ ♔g7 32 ♖g5 ♖f7 1-0.

b2) 12...♗a6 13 ♗f4 ♖fc8 14 ♘e3 ♕d8 (14...♘d4? 15 ♘xd4 cxd4 16 ♘xd5! is good for White again) 15 ♖ac1 (15 h5!?) 15...b4 16 c4 bxc3 17 bxc3 ♖ab8? (Uhlmann suggests

17...♘f8)

18 ♘xd5! (here we go again – it's really surprising how many black players have fallen for this trick) 18...exd5 19 e6 ♘f8 20 exf7+ ♔xf7 21 ♘e5+ ♘xe5 22 ♕xe5 ♗b7 23 ♖b1 ♘g6 24 ♕e6+ ♔e8 (24...♔f8 loses to 25 ♗xb8 ♖xb8 26 ♖xb7 ♖xb7 27 ♗xd5) 25 ♕g8+ ♘f8 (or 25...♔d7 26 ♗h3+ ♔c6 27 ♕e6+ ♗d6 28 ♕xd5+!! ♔xd5 29 ♗g2 mate) 26 ♕xg7 ♖c7 27 ♗xc7 ♕xc7 28 ♗xd5 ♘g6 29 h5 ♘f8 30 ♗c6+ ♔d8 31 ♕xf8+ 1-0 Bednarski-Doroshkievich, Polanica Zdroj 1971.

12 h4 a5 13 ♗f4 ♗a6

After 13...a4 White can prevent Black from playing ...a4-a3 with 14 a3!?, for example 14...♗a6 15 ♘e3 bxa3 16 bxa3 ♘d4 (16...♖ab8 17 ♘xd5 exd5 18 e6 ♗d6 19 ♗xd6 ♕xd6 20 exd7 ♕xd7 21 ♘e5 ♘xe5 22 ♕xe5 ♗b7 23 ♕e7 was better for White in Paragua-Roiz, St Lorenzo 1995) 17 ♘xd4 cxd4 18 ♘xd5 exd5 19 e6 ♗d6 20 ♗xd6 ♕xd6 21 exd7 ♕xd7 22 ♕e5! and both Black's d-pawns are weak.

14 ♘e3

Lining up ♘xd5 ideas, as well as ♘g4.

14...a4

Or:

a) 14...♖fc8 15 ♘xd5! exd5 16 e6 ♗d6 17 ♗xd6 ♕xd6 18 exd7 ♕xd7 19 ♘g5! ♘d4 (19...h6 20 ♗h3 f5 21 ♘e6!) 20 ♕h5 h6 21 ♘xf7 and White wins a pawn, D.Gross-Petrik, Guarapuava 1995

b) 14...♘b6 (this stops ♘xd5 tricks but

removes a defender from the kingside) 15 ♘g4 ♕a7 16 h5 ♖fc8 17 h6 g6 18 c3 bxc3 19 bxc3 ♘d7 20 ♗g5 and White has annoying pressure on the dark squares around the black king, Benko-Csom, Palma de Mallorca 1971.

15 b3

Uhlmann gives 15 ♘xd5 exd5 16 e6, with a slight plus top White, while 15 a3!? transposes to note to Black's 13th.

After 15 b3, the game Vasiukov-Uhlmann, Berlin 1962, continued 15...♖a7 16 h5 ♖fa8? 17 h6 g6 18 ♘xd5! exd5 19 e6 ♕d8 20 exf7+ ♔h8 (20...♔f8 21 ♘g5! ♗xg5 22 ♗xg5 ♕xg5 23 ♕e8+ or 20...♔xf7 21 ♕e6+ ♔f8 22 ♘g5 ♗xg5 23 ♗d6+ are winning for White) 21 ♘e5 ♘cxe5

22 ♕xe5+! ♗f6 (22...♘xe5 loses after 23 ♗xe5+ ♗f6 24 ♗xf6+ ♕xf6 25 ♖e8+) 23 ♕e8+ ♘f8 24 ♗e5 ♕b6 25 ♗xd5 ♖c8 26

♗e6! ♗xe5 27 ♗xc8 ♗d6 28 ♗xa6 ♖xa6 29 bxa4 ♖a7 30 ♖e6 ♕c7 31 ♖ae1 c4 32 ♖xd6 ♕xd6 33 ♖e6 and Black resigned on account of 33...♕c5 34 d4.

A23)
8...b6

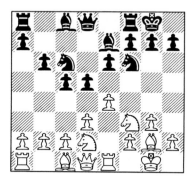

This move shouldn't concern White too much. Indeed, Black often winds up playing ...b6-b5, arriving a tempo down on Variation A24. These positions are worth studying, however, as Black often stumbles into them after having played an earlier ...b7-b6, before deciding to castle short.

9 e5 ♘d7

Or 9...♘e8 10 ♘f1 f5 11 exf6 ♗xf6 12 ♘e3 ♘d6 (Jansa-Kostro, Polanica Zdroj 1968), and now Uhlmann recommends 13 c3, intending ♘g4.

10 ♘f1 ♗a6

Or 10...♗b7 11 h4 and now:

a) 11...b5 12 ♘1h2 a5 13 ♘g4 a4 14 a3 b4 (Ciocaltea-Zivkovic, Bar 1977), and now 15 h5, intending h5-h6, looks stronger than the game continuation of 15 ♗g5.

b) 11...h6 12 ♘1h2 ♖e8 13 ♘g4 ♘f8 14 c3 ♖c8 15 ♗h3 a5 16 ♗d2 b5 17 d4 and White was doing well in Liberzon-Murey, Reykjavik 1975. The rest of the game is interesting; White successfully sacrifices on the kingside and crashes through: 17...cxd4 18 cxd4 ♕b6 19 ♗xh6 gxh6 20 ♕d2 ♘h7 21 ♕f4 ♘d8 22 ♗f1 ♔h8 23 ♗d3 ♖g8 24

♕xh6 ♖g6 25 ♗xg6 fxg6 26 ♘f6 ♗xf6 27 exf6 ♕c7 28 ♘e5 ♔g8 29 ♖ac1 1-0

11 h4 ♖c8

Or 11...♕e8 12 ♗h3 ♗d8 13 ♗f4 ♗c7 14 ♘1h2 ♘d8 15 ♕d2 and White gradually builds up the pressure, Petrosian-Barcza, Budapest 1952.

12 ♘1h2 b5 13 ♗g5

13 h5!? also comes into consideration.

13...b4

We are following the game Ljubojevic-Korchnoi, Sao Paulo 1979. Here Korchnoi erred with 14 ♕d2?, and after 14...c4 15 d4 c3! 16 bxc3 bxc3 17 ♕f4 ♘b4 18 ♖ec1 ♗e2 19 a3 ♘c6 20 ♖e1 ♗a6 Black was doing well. Instead White should continue actions on the kingside with 14 ♕c1! or 14 ♘g4 (Cabrilo).

A24)
8...b5

Black's most popular and ambitious move. Queenside operations are not delayed any further.

9 e5

After 9 e5 Black has a choice of knight retreats:

A241: 9...♘e8
A242: 9...♘d7

A241)
9...♘e8

This is much less popular than 9...♘d7, although it is not clear whether there is any particular reason for this.

10 ♘f1

White carries on operations on the kingside.

10...b4

Alternatively:

a) 10...♘c7 11 h4 ♗d7 12 h5 b4 13 h6 g6 14 ♗f4 ♘b5 15 ♕c1 was unclear in Reinderman-Bischoff, Venlo 2000.

b) 10...f6?! (this seems premature) 11 exf6 ♗xf6 (11...gxf6 12 ♗h6 ♖f7 13 c4 ♘c7 14 cxd5 ♘xd5 15 a3 ♖b8 16 ♖c1 and Black's pawn structure leaves a lot to be desired, Borik-Sonntag, German Bundesliga 1995) 12 ♘e3 ♕d6 (12...e5 13 ♘xe5!) 13 c4! ♘c7 14 ♘g4 e5 15 ♘xf6+ gxf6 (15...♕xf6?! 16 cxd5 ♘xd5 17 ♘xe5! is strong for White) 16 cxd5 ♘xd5 17 ♘d2! ♗e6 18 ♘e4 ♕e7 19 ♗h6 ♖fd8 20 ♖c1 c4 21 ♕h5 and Black's position was full of weaknesses, Dolmatov-Meyer, Philadelphia 1991.

11 h4 a5 12 ♘1h2

12 ♗f4 a4 13 a3 (Fischer's recipe – see also Variation A2421) 13...bxa3 14 bxa3 ♘c7 15 h5 ♘b5 16 h6 g6 17 c4 ♘bd4 18 ♘xd4 ♘xd4 19 ♘e3 ♗b7 20 ♖b1 ♗c6 was equal in Sandipan-Davies, Dhaka 2001.

12...a4

13 ♘g5

Or:

a) 13 a3 (to prevent ...a4-a3) 13...bxa3 14 bxa3 ♘c7 15 ♗g5 ♗a6 16 ♕d2 ♖b8 17 ♘g4

♔h8 18 ♗xe7 ♕xe7 19 h5 h6! (preventing h5-h6) was unclear in McShane-Davies, British League 1997.

b) 13 ♘g4 a3 14 h5 f5 15 exf6 gxf6 16 bxa3 bxa3 17 ♘h6+ ♔g7 18 c4!, with a complicated position, Szabo-Darga, Winnipeg 1967.

13...a3 14 bxa3 ♘d4

The more miserly 14...bxa3 should be considered.

After 14...♘d4 15 axb4 cxb4 16 ♘gf3 ♘b5 Black has some compensation for the pawn, but it's probably not quite enough, Musil-Velimirovic, Portoroz/Ljubljana 1975.

A242)
9...♘d7

This is by far Black's most popular retreat.

10 ♘f1 a5 11 h4 b4

Or:

a) 11...a4 12 a3! b4 13 ♗f4 transposes to Variation A2421.

b) 11...♗b7 12 ♘1h2 a4 (Pavlov-Sveshnikov, Moscow 1977) and now White should play 13 a3!.

12 ♗f4

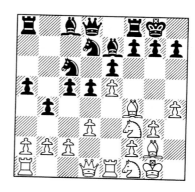

Here we will look at two possible ideas for Black, which are closely linked.

A2421: 12...a4
A2422: 12...♗a6

A2421)
12...a4

This move has been criticised, perhaps unfairly, in some texts.

12...a4 13 a3!?

Bobby Fischer's important move, which breathed new life into this variation for White. The main point is that Black is prevented from playing ...a4-a3 and thus weakening the c3- and d4-squares. From a practical viewpoint White has scored very well from this position.

13...bxa3

Given as the 'main line', but in my opinion this may be a slight inaccuracy. 13...♗a6!? loses a pawn after 14 axb4 cxb4 15 ♖xa4, but Black's compensation is considerable after 15...♘c5 16 ♖a1 b3. In which case, White might have nothing better than to transpose to Variation A2422 with 14 ♘e3 or 14 ♘1h2.

14 bxa3 ♗a6

14...♘d4 15 c4! ♘b6? (better is 15...♘xf3+) 16 ♘xd4 cxd4 17 ♕g4 gave White a strong attack in Sasikiran-Reefat, Kelamabakkam 2000.

15 ♘e3 ♘a5

Or:

a) 15...♗b5?! 16 c4! is strong – compare with Variation A2422.

b) 15...♘d4 16 c4! ♘b3 (after 16...♘b6 17 cxd5 ♘xd5 18 ♘xd5 exd5 19 ♘xd4 cxd4 20 ♕xa4 ♗xd3 21 ♕xd4 White was simply a pawn up in Geurink-Tondivar, Leeuwarden 1995) 17 cxd5! ♘xa1 18 ♕xa1 exd5 19 ♘xd5 and White has excellent compensation for the exchange, for example 19...♗xd3 20 e6 fxe6 (20...♘f6 21 ♘xe7+ ♕xe7 22 ♘e5 ♗g6 23 ♘c6 ♕b7 24 ♗d6 was very good for White, Gheorghiu-Uhlmann, Sofia 1967) 21 ♖xe6 ♗f6 (Vogt-Schauwecker, Swiss League 1994)

---

see following diagram

---

and now 22 ♕a2! looks strong, for example 22...♔h8 (22...c4 23 ♗c7 ♕c8 24 ♖xf6!) 23 ♘xf6 ♖xf6 (23...gxf6 24 ♗h6 ♖e8 25 ♘g5!; 23...♘xf6 24 ♖d6!) 24 ♖xf6 ♘xf6 25

♘e5 ♖a7 26 ♕d2 c4 27 ♘xc4! and despite being the exchange up, Black has serious problems dealing with the threat of ♘e5.

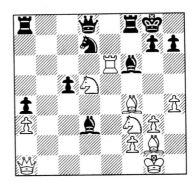

16 ♗h3

16 ♘g5!? also looks good, for example 16...♖b8 17 ♗h3 ♖b6 (17...h6 18 ♘xf7!?) 18 ♕g4 ♗c8 19 ♕h5 ♗xg5 20 hxg5 g6 21 ♕h6 ♕e7 22 ♘g4 ♖e8 23 ♘f6+ ♘xf6 24 gxf6 ♕f8 25 ♕h4 and White's attack is looking very dangerous, Eisenmann-Drechsler, correspondence 1988.

16...d4 17 ♘f1!

Strange at first sight, but 17 ♘g4 would block the queen's route to the kingside.

17...♘b6 18 ♘g5

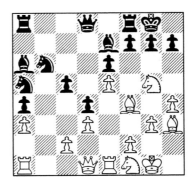

White has a very menacing attack. We are following the stem game Fischer-Miagmasuren, Sousse Interzonal 1967, which continued 18...♘d5 19 ♗d2 ♗xg5 20 ♗xg5 ♕d7 21 ♕h5 ♖fc8 22 ♘d2 ♘c3 23 ♗f6! ♕e8

(23...gxf6 24 exf6 ♚h8 25 ♘f3 ♘d5 26 ♕h6! ♖g8 27 ♘e5 ♕c7 28 ♗g2! – Black has no good defence to ♗e4 – 28...♖ae8 29 ♗e4 ♘xf6 30 ♕xf6+ ♖g7 31 ♖ab1 ♕e7 32 ♘g4 and White has a winning advantage) 24 ♘e4 g6 25 ♕g5 ♘xe4 26 ♖xe4 c4 27 h5 cxd3 28 ♖h4 ♖a7 (or 28...dxc2 29 hxg6 c1♕+ 30 ♖xc1 ♖xc1+ 31 ♚h2! fxg6 32 ♖xh7 ♚xh7 33 ♕h4+ ♚g8 34 ♕h8+ ♚f7 35 ♕g7 mate) 29 ♗g2! dxc2 30 ♕h6 ♕f8

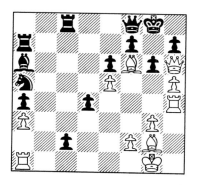

31 ♕xh7+!! 1-0 (31...♚xh7 32 hxg6+ ♚xg6 33 ♗e4 is mate).

A2422)
12...♗a6

This move has taken over the mantle of being the main line.

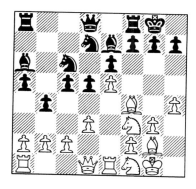

13 ♘1h2

Also interesting is 13 ♘g5!? and now:
a) 13...♗xg5? (this gives White a free at-
tack) 14 hxg5 ♕c7 15 ♕h5 ♗b7 16 ♘h2 ♘d4 17 ♘g4 ♘xc2 18 ♘f6+! ♘xf6 19 gxf6 ♚h8 20 fxg7+ ♚xg7 21 ♕g5+ 1-0 Minkov-Hanzel, correspondence.

b) 13...h6 14 ♘h3, followed by ♕g4 or ♕h5.

c) 13...♕e8! (the best defence) 14 ♕g4 (14 ♕h5 ♗xg5 15 hxg5?! f5! blocks the White attack; players should be aware of this defence) 14...♚h8! (14...a4? 15 ♘xe6! 1-0 was the abrupt conclusion of Bronstein-Uhlmann, Moscow 1971, while 14...♘b6 15 h5 ♗b5 16 ♘f3 ♚h8 17 h6 g6 18 ♗g5 a4 19 ♕f4 ♗xg5 20 ♘xg5 ♕e7 21 ♘e3 ♖a7 22 ♘g4 gave White a strong attack on the dark squares, Van der Weide-Visser, Dutch League 1995) 15 ♘h2 ♗xg5?! (Black should play 15...♘d4 or 15...a4) 16 hxg5 ♘d4 17 ♖ac1 a4 18 ♘f3 b3 19 axb3 axb3 20 ♘xd4 cxd4 21 ♗d2 and the d-pawn is dropping off, Baur-Schneider, Badenweiler 1994.

It's also possible to play as in Variation A2421 with 13 ♘e3 a4 14 a3 ♗b5! (14...bxa3 15 bxa3 transposes to Variation A2421) 15 h5 (after 15 c4 we see the point of Black not exchanging on a3; he can play 15...bxc3! 16 bxc3 ♘a5 17 ♖b1 ♗c6 18 c4 dxc4 19 dxc4 ♖b8 and Black is even better, Damjanovic-Uhlmann, Monte Carlo 1968) 15...♖c8 16 ♘g4 c4 17 d4 c3 18 bxc3 bxa3 19 h6 and once again we have a very finely balanced position, J.Kristiansen-Sorensen, Lyngby 1989.

13...a4 14 a3

Once again following Fischer's idea of preventing Black from playing ...a4-a3. An example of White allowing the advance is the following: 14 ♖c1!? a3 15 b3 ♖c8 (15...♘a7 16 ♘g5 ♘b5 17 ♕h5 h6 18 ♘gf3 ♕e8 19 ♕g4 ♚h8 20 ♗f1 ♘b8 21 ♗d2 ♘c6 22 ♗h3 was unclear in Polugaevsky-Guyot, France 1993) 16 ♘g4 ♘d4 17 ♘xd4 cxd4 18 ♘h2 ♕c7 19 ♕g4 ♚h8 20 ♘f3 ♕c3 21 ♗g5 ♗xg5 22 ♘xg5 h6. Now in the game P.Claesen-Muir, European Team Championship, Batumi 1999, White played passively with 23 ♘f3?, and after 23...♕b2! Black went on to win. Instead Horn analyses the following variation to a draw: 23 ♘xf7+! ♖xf7 24 ♕xe6 ♖cf8 25 ♕xa6 ♖xf2 26 ♕d6 ♕d2 27 ♗xd5 ♖h2 28 ♖f1 ♖ff2 29 ♕c6 ♕e3 30 ♕a8+ ♘f8 31 ♕xf8+ ♖xf8+ 32 ♔xh2.

14...♗b5

Alternatively:

a) 14...c4!? 15 d4 c3 16 bxc3 bxc3 17 ♘g5 ♘b6? (Kaidanov suggests that 17...h6 is stronger, against which White should play 18 ♘h3 and ♕h5) 18 ♕h5 and now:

a1) 18...h6 19 ♘g4!

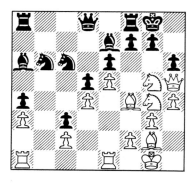

19...hxg5 (or 19...♘xd4 20 ♘xh6+ gxh6 21 ♕xh6 ♗xg5 22 ♗xg5 f6 23 ♗xf6 ♖xf6 24 exf6 ♕c7 25 ♖e5 and White wins) 20 hxg5 g6 (20...♘xd4 loses after 21 ♘f6+ gxf6 22 gxf6 ♗xf6 23 exf6 ♕xf6 24 ♗e5!) 21 ♕h6 ♘xd4 22 ♘f6+ ♗xf6 23 gxf6 ♘f5 24 ♕h3 and Kaidanov assesses this as winning for White, which seems correct. After 24...♘d7 25 g4 ♘d6 26 ♕h6 ♘e8 27 ♖e3 ♘exf6 28 ♖h3 Black has no good defence.

a2) 18...♗xg5 19 ♗xg5 ♕e8 20 ♗f6! ♘xd4? (20...gxf6 is more resilient, but Kaidanov's 21 ♘g4 ♘d7 22 ♗xd5 exd5 23 exf6 ♔h8 24 ♖xe8 ♖axe8 25 ♕xd5 ♘cb8 is still clearly better for White) 21 ♘g4 and White's attack proved to be much too strong, Kaidanov-Nijboer, Elista Olympiad 1998. The game concluded 21...♘f5 22 ♕g5 ♔h8 23 ♗xg7+ ♘xg7 24 ♘f6 ♕d8 25 ♕h6 ♖xf6 26 ♕xf6 ♖ae8 27 g4 ♘d7 28 ♕f4 ♗c4 29 h5

♖c8 30 ♖ab1 f5 31 exf6 1-0.

b) 14...bxa3 15 bxa3 ♖b8 16 ♘g5 ♕e8 17 c4! ♘b6 18 cxd5 ♘xd5 19 ♗xd5 exd5 20 e6! and the complications favour White, Kaidanov-S.Anderson, Dallas 1996.

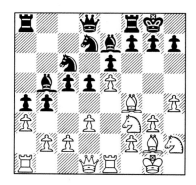

The position after 14...♗b5 is rich in possibilities and gives both sides ample opportunity to play for the win. Here are some examples:

a) 15 ♗h3 ♕e8 16 ♘g4 ♖c8 17 ♕c1?! (17 h5!? or 17 ♗g5 look stronger) 17...♘d4! 18 ♘xd4 cxd4 19 ♕d1 bxa3 20 bxa3 ♖c3 21 ♗c1 ♖c8 22 ♖e2 ♕c7 23 ♗b2 ♖c8 24 ♗xc3 ♕xc3 and Black has more than enough compensation for the exchange in C.Hansen-Ye Jiangchuan, Istanbul Olympiad 2000.

b) 15 ♘g5!? and now:

b1) 15...♘d4!? 16 c3 ♘b3 17 ♖a2 (incarcerating the rook!) 17...♖c8?! (17...♕c7!? may be stronger; the position is unclear after 18 c4 dxc4 19 ♗xa8 ♖xa8 20 dxc4 ♗xc4 21 ♕c2 ♗xg5 22 ♕xc4 ♘b6 23 ♕e4) 18 c4 dxc4 19 dxc4 ♗c6 20 ♗xc6 ♖xc6 21 axb4 ♘b6 22 ♕c2 g6 23 b5 ♖c7 24 ♘g4 and White was better in Jansa-Krallmann, Hamburg 1995.

b2) 15...♕e8 16 ♕h5 ♗xg5 (16...h6 17 ♘g4! hxg5 18 hxg5 gives White a powerful attack) 17 ♕xg5 (17 hxg5 f5! is a defensive trick) 17...♘d4 (Fleitas-Perez, Cuba 1998) and now, according to Perez, White can keep the advantage with 18 ♘g4 ♕d8 19 ♘e3.

B)

5...g6

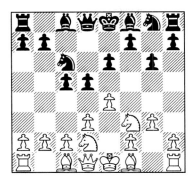

5...g6 is an ambitious move and a popular choice, especially at grandmaster level. From g7 Black's fianchettoed bishop controls the vital e5-sqare, and thus puts pressure on White's spearheading pawn, if and when it arrives there. The bishop also provides protection to the black king, if he castles short. On the other hand, the move ...g7-g6 does weaken the dark squares on the kingside, and White can always hope to take advantage of this later on.

6 ♗g2 ♗g7 7 0-0 ♘ge7

7...♘f6 has always been less popular, perhaps because it blocks the bishop on g7. More recently, however, it's been used by some strong grandmasters, so we should take a quick look. One possibility is 8 exd5!?, when 8...exd5 9 ♖e1+ is annoying for Black, while 8...♘xd5 transposes to Variation B1.

Instead, Adams-Khalifman, Dortmund 2000, continued 8 c3 0-0 9 e5 ♘d7 10 d4 b5 11 ♖e1 b4 12 ♘f1 ♗a6 13 h4 bxc3 14 bxc3 ♕a5 15 ♗d2 ♘b6 16 c4 ♕a4 17 cxd5 ♕xd1 18 ♖axd1 ♘xd5 19 dxc5 and White held a slight plus.

After 7...♘ge7 I'm giving White a choice of two different approaches. Variation B1 is tricky, but Variation B2 offers White more serious chances for an opening advantage.

B1: 8 exd5!?

B2: 8 ♖e1

B1)

8 exd5!?

Immediately releasing the tension, White plans to open the centre as quickly as possible, perhaps making use of Black's uncastled king. This is a deceptively tricky line, although Black should be okay, if he knows what he's doing.

8...exd5

For a long time the natural looking 8...♘xd5!? was considered wrong after 9 ♘b3 b6 10 c4 ♘de7 11 d4, when apparently the position opens up to White's advantage. For example, Csom-Ivkov, Ljubljana/Portoroz 1973, continued 11...cxd4 12 ♘fxd4 ♗d7 13 ♗g5 f6 14 ♗e3 0-0 15 ♕e2 e5 16 ♘b5 and White's pieces were much more active than their counterparts. However, 11...♗a6! is much stronger, after which Black seems to be fine. Perhaps White should consider diverging with 9 ♘e4!?.

9 d4!?

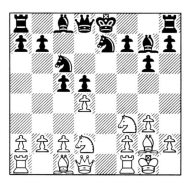

I believe this is an idea of the well-known Russian International Master and trainer Mark Dvoretsky. White offers a pawn to mess up Black's pawn structure. If this pawn can be regained then White usually keeps an advantage.

9...cxd4

9...♘xd4 leads to a similar position to the text after 10 ♘xd4 cxd4 (10...♗xd4 11 ♘b3! is annoying for Black; after 11...♗g7 12 ♘xc5 White has an edge due to the weakness of the isolated d5-pawn) 11 ♘b3 ♘c6!? (11...♛b6 12 ♖e1 ♗e6 13 ♗g5! is strong) 12 ♖e1+ ♗e6 13 ♗f4 0-0 14 ♘c5 and White has reasonable compensation for the pawn.

For those black players not willing to accept the sacrifice there's the enticing 9...c4, gaining space on queenside. However, this move has its own drawback in that it leaves the d5-pawn backward and inevitably vulnerable. Here's an excellent example of White exploiting this: 10 c3 ♗f5 11 ♖e1 0-0 12 ♘f1 h6 13 h4 (preventing ...g6-g5) 13...♖e8 14 ♗f4 ♛d7 15 ♘e5! ♘xe5 16 ♗xe5 f6 17 ♗f4 g5 18 hxg5 hxg5 19 ♗d2 ♗g4 20 ♗f3 ♗xf3 21 ♛xf3 g4 22 ♛h1! f5 23 ♛h5 ♖f8 24 ♗g5

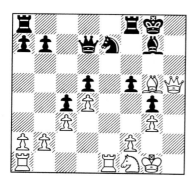

(Black has problems defending all his weak points) 24...♖ae8 25 ♘e3 ♘c8 26 ♔g2 ♖f7 27 ♗h6 ♗xh6 28 ♛xh6 ♖ef8 29 ♖h1 ♖g7 30 ♖h5 ♘e7 31 ♖g5 ♖ff7 32 ♖h1 ♔f8 33 ♖xg7 ♖xg7 34 ♛f6+ ♔g8 35 ♖h5 ♛c6 36 ♛e5 1-0 Gormally-Zagorskis, Copenhagen 1998 – f5 is dropping and then Black's whole position collapses.

10 ♘b3 ♛b6

Black should definitely try to hang on to his pawn, otherwise he will simply be worse due to his weakened pawn structure:

a) 10...0-0 11 ♘fxd4 ♘f5 12 ♘e2! (12 ♘xc6? bxc6 13 c3 a5! was better for Black in Moskovic-Emms, Barking 1994) 12...d4 13 ♘f4 ♖e8 14 ♘d3 and White is better here – the knight is well placed on d3 and the d4-pawn can eventually become vulnerable.

b) 10...♗g4!? 11 h3 ♗xf3 12 ♛xf3 0-0 13 ♗f4 'and White retains positional compensation for the sacrificed pawn' – Dvoretsky.

11 ♗f4

In the stem game Dvorietzky-Vulfson, USSR 1986, White played 11 ♗g5!? ♘f5 12 ♖e1+ ♗e6 13 g4! ♘d6 14 ♘fxd4! ♗xd4 15 ♘xd4 ♛xd4 16 ♗xd5 0-0 17 ♗xc6 ♛c5 18 ♗f3 and emerged from the complications with an edge. Dvoretsky, however, gives 11...0-0! as an improvement, with the continuation 12 ♘fxd4 ♘f5!, when White's pressure on d5 is compensated by Black's pressure on b2.

11...0-0

11...d3!? 12 c3 ♗f5 is similar to the text. White could also try 12 cxd3!? ♗xb2 13 ♖b1 ♗g7 14 ♘bd4 ♛a5 15 ♘b5, although after 15...0-0 the best I can see is a draw by repetition after 16 ♘c7 ♖b8 17 ♘b5.

12 ♗d6

In the excellent book *Opening Preparation* Dvoretsky claims White has the better chances here, but it's certainly not clear-cut.

12...d3 13 c3!

White must allow Black a passed pawn on d3 for the moment. 13 cxd3?! ♗xb2 would actually lead to a position which is normally reached (with colour reversed) via the move order 1 e4 c6 2 d4 d5 3 exd5 cxd5 4 c4 ♘f6 5 ♘c3 g6 6 ♛b3 ♗g7 7 cxd5 0-0 8 ♘ge2 ♘bd7 9 g3 ♘b6 10 ♗g2 ♗f5 11 0-0 ♗d3 12 d6 exd6 13 ♗xb7. The position after 13

♗xb7 is known to be good for White, so 13 cxd3 certainly cannot be recommended!

13...♗f5

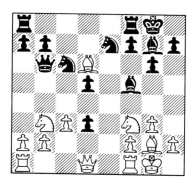

This is a critical position for the assessment of 8 exd5. White has some compensation and certainly if he picks up the d3-pawn he will be better, but that's quite a big 'if'.

a) 14 ♗c5 ♕b5 achieves little for White.

b) 14 ♘h4 ♖fd8 (or 14...♗e4 15 ♗c5 ♕b5 16 f3 f5!?) 15 ♗c5 ♕c7 16 ♖e1 ♗e4 17 f3 ♗f5 18 ♘xf5 ♘xf5 19 ♗h3 20 hxg3 ♕xg3+ 21 ♗g2 d4 was unclear in Vinke-Bergstrom, Lindesberg 1993

c) 14 ♖e1 ♖fe8 15 ♗c5 ♕c7 16 ♘h4 ♗e6 17 ♕xd3 (17 ♘f3 ♗f5 18 ♘h4 ♗e6 19 ♘f3 ½-½ was the end of Poettinger-Novkovic, Vorarlberg 1995) 17...♘e5 18 ♕c2; White has succeeded in regaining the pawn and keeps an edge due to his better structure. However, in this last line Black could try the interesting 16...♗e4!?, when both 17 f3 f5!? and 17 ♗xe4 dxe4 18 ♖xe4 ♖ad8 are unclear.

In conclusion, 8 exd5 is very tricky and certainly worth a try, but it seems more logical to delay this capture until Black has committed himself. .

B2)

8 ♖e1

This flexible move, maintaining the tension in the centre, is White's most popular choice.

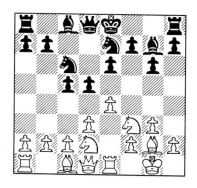

Now Black must make an important decision: whether to castle or to leave his king in the centre and develop elsewhere.

B21: 8...0-0

B22: 8...b6

Alternatively:

a) 8...♕c7 (the queen is not necessarily well placed here) 9 exd5! exd5 (9...♘xd5?! 10 ♘b3 b6 11 c4! ♘de7 12 d4 exploits White's pressure on the long diagonal) 10 d4 c4 (10...♘xd4? 11 ♘xd4 ♗xd4 12 ♘b3 ♗g7 13 ♗f4 ♕d8 14 ♕xd5 ♕xd5 15 ♗xd5 ♗xb2 16 ♖ab1 ♗f6 17 ♘xc5 leaves White with a dominating position, while after 10...cxd4 11 ♘b3 ♗g4 White gains time on the black queen with 12 ♗f4) 11 ♘f1 0-0 12 c3 and White will follow up with ♗f4.

b) 8...dxe4?! 9 ♘xe4 b6 10 ♗g5 ♗b7 (10...♗xb2 11 ♘f6+ ♗xf6 12 ♗xf6 0-0 13 ♘e5 is horrible for Black) 11 ♕d2 and the dark squares around the black king are looking very shaky. Abello-Riff, Bescanon 1999, concluded 11...♕c7 12 ♗f6 ♖g8 13 ♗xg7 ♖xg7 14 ♘f6+ ♔f8 15 ♕h6 ♘f5 16 ♘xh7+ ♔e7 17 ♕g5+ ♔d7 18 ♘f6+ ♔c8 19 ♘e8 and Black resigned.

c) 8...d4 (an obvious space gaining move which blocks the centre; there is, however, a major drawback to this move) 9 e5! (now that White has possession of the e4- and c4-squares, this advance is stronger than normal) 9...♕c7 10 ♘c4 0-0 11 a4 and White's pieces are well placed.

d) 8...h6 (the idea of this move is to support the pawn thrust ...g6-g5-g4 which can be effective when White has pushed e4-e5 – the e5-pawn can become vulnerable) 9 exd5!? (White is aiming for a more favourable version of Variation C1, with ♖e1 being more useful than ...h7-h6; 9 h4 is the most popular move, transposing after 9...b6 to Variation B222) 9...exd5 (9...♘xd5 10 ♘b3 b6 11 c4 ♘de7 12 d4 cxd4 13 ♘fxd4 again causes Black problems along the long diagonal) 10 d4 cxd4 11 ♘b3 ♗g4 (11...♕b6 12 ♗f4 0-0 13 ♗d6! – here the inclusion of ♖e1 and ...h7-h6 really helps White – 13...♖e8 14 ♗c5 ♕c7 15 ♘fxd4 and Black has no compensation for his weak isolated d5-pawn) 12 h3 ♗xf3 13 ♕xf3 0-0 14 ♗f4 and White has the usual positional compensation for the pawn.

B21)
8...0-0

'Castling is bad for Black; White's attack is very dangerous' – Dvoretsky. I wouldn't necessarily agree that castling is 'bad'. After all, some good Grandmasters have been fully aware of the dangers and have still chosen the move. Black does, however, have to play very carefully in order not to be blown off the board, and there's more good news in that in some lines White's position virtually plays itself.

9 h4

Previously the more direct 9 e5 ♕c7 10 ♕e2 was thought to be strong, but Black's play in variation 'b' casts doubt upon this.

a) 10...b6 11 ♘f1 ♗a6 12 ♗f4 ♖ad8 13 h4 d4 14 ♘1h2 ♘b4 15 ♕d2 (White's attack is automatic) 15...fe8 16 ♘g4 ♘ed5 17 ♗h6 ♗h8 18 ♗g5 ♖d7 19 a3 ♘c6 20 ♗f6 ♘xf6 21 exf6 h5 22 ♘h6+ ♔f8 23 ♘g5 ♗xf6 24 ♘h7+ ♔g7 25 ♘xf6 ♔xf6

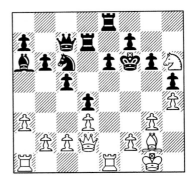

26 ♘f5!! exf5 (it's mate after 26...gxf5 27 ♕g5, 26...♔xf5 27 ♕g5, or 26...e5 27 ♕g5+ ♔e6 28 ♘g7+ ♔d6 29 ♕f6+ ♖e6 30 ♘e8) 27 ♖xe8 ♔g7 28 ♖ae1 ♘d8 29 ♕g5 c4 30 ♖h8 ♘e6 31 ♕h6+ ♔f6 32 ♖e8 1-0 Ciocaltea-Ilijin, Romania 1976.

b) 10...g5! 11 h3 (11 ♘xg5 ♕xe5 looks okay for Black) 11...h6 (11...♘g6!?) 12 ♘b3 b6 13 d4 ♘g6 14 ♗e3 cxd4 15 ♗xd4 ♘xd4 16 ♘bxd4 ♗d7 with an unclear position, Movsesian-Ulibin, Dresden 1994.

9...h6

This move nearly always seems to follow h2-h4, but Black does have other options:

a) 9...e5 certainly prevents White from playing e4-e5, but loosens the centre. White can claim an edge using quieter means, for example 10 exd5 ♘xd5 11 c3 b6 12 ♘c4 ♖e8 13 ♕b3 ♗b7 14 ♘g5 ♕d7 15 ♘e4 ♖e6 16 a4 ♖d8 17 a5, as in Lau-Löffler, German Bundesliga 1989.

b) 9...♕c7 10 h5! h6?! (10...b6 looks stronger) 11 hxg6 fxg6 12 c3 ♔h7 13 ♘b3 d4 14 cxd4 cxd4 15 e5 ♗d7 16 ♘c5 and

Black has many weaknesses, Mortensen-Agdestein, Espoo 1989.

c) 9...d4 10 e5! ♕c7 11 ♕e2 ♘d5 12 ♘f1 and White will continue with ♘1h2-g4.

10 e5 f5!?

Recently it's been shown that Black should strike back on the kingside before falling into a passive position, in which White's play is automatic. The quieter alternative is 10...♕c7 11 ♕e2 and now:

a) 11...g5? (with the addition of h2-h4 and ...h7-h6 this just doesn't work) 12 hxg5 hxg5 13 ♘xg5 ♕xe5 14 ♘de4! ♘d4 (14...dxe4 loses to 15 ♕h5) 15 ♕d1! (15 ♕h5? ♕f5! stops White's attack) 15...f6 (or 15...dxe4 16 ♕h5 ♕f5 17 ♗xe4 and Black can resign) 16 ♗f4 ♕f5 17 ♘d6 ♕g6 18 ♘xc8 ♖axc8 19 ♘xe6 with a winning position, Nanu-Puscas, Baile Tusnad 1999.

b) 11...b5 12 ♘f1 b4 13 ♘1h2 ♔h8 14 ♗f4 ♘g8 15 ♘g4 ♕e7 16 ♕d2 h5 17 ♘gh2 and White will continue the attack with ♘g5 and ♘hf3, Iordachescu-Prasad, Yerevan Olympiad 1996.

c) 11...b6 12 ♘f1 d4 13 ♘1h2 ♔h7 14 ♘g4 ♘d5 and now Dvoretzky-Feuerstein, Parsippany 2000, continued 15 ♕d2 h5 16 ♘f6+ ♔h8 17 ♕g5 ♕d8 18 ♘xd5 exd5 19 ♗f4, with an edge to White. However, the more direct 15 h5! looks even stronger; after 15...g5? 16 ♗xg5! hxg5 17 ♘xg5+ ♔g8 18 ♕e4 f5 19 exf6 ♘xf6 20 ♕g6 White has a winning position.

d) 10...b5 (Black begins his queenside counterplay) 11 ♘f1 a5 12 ♗f4 ♗a6 13 ♕d2 ♔h7 14 ♘1h2 ♘d4 15 ♘xd4 cxd4 16 ♘g4 ♘f5 17 ♗f3 ♖c8 18 ♔g2 a4 19 a3 ♖c6 20 ♖ac1 ♕e7 21 ♗g5!.

see following diagram

After this move Black cannot defend his position:

d1) 21...♕c7 22 ♘f6+ ♗xf6 (or 22...♔h8 23 g4! hxg5 24 hxg5 ♘h4+ 25 ♔g3 ♗xf6 26 gxf6 ♔h7 27 ♔xh4) 23 ♗xf6 ♖c8 24 ♗d1 ♘g7 25 ♕f4 ♕a5 26 ♖h1 b4 27 ♗xg7 ♔xg7

28 h5 and Black resigned, Solomunovic-Horther, Germany 1999.

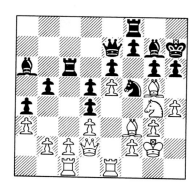

d2) 21...hxg5 forces White to show the true depth of his idea. 22 hxg5 ♕c7 23 ♘f6+ ♗xf6 24 gxf6 ♖c8 25 g4! and now:

d21) 25...♖xc2 26 ♖h1+ ♔g8 27 ♖xc2 ♕xc2 28 ♕f4! ♘e3+ 29 ♔g3 and White wins.

d22) 25...♘h4+ 26 ♔g3 ♖xc2 27 ♕g5! ♖h8 28 ♖h1 ♔g8 29 ♖ce1! ♕a5 (what else? – 29...♔f8 loses after 30 ♖xh4 ♖xh4 31 ♕xh4 ♔e8 32 ♕h7 ♕c5 33 ♖h1 ♕f8 34 ♕g7) 30 ♖d1!! ♕c7 31 ♖xh4 ♖xh4 32 ♕xh4 ♕xe5+ 33 ♔g2 and ♖h1 will be decisive.

d23) 25...♘e3+ 26 ♖xe3 ♖xc2 (Black will be mated after 26...dxe3 27 ♖h1+ ♔g8 28 ♕xe3) 27 ♗e2!! (another diagram please!)

27...♖xd2 28 ♖h3+ ♔g8 29 ♖ch1 and it's mate next move.

11 exf6 ♖xf6

Now White's spearhead pawn on e5 has been eliminated so Black is less likely to come under the same sort of pressure on the kingside. Black's pieces could become active and he has use of the semi-open f-file. On the other hand, there are other causes for concern, including Black's airy kingside and the pressure down the half-open e-file.

12 ᐅb3

Planning ♗f4. Also possible is 12 ᐅh2 (planning ᐅg4) 12...♖f7 13 ᐅg4 ♕d6 (13...e5 14 c4! looks good for White) 14 ᐅb3 ♔h7 15 c4 and now in Oratovsky-Maiwald, Vejen 1993, Black erred with 15...♗d7?!, allowing White to claim an advantage with 16 ♗e3 b6 17 d4!. Oratovsky suggests 15...b6 as an improvement, giving 16 ♗e3 ♗b7 17 ♕c1 as unclear.

12...♕d6

12...b6?! is too slow; White simply plays 13 ♗f4, followed by ♕d2. 12...e5 is playable, however. White should continue with 13 ᐅh2 ♕d6 14 ᐅg4 ♗xg4 15 ♕xg4 ♖af8 16 ♖e2, when the bishop pair promises an edge.

13 d4

13 ♗f4?! ♖xf4 14 gxf4 ♗xb2 gives Black excellent compensation for the exchange, while 13 ♗e3 b6 14 ♕d2 ♔h7 15 ♗f4 is once again answered by 15...♖xf4! 16 gxf4 ♗d7 17 d4 ♖f8 with an unclear position, Sheremetieva-M.Socko, Kishinev 1995.

13...cxd4 14 ᐅfxd4 e5 15 ᐅb5

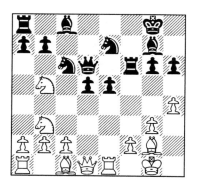

French GM Joel Lautier assesses this dou-

double-edged position as slightly better for White, but White must play accurately to bear this assessment out. The game Skorchenko-Kiseleva, Krasnodar 1998, continued 15...♕d8 16 c4 ♕b6! 17 ♕e2?! dxc4 18 ♕xc4+ ♗e6 19 ♕e2 ᐅf5 20 ♔h1 ♖af8 and Black was very active. Instead of 17 ♕e2, White should play 17 ♗e3! d4 18 ♗d2 ♗e6 19 ᐅd6 ♖af8 20 ᐅe4 ♖6f7 21 ᐅbc5 ♗f5 22 b4 and I prefer White.

B22)
8...b6

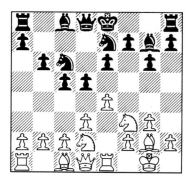

This is Black's most popular move. For the time being he keeps White guessing about where his king will go and instead prepares to fianchetto the c8-bishop. White now has three very playable alternatives:

B221: 8 exd5
B222: 8 h4
B223: 8 c3

9 e5?! releases the tension too early and allows Black an easy plan of undermining the support of the pawn: 9...♕c7 10 ♕e2 h6! (preparing ...g6-g5) 11 h4 g5! (anyway) 12 hxg5 hxg5 13 ᐅxg5 ♕xe5 14 ♕xe5 ♗xe5 and Black is better – Dvoretsky.

B221)
8 exd5

This move is very direct.

9...ᐅxd5

After 9...exd5 10 d4! White once again reaches a more favourable version of Variation B1 – ♖e1 is more useful than ...b7-b6. Black has three possible replies:

a) 10...cxd4 11 ♘b3 ♗g4 12 ♗g5 0-0 13 ♗xe7 ♘xe7 14 ♘bxd4 and the isolated pawn on d5 is more of a weakness than a strength

b) 10...♗f5!? (this is tricky) 11 c4! ♘b4! (11...cxd4 12 cxd5 ♘a5 13 ♘xd4 and 11...dxc4 12 ♘xc4 0-0 13 dxc5 ♕xd1 14 ♖xd1 bxc5 15 ♗e3 are both clearly favourable for White) 12 cxd5 ♘c2 13 d6! ♕xd6 14 ♘h4 ♘xe1 15 ♘xf5 ♘xf5 16 ♗xa8 ♘d3 17 ♕e2+ ♔d7 18 dxc5 ♘xc5 19 ♘e4 ♘xe4 20 ♗xe4 and Black's vulnerable king on d7 gives White an advantage.

c) 10...0-0 11 dxc5 bxc5 12 ♘b3 ♕b6 13 c3 c4 14 ♘bd4 and White has a nice outpost on d4, Oratovsky-Kiriakov, Vejen 1993.

10 d4!?

Again a sharp response, as White tries to exploit Black's unfinished development and the long h1-a8 diagonal. 10 ♘c4 would be the solid approach.

10...cxd4

10 ...♘xd4 11 ♘xd4 cxd4 12 ♘b3 transposes to the text, although White also has the extra option of 11 c4 ♘c7 12 ♘xd4 cxd4 13 ♗xa8 ♘xa8 14 ♕f3.

11 ♘b3 0-0

A major alternative is 11...♗b7 12 ♘fxd4 ♘xd4 13 ♘xd4 ♖c8 (preventing c2-c4).

Now White has the unexpected blow 14 ♖xe6+!?, leaving Black with two options:

a) 14...fxe6? 15 ♘xe6 ♕d7 16 ♘xg7+ ♕xg7 (16...♔f7 17 ♗h6 left Black in big trouble, Howell-Soln, Bled 1995) 17 ♗xd5 ♗xd5 18 ♕xd5 ♕d7 19 ♕e5+ ♔f7 20 ♗h6 and White has a very strong attack, Komliakov-Moskalenko, Noyabrsk 1995.

b) 14...♘e7!! (Peter Horn – this surprisingly calm retreat, exploiting the pin on the d-file, is enough to keep a balanced position) 15 ♗xb7 fxe6 16 ♗e3 (16 ♗xc8? loses to 16...♗xd4, when Black threatens both to capture on c8 and ...♗xf2+) 16...♖c4 17 ♘xe6 ♕xd1+ 18 ♖xd1 with an equal position. In fact, best play from here looks to be 18...♗xb2 19 ♖d8+ ♔f7 20 ♘g5+ ♔g7 21 ♘e6+ with a draw by perpetual check.

Given Black's resources in the above line, maybe White should consider a more positional route with 14 c3, for example 14...0-0 15 a4 e5 16 ♘b5 a6 17 ♘a3 ♗c6 18 ♕e2 and the pressure on Black's queenside ensures that White maintains a slight plus, Tringov-Janosevic, Belgrade 1969.

12 ♘bxd4 ♘xd4 13 ♘xd4 ♗a6

Following 13...♕c7 White can play quietly with 14 c3, or else try 14 ♗xd5!? exd5 15 ♗f4 ♕c4 16 ♗e5.

Here White can win a pawn with 14 ♘c6!? ♕d7 15 ♗xd5 exd5 16 ♕xd5, but after Horn's suggestion of 16...♖ae8!! White has nothing better than to force a draw with 17

♕xd7 (17 ♖xe8 ♕xe8! threatens ...♗b7 and ...♕e1+) 17...♖xe1+ 18 ♔g2 ♗f1+ 19 ♔f3 ♗e2+ with a perpetual, as 20 ♔f4? loses to 20...♗h6+ 21 ♔e4 ♗g4+.

If White is playing to win, then he should consider 14 h4!?, for example 14...♖c8 (14...h6 transposes to Variation B222) 15 ♗g5 ♕d7 16 ♕d2 ♖c4 17 c3 ♗xd4?! (17...♖fc8 look safer) 18 cxd4 f6 19 ♗h6 ♖e8 20 ♗f1 ♖a4 21 ♗h3 and White's bishops look dangerous, Boyd-Sulava, Cannes 1996.

B222)
9 h4

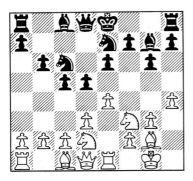

A multi-purpose move. White prevents ...g6-g5 and in some positions he can soften up the black kingside with h4-h5. As well as this, White is not committing himself just yet in the centre.

9...h6

The most common reply, keeping White's pieces out of g5 and preparing to answer h4-h5 with ...g6-g5!.

10 c3

The move c2-c3 is useful in that some lines White is ready to play e4-e5, quickly followed by d3-d4. On the other hand Black can try to benefit from the fact that the d3-pawn is now more vulnerable.

After 10 exd5!? Black must be very careful – the insertion of h2-h4 and ...h7-h6 is sometimes to White's advantage.

a) 10...exd5!? (this is probably Black's saf-

est move) 11 d4!? (we've seen this idea before) 11...cxd4 12 ♘b3 ♗g4 13 ♗f4 0-0 14 ♕d2 ♗xf3 15 ♗xf3 ♔h7 16 ♖e2 ♕d7 17 ♖ae1 and White has the usual structural compensation for the pawn, Shirov-G.Hernandez, Merida 2000.

b) 10...♘xd5 (this can lead to great complications) 11 d4! cxd4 12 ♘b3 and now:

b1) 12...♗b7 13 ♘fxd4 ♘xd4 (13...♘de7 14 ♘b5 0-0 15 ♘d6 is annoying for Black, but is probably better than the text) 14 ♘xd4 ♖c8 15 ♘xe6!

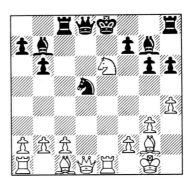

Here we see an important difference to Variation B221. The insertion of h2-h4 and ...h7-h6 has left the g6-pawn very weak. After 15...fxe6 16 ♖xe6+ ♔f7 17 ♕g4 ♗f6 (or 17...♘f6 18 ♖xf6+ ♕xf6 19 ♗xb7 ♖xc2 20 ♗d5+ ♔f8 21 ♗f4 and Black is unlikely to survive against White's queen and rampaging bishops) 18 c4 h5 19 ♕e4 ♖xc4 20 ♖xf6+ ♘xf6 21 ♕xc4 White had reached a winning position in Kaiszauri-Mortensen, Gladsaxe 1979.

b2) 12...0-0! 13 ♘fxd4 ♘xd4 14 ♘xd4 ♗a6 and now once again White can win a pawn with 15 ♘c6 ♕d7 16 ♗xd5 exd5 17 ♕xd5, but Black has sufficient counterplay after either 17...♕xd5 18 ♘e7+ ♔h7 19 ♘xd5 ♖fe8 or 17...♖fd8!? 18 c4 ♕xd5 19 cxd5 ♖d7 (notice though that in comparison to Variation B221, 17...♖ae8? now loses as the white king has the h2-square). In view of this, White should consider instead both 15 c3 and 15 h5!?.

10...a5

Another common move by Black, who continues to gain space on the queenside. If allowed Black will follow up with ...a5-a4(-a3), but normally White puts a stop to this advance straight away. Another point to Black's move is that it prepares ...♗a6.

Notice that Black is still in no hurry to commit his king to the kingside. After 10...0-0?! White is now ready to advance with 11 e5, knowing that Black will hardly be able to undermine White's protection of e5 with ...g6-g5 now that the king is stuck on the kingside. After 11 e5, White's attack should flow smoothly, for example 11...♗a6 12 ♘f1 b5 13 ♗e3 d4 14 cxd4 cxd4 15 ♗d2 b4 16 ♕e2 ♖c8 17 ♘1h2 ♘d5 18 ♘g4 ♔h7 19 h5!

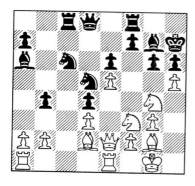

and White has good pressure on the kingside, Vavra-Sulava, Charleville 2000.

11 a4

Preventing Black's expansion plans and claiming the b5-square.

11...♗a6

A natural move, targeting the vulnerable pawn on d3.

Black's other common choice here is the slightly strange looking 11...♖a7!?, vacating the dangerous h1-a8 diagonal and thus avoiding many tactical problems. White should now continue 12 exd5 exd5 (12...♘xd5 leads to similar lines to text) 13 ♘b3 d4 (a point of ...♖a7 – 13...0-0 14 d4! c4 15 ♘bd2, followed

and b2-b3, gives White an advantage) 14 cxd4 cxd4 15 ♗f4 0-0 16 ♘e5! and White keeps a small advantage. Yudasin-Jukic, Bern 1989, continued 16...♘xe5 17 ♗xe5 ♗xe5 (17...♗b7!?) 18 ♖xe5 ♕d6 19 ♕e2 ♗e6 20 ♘d2 ♘c6 21 ♖xe6! fxe6 22 ♘c4 ♕d7 23 ♘xb6 ♕e8 24 ♖c1 and Black's weakened position more than compensates for the sacrificed material.

12 exd5 ♘xd5

After 12...exd5 White plays for d3-d4 with 13 ♘b3! and now:

a) 13...d4 14 ♘fxd4! ♘xd4 15 cxd4 is strong for White.

b) 13...0-0 14 d4! c4 15 ♘bd2 (now the bishop on a6 is misplaced) 15...♗c8 16 ♘f1 ♗e6 17 ♗f4 ♕d7 18 b3! and White will increase the pressure with ♘e3, Benjamin-Eingorn, Saint John 1988.

13 ♘c4

By recapturing on d5 with the knight, Black has neutralised any d3-d4 ideas by White, but in return White's knight mow has a very favourable outpost on c4. Black will always have to think twice about playing ...♗xc4, as this would leave him vulnerable on the light squares and prone to tactics along the long diagonal. Here are two possible continuations:

a) 13...0-0 14 ♕b3 ♖b8 15 ♗d2 ♖e8 16 ♖ad1 ♗b7 17 ♗c1 ♗a8 18 ♘a3 e5 19 ♘d2 ♘de7 20 ♘dc4 ♘c8 21 ♘b5 and White has made good use of his outposts, Lau-Jackelen,

Bad Wörishofen 1989.

b) 13...♕c7 14 ♕b3 (14 h5?! g5! 15 ♘xg5 hxg5 16 ♗xd5 0-0-0! is not what White wants, while 14 ♘a3?! ♖d8 15 ♘b5 ♗xb5 16 axb5 ♘ce7 was fine for Black in Kholmov-Pähtz, Varna 1987; 14 ♕e2 looks okay though) 14...♖d8 15 ♗d2 0-0 16 ♖ad1 and White has a small advantage.

B223)
9 c3

Here White follows a more positional course than with 9 exd5 or 9 h4.

9...a5

We've already discussed the ideas behind this move. Black does, however, have many alternatives:

a) 9...♕c7?! (Black's queen is misplaced and there are now some tricks both along the e-file and the possibility of a later ♗f4) 10 exd5! exd5 (10...♘xd5 11 d4! cxd4 12 ♘xd4 ♘xd4 13 ♗xd5 ♘c6 14 ♘c4 0-0 15 ♗f4 ♕b7 16 ♗g2 left Black with a horrible pin along the long diagonal, Filipowicz-Jaracz, Mikolajki 1991) 11 ♘f1 0-0 12 ♗f4 ♕d7 and Black's pieces aren't ideally placed, Yurtaev-Dvoretzky, Frunze 1983. Here Dvoretsky suggests 13 h4.

b) 9...h6 10 d4!? (White doesn't have to resort to these violent means; 10 h4 transposes to Variation C222, while 10 exd5!? exd5 11 d4 cxd4 12 ♘xd4 ♘xd4 13 cxd4 0-0 looks equal) 10...cxd4 11 ♘xd4 ♘xd4 12 cxd4

dxe4 (12...0-0 is safer – 13 e5 ♗a6 14 ♘f3 ♕d7 15 h4 ♖fc8 16 ♗f4 ♔h7 17 ♕d2 was slightly better for White in Van der Weide-Podzielny, Essen 2000) 13 ♘xe4 ♘d5 (13...♗b7 14 ♗f4 0-0 15 ♘f6+! wins material) 14 ♕a4+ ♔f8 (14...♕d7 15 ♕a3!) 15 b3 ♔g8 16 ♗a3 ♗d7 17 ♕c4 ♖c8 18 ♕d3 ♗c6 19 ♘d6! ♖c7 20 ♖ac1 and White has a good initiative. Kochetkov-Kalegin, Minsk 1994, continued 20...♗f8?

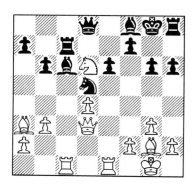

21 ♖xe6! and White had a crushing attack.

c) 9...♗b7 looks sensible. Now White could continue with noncommittal moves such as 10 ♕e2 or 10 h4, but there is a case for 10 e5!? here, even though Black has yet to castle and can arrange ...g6-g5. After 10 e5 we have:

c1) 10...♕c7 11 d4! (the point of 9 c3 – White builds the pawn chain) 11...0-0-0 (or 11...cxd4 12 cxd4 ♘b4 13 ♕a4+ ♘ec6 14 ♖e3 and the knight will be pushed away with a2-a3) 12 ♘f1 h6 13 h4 ♔b8 14 ♗f4 ♖c8 15 ♖c1 ♘f5 16 ♕d2 ♗f8 17 ♘e3 cxd4 18 cxd4 ♘xe3 19 ♕xe3 and White has a comfortable edge, Van der Weide-Baklan, Groningen 1996.

c2) 10...g5!? (the critical move) 11 ♘xg5 ♘xe5 12 ♘df3 ♘5g6 (12...♘xf3+?! 13 ♕xf3 0-0 14 ♕h5 is very good for White according to Moiseev) 13 d4 h6 14 ♘h3 ♕d7 15 a4 (Black's king won't want to be on the kingside, so White discourages queenside castling) 15...♘c6 (15...a5!? – Moiseev) 16 ♘f4

♘xf4 17 ♗xf4 and Black's king has problems finding a really safe place, Yurtaev-Gulko, Moscow Olympiad 1994.

d) 9...0-0 and now:

d1) 10 exd5!? ♘xd5 (10...exd5 11 ♘b3 h6 12 a4 a5?! 13 d4 c4 14 ♘bd2 ♗g4 15 b3 cxb3 16 ♕xb3 ♖b8 17 ♗a3 was very pleasant for White in Spraggett-Munoz Sotomayor, Elista Olympiad 1998 – both d5 and b6 are sensitive) 10...♘xd5 11 ♘c4 ♕c7 12 a4 ♗b7 13 h4 h6 14 ♗d2 ♖ae8 15 ♕c1 ♔h7 16 ♕c2 ♔h8 with an unclear position, Todorcevic-Miralles, Marseille 1987.

d2) 10 e5 (this is the move which 10...0-0 encourages, but Black can still hit out with ...g6-g5; if White is not happy playing this line he could choose either 10 h4 or 10 ♕e2) 10...♕c7 11 ♕e2 (11 d4 cxd4 12 cxd4 ♘b4! gives Black counterplay) 11...g5!? 12 ♘xg5!? (12 h3 is also possible, for example 12...h6 13 ♘f1 ♘g6 14 d4 a5 15 ♗e3 cxd4 16 cxd4 ♗a6 17 ♕d2 with a small plus for White, Iuldachev-Murugan, Kuala Lumpur 1993) 12...♕xe5 13 ♘de4!?

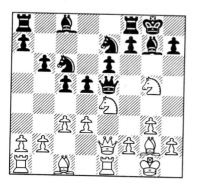

First played by the Belarussian IM German Kochetkov, this move is much stronger than the previous choice of 13 f4? ♕xe2 14 ♖xe2 ♗a6, when Black was clearly better in Höhn-Pedersen, Duisburg 1992. After 13 ♘de4 Black must make another decision:

d21) 13...h6 14 ♗f4 ♕f5 15 ♘d6 ♕g6 16 ♘xc8 hxg5?! (16...♖axc8 17 ♘f3 reduces White's advantage) 17 ♘xe7+ ♘xe7 18 ♗d6

♖fe8 19 ♗xe7 ♖xe7 20 ♗xd5 and White was a clear pawn to the good in Van der Weide-Van de Mortel, Leeuwarden 1996.

d22) 13...dxe4!? has only been 'refuted' by some dodgy published analysis, and it looks quite playable to me. White plays 14 ♗f4 ♕f6 (14...♕d5? loses after 15 ♗xe4 ♕d8 16 ♗xh7+ ♔h8 17 ♕h5) and now 15 ♘xh7!? ♔xh7 16 ♗xe4+ ♘g6 17 ♕h5+ ♔g8 18 ♗g5 ♕e5 19 ♗xc6 ♕b8! is very unclear, as is 15 ♗xe4!? e5 16 ♗xh7+ ♔h8 17 ♕h5 (17 ♘e4?! ♕e6 18 ♕h5?? – the refutation – loses to the simple 18...♕g4) 17...♗g4! 18 ♕xg4 exf4 19 ♗e4.

d23) 13...♘g6 14 f4! ♕c7 15 ♘f2 h6 16 ♘f3 f5 17 ♗e3 ♗a6 18 ♕d1 and White has a slight pull, Maje-Tu Hoang Thong, Elista Olympiad 1998.

e) 9...♗a6!? is yet another playable move, immediately putting pressure on the d3-pawn.

White now has:

e1) 10 ♕a4!? is a tricky move. Black should play 10...♗b7, rather than 10...♗xd3?! 11 exd5 b5 12 ♕a6 ♘b8 13 ♕b7, which is good for White.

e2) 10 exd5 and now 10...exd5?! 11 d4! cxd4 (11...0-0 12 dxc5 bxc5 13 ♘b3 c4 14 ♘bd4 left White better in Bates-G.Buckley, Hampstead 1998) 12 ♕a4 ♗b7 13 ♘xd4 0-0 14 ♘2f3 leaves White with the usual pressure against the isolated d5-pawn. Perhaps Black should play 10...♘xd5, when 11 ♕a4 ♗b7

12 d4 cxd4 13 ♘xd4 ♕d7 looks equal.

e3) 10 ♗f1!? 0-0 11 e5 h6 12 h4 ♕c7 13 ♕a4! ♗c8 14 d4 and White has an edge, Minic-Marjanovic, Bar 1980.

10 a4 ♗a6

Alternatively:

a) 10...h6 11 exd5 (for 11 h4 see Variation C222) 11...exd5 12 ♘b3! 0-0 13 d4 c4 14 ♘bd2 and White will follow up with b2-b3.

b) 10...♖a7 11 exd5 exd5 12 ♘b3! (the plan of ♘b3 and d3-d4 is particularly effective when Black has played ...a7-a5) 12...0-0 13 d4 c4 14 ♘bd2 ♗f5 (or 14...♗e6 15 b3 cxb3 16 ♕xb3 h6 17 ♗a3 with advantage, Ostermeyer-Jackelen, Porz 1988) 15 b3 ♗d3 (15...cxb3 16 ♕xb3 leaves Black with pawn weaknesses on d5 and b6, the second weakness being a consequence of ...a7-a5) 16 ♗f1 (16 bxc4 dxc4 17 ♗a3!? and 16 ♘f1!? should be considered) 16...♗xf1 17 ♔xf1 cxb3 18 ♕xb3 and White is slightly better, Zolnierowicz-Gleizerov, Bydgoszcz 2000.

11 exd5 ♘xd5

Giving White an outpost on c4, but after 11...exd5 White reverts to Plan A with 12 ♘b3 0-0 (12...d4 13 ♘fxd4! makes good use of the pins) 13 d4, for example 13...c4 14 ♘bd2 ♘f5 15 b3! cxb3 16 ♕xb3 ♖b8 17 ♗a3 and White is clearly better, M.Müller-Glek, Berlin 1994.

12 ♘c4

The knight is very well placed here and I feel this is enough to give White the edge in the position. .

12...0-0 13 h4

13 ♕e2 ♕c7 14 ♗d2 h6 15 h4 ♖ad8 16 h5!? g5 17 ♘xg5!? was interesting in Vogt-Kindermann, Biel 1990, which continued 17...hxg5 18 ♗xg5 f6! (18...♖de8? 19 h6 ♗h8 20 h7+! ♔xh7 21 ♕h5+ ♔g8 22 ♗e4 f6 23 ♗xd5 fxg5 24 ♖xe6 ♖xe6 25 ♗xe6+ ♔g7 26 ♕xg5+ ♔h7 27 ♔g2! wins for White, as does 18...♘f6? 19 ♗xf6 ♗xf6 20 ♕f3) 19 ♕xe6+ ♕f7 20 ♗h4 ♘e5! with a very unclear position.

13...♕c7 14 h5! ♖ad8 15 ♕e2 ♖fe8 16

hxg6 hxg6 17 ♘g5

White has considerable attacking chances on the kingside. We've been following the game Kaidanov-Zapata, New York 1993, which now continued 17...e5!? 18 ♕e4 ♗b7 19 ♕h4 ♘f6 20 ♘e4 ♘h7! (20...♘xe4? 21 dxe4, intending ♗g5 and ♘e3-d5) 21 g4! (planning ♖e3-h3) 21...♖xd3 22 ♗f1 ♖d7 23 ♖e3 ♘d8? (according to Dimitry Gurevich, 23...g5! keeps the balance) 24 ♖h3! ♗xe4 25 ♕xh7+ ♔f8 26 ♗h6 f6 27 ♖e1 ♕b7 28 g5! fxg5 29 ♕h8+ and Black resigned.

C)
5...♗d6

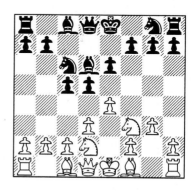

5...♗d6 introduces another reliable system for Black, who intends to follow up with ...♘ge7 and 0-0. In many ways this line is similar to Variation C, the only difference being that the bishop is developed on d6

rather than g7. It's less active on d6, but on the other hand Black has not had to weaken his dark squares on the kingside with ...g7-g6.

6 ♗g2 ♘ge7 7 0-0 0-0 8 ♘h4

This ambitious move, planning kingside expansion with f2-f4, was introduced at the highest level by Bobby Fischer. Although less common than 8 ♖e1, 8 ♘h4 has scored better and I believe it reaches more complex positions. For the record I believe 8 ♖e1 is playable, but the line 8 ♖e1 ♕c7 9 c3 ♗d7 10 ♕e2 f6! seems to be extremely solid for Black – White simply cannot advance with e4-e5.

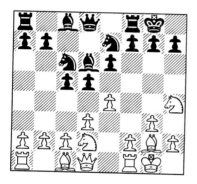

After 8 ♘h4 we will look at the following black options:

C1: 8...b6
C2: 8...♗c7
C3: 8...♗d7

Black also has some other possibilities:

a) 8...f5 9 f4 ♗d7 transposes to Variation C3.

b) 8...g5!? (outrageous, but not that bad!) 9 ♘hf3 (not 9 ♕g4?! f6 10 ♘hf3 ♕e8 11 ♘e1 e5 and White is driven back, Sadiku-Nikcevic, Pula 1990) and now

b1) 9...♘g6 10 ♘b1!? (for those not so keen on this redevelopment, 10 ♘b3!? looks worth a try) 10...f6 11 exd5 exd5 12 ♖e1 ♗f5 13 ♘c3 ♘ce7 14 d4 c4 15 ♗xg5! fxg5 16 ♘xg5 ♗b4 17 ♕h5 ♘h8 18 ♖e5 and White had a strong attack, Nevednichy-Vasilescu,

Bucharest 1992.

b2) 9...f6 10 exd5 exd5 11 c4 ♗e6 12 ♖e1 ♗f7 13 cxd5 ♘xd5 14 ♘e4 ♗e7 15 h4 h6 16 d4 c4 17 ♘c5 and Black hasn't entirely justified weakening his kingside, Sedina-Mrdja, Porto San Giorgio 1996.

c) 8...b5 9 f4 and now:

c1) 9...c4 10 e5 ♗c5+ 11 ♔h1 ♗a6 12 dxc4 bxc4 13 c3! ♕b6 14 ♕h5 and White can build up an attack on the kingside. Nevednichy-Saltaev, Tiraspol 1994, continued 14...g6 15 ♕g5 ♖ad8 16 ♘df3 ♘f5 17 ♘xf5 exf5 18 ♕h6 ♗e7 19 ♖e1 ♗c8 20 ♗e3!

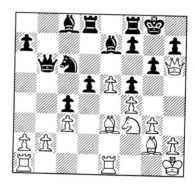

and now 20...♕xb2? loses immediately to 21 ♗c5! ♗xc5 22 ♘g5.

c2) 9...f6 (restraining White's e-pawn) 10 ♔h1 (avoiding any trouble along the g1-a7 diagonal) 10...c4 11 ♘df3 dxe4 12 dxe4 e5 (12...♗b7!?) 13 a4 b4 14 ♘f5 and now Wolff-Spangenberg, Buenos Aires 1997, continued 14...♗c5? 15 ♘xe7+ ♗xe7 16 ♕d5+! ♕xd5 17 exd5 ♘a5 18 ♘xe5! ♗f5 19 d6 ♗xd6 20 ♗d5+ ♔h8 21 ♗xa8 fxe5 22 fxe5 ♗xc2 23 ♗g5 and White won. Horn gives 14...♗xf5 as an improvement, continuing 15 exf5 exf4 16 ♘d4! ♘xd4 17 ♕xd4 ♖c8 18 ♗xf4 ♗xf4 19 ♕xf4, when White has an edge – on an open board the bishop on g2 is stronger than the knight on e7.

c3) 9...f5!? (blocking the f4-pawn; this is a common idea for Black) 10 exd5 (10 c3 ♖b8 11 exf5 exf5 12 ♘df3 b4 13 c4 d4 14 ♖e1 h6

15 &d2 was unclear in Meier-Bönsch, Berlin 1992) 10...exd5 11 ♘df3 h6 12 ♖e1 ♕b6 13 &e3 d4 14 &f2 &d7 15 c3! ♖ae8 16 cxd4 cxd4 17 ♖c1 with a tense position in Stripunsky-Goldin, Philadelphia 2000 – it's not clear whether Black's pawn on d4 is a strength or a weakness.

d) 8...♕c7 9 f4 f6 10 c3 &d7 11 ♖e1!? (Nevednichy-Horvath, Odorheiu Secuiesc 1993, continued 11 ♘b3 d4 12 c4 a6 13 &d2 ♖ab8 14 ♖c1 &e8 15 ♕e2 &f7 and now White should have played 16 ♔h1) 11...♖ae8 12 ♘f1 b5 13 a4 a6 14 axb5 axb5 15 exd5 ♘xd5 16 f5 and White was slightly better, Vujosevic-Fogarasi, Budapest 1990.

C1)
8...b6

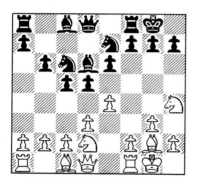

A sensible move. Black prepares to activate his bishop via either b7 or a6.
9 f4 dxe4
Alternatively:

a) 9...f5 (we've already seen the motives behind this move) 10 exf5 exf5 11 ♘df3 ♕c7 12 c3 &a6 13 ♖e1 ♖ae8 14 &e3 h6 15 d4 ♖d8 16 &f2 and White was better in Dvoretzky-Chekhov, Sverdlovsk 1987. Both sides have outposts, but it's easier for White to use e5 than it is for Black to use e4.

b) 9...f6 10 ♘df3 &c7 11 ♕e1 (White is slowly building up on the kingside) 11...♖b8 12 &e3 e5 13 f5 &a6 14 ♘d2 c4!? (after 14...d4 15 &f2 White will continue with g3-

g4, ♘hf3, h2-h4 and g4-g5) 15 dxc4 d4 (15...dxc4 16 c3 makes the bishop on a6 look rather silly) 16 &f2 b5 17 c5! b4 18 ♕d1 &xf1 19 &xf1 and White has good light square control for the exchange. Jaracz-Haba, Koszalin 1999, continued 19...♘a5 20 ♘b3 ♘ec6 21 &e1 ♖f7 22 ♘xa5 ♘xa5 23 a3! bxa3 24 b4! ♘c6 25 b5 d3 26 &xd3 ♘b4 27 &c4 ♘xc2 28 ♕xc2 ♕d4+ 29 ♔g2 ♕xa1

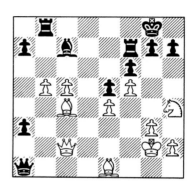

30 &xf7+ ♔xf7 31 ♕c4+ ♔f8 32 ♘g6+ hxg6 33 fxg6 ♔e8 34 ♕e6+ ♔d8 35 c6 1-0.
10 dxe4 &a6
Naturally gaining a tempo on the f1-rook, although interestingly the Slovakian GM Ftacnik gives this move a dubious sign.
11 ♖e1 &c7
Alternatively:

a) 11...c4 12 c3! (once again this kills the bishop on a6 – 12 e5 &c5+ 13 ♔h1 c3! 14 bxc3 ♖c8 was Black's idea) 12...♘a5?! (12...&c5+ 13 ♔h1 e5 14 f5 ♘c8 was still good for White in Dvoretsky-Mikhalcisin, Tbilisi 1980; Dvoretsky suggests 15 ♕h5, followed by g3-g4-g5) 13 e5! &c5+ 14 ♔h1 ♘d5 15 ♘e4 &b7 16 ♕h5! ♘e7 17 g4! with a very strong attack, Fischer-Ivkov, Santa Monica 1966. The rest of game is quite instructive: 17...&xe4 18 &xe4 g6 19 ♕h6 ♘d5 20 f5 ♖e8 21 fxg6 fxg6 22 ♘xg6! ♕d7 23 ♘f4 ♖ad8 24 ♘h5 ♔h8 25 ♘f6 ♘xf6 26 exf6 ♖g8 27 &f4 ♖xg4 28 ♖ad1 ♖dg8 29 f7! and Black resigned on account of 29...♕xf7 30 &e5+ ♖4g7 31 ♕xh7 mate.

b) 11...e5!? 12 f5 f6 13 ♗f1 ♗xf1 14 ♘xf1 (14 ♖xf1!? prevents ...c5-c4) 14...c4 15 c3 (15 ♕g4!?) 15...♗c5+ 16 ♗e3 ♗xe3+ 17 ♘xe3 ♘a5 18 ♕xd8 and the players agreed a draw in Koch-Hauchard, Vichy 2000.

12 c3

12 e5!? is interesting. Following 12...♕d7 (12...♕d4+!?) 13 ♕h5! Black has two choices:

a) 13...♕d4+ 14 ♔h1 ♕f2 15 ♘hf3 ♖ad8? (15...♗e2 is a stronger defence) 16 ♘e4! ♕xc2 17 ♘fg5 h6 18 ♘f6+! gxf6 19 ♗e4 ♗d3 (19...♕f2 20 ♗e3!) 20 ♕xh6! ♗xe4+ 21 ♘xe4 ♘d5 22 exf6 and Black resigned, Gottardi-Harding, correspondence 1990

b) 13...♘d4! and now:

b1) 14 ♗xa8 ♖xa8 (but not 14...♘xc2 15 ♗e4 g6 16 ♕d1 ♘xa1 17 ♘df3 and the knight on a1 is trapped) 15 ♕d1 ♗b7 gives Black good compensation for the exchange, according to Chekhov.

b2) 14 ♗e4 ♘ef5 15 ♘hf3 ♖ad8 16 c3 ♘e2+ 17 ♔f2 ♘xc1 18 ♖axc1 f6!, with an unclear position, Bologan-J.Horvath, Vienna 1996.

12...♗d3

12...♕d7 13 e5 ♖ad8 14 ♕h5 was good for White in Lerner-Dolmatov, Kharkov 1985. Now Black compounded his difficulties with 14...f5? and after 15 exf6 ♖xf6 16 ♘e4 ♖h6? 17 ♕xh6! White was winning

13 e5 ♕d7?!

Dolmatov suggests 13...b5!? as an improvement, although I still prefer White's attacking chances on the kingside to those of Black's on the queenside after 14 ♘e4 c4 15 ♕g4 ♗b6+ 16 ♔h1.

14 ♘e4 ♖ad8 15 ♕g4

Black is facing a rather daunting attack on the kingside. The game Dolmatov-Lautier, Polanica Zdroj 1991, continued 15...♗xe4?! (Dolmatov suggests 15...♔h8) 16 ♗xe4 ♘g6 17 ♘f3 ♘ce7 18 ♗c2 ♘f5 19 ♘g5 20 ♕h5 ♘h6?! (Dolmatov gives the line 20...h6!? 21 ♘xe6 ♘xe5 22 ♕xf5 g6 23 ♕e4 ♖xe6 24 fxe5 ♖xe5 25 ♕xe5 ♗xe5 26 ♖xe5 ♖e8 27 ♖xe8+ ♕xe8 28 ♔f2!, when White's rook

and two bishops outweigh Black's queen) 21 h4 b5?! 22 ♔h2 b4 23 ♕e2 ♘f5 24 h5 ♘f8 25 ♘e4! ♕c6 26 g4 ♘e7 27 h6 ♘d7 28 hxg7 ♔xg7 29 ♔g3 and Black was positionally lost.

C2)

8...♗c7

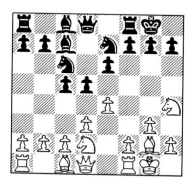

A non-committal move. Black puts his bishop on a safer square and awaits White's plan.

9 f4 f5

Black chooses to block White's f-pawn. Alternatives are:

a) 9...dxe4 10 dxe4 b6 (10...f5?! doesn't work very well with ...dxe4; after 11 c3 ♖b8 12 exf5 exf5 13 ♖e1 Black's position was full of weak squares in Nevednichy-Florescu, Bucharest 1998) 11 c3! ♗a6 12 ♖e1 and we have reached Variation C1.

b) 9...f6 10 ♘df3 (10 exd5!? exd5 11 ♖e1 b6 12 c3 ♕d7 13 ♘b3 ♗b7 14 d4 c4 15 ♘d2 ♖fe8 16 ♘f1 b5 17 ♘e3 was better for White in David-Rodgaard, Moscow Olympiad 1994 – Black's d5-pawn looks rather vulnerable) 10...dxe4 11 dxe4 ♕xd1 12 ♖xd1 and the extra space on the kingside grants White an edge in this ending, Szmetan-Rubinetti, Buenos Aires 1977.

c) 9...♘g6!? 10 ♘xg6 (10 ♘hf3!?) 10...hxg6 11 ♘f3 (11 e5!?) 11...dxe4 12 dxe4 b6 13 ♗e3 (13 ♕e2!? is more ambitious) 13...♗a6 14 ♖f2 ♕xd1+ 15 ♖xd1 ♖ad8 with a level position, Radulov-Damjanovic, Sarajevo 1971.

10 c3 ♔h8 11 exf5 exf5 12 ♘df3 ♗e6 13 ♖e1 ♗g8

Sznapik-Holm, Polanica Zdroj 1972, continued instead with 13...♕d7 14 ♘g5 ♗g8 15 ♕h5 ♖f6 16 ♗d2 ♖af8 17 ♖e2 ♖h6 18 ♕f3 ♘c8 19 ♖ae1 ♘d6 20 a3 c4 21 dxc4 ♘xc4 22 ♗c1 d4 23 ♕d3 ♗b6 24 ♔h1 ♖d6 and now White should probably capture on d4. Instead he played for tricks with 25 g4!? and was rewarded after 25...dxc3?? (25...♘e3!) 26 ♘g6+!.

14 ♗d2 ♕d7 15 a3 a5 16 a4!

We are following the game Ciocaltea-Liberzon, Netanya 1983. White's position is slightly more comfortable than Black's – he has both e5 and b5 under his control.

C3)
8...♗d7 9 f4 f5

This is a solid approach: Black stops White advancing too far on the kingside. The price for luxury is giving away the e5-square, although it's not that easy for White to take advantage of this

10 exd5

Great complications were created in the game Vasiukov-Krasenkov, St. Petersburg 1994, after 10 c4!? b5!? (10...d4 is safer) 11 cxd5! exd5 12 exf5 ♘b4 13 ♘df3! c4!? 14 dxc4 ♗c5+ 15 ♔h1 dxc4! 16 ♘g5 ♘xf5! 17 ♗d2! (17 ♗d5+ ♔h8 18 ♘xh7 ♘xd5 19

♘xf8 ♗c6 gives Black good compensation) 17...♘xh4 18 ♗xb4 ♗xb4 (18...♘xg2? loses to 19 ♕d5+) 19 ♕d5+ ♔h8 20 gxh4 and now, according to Krasenkov, Black's only way to stay in the game is with 20...♕e8.

10...exd5 11 c3

Or 11 ♘df3!? ♕b6 12 c3 ♖ae8 13 ♖e1 d4 14 ♘g5 g6 15 ♗d2 ♘d8?! (15...h6 16 ♘gf3 ♕xb2 is more critical) 16 cxd4 cxd4 17 b4 ♗b8 18 ♕b3+ ♔g7 19 ♕b2 and Black has problems along the long diagonal, An.Rodriguez-Milos, Villa Gesell 1996.

11...♕b6 12 ♔h1 ♖ae8 13 ♘df3

Artishevsky-Cherepkov, Minsk 1985, continued 13...d4 14 c4 ♕c7 15 ♖e1 a6 16 ♗d2, with a fairly level position.

Main Line 2:
Black plays ...d7-d5, but not ...c7-c5

1 e4 e6 2 d3 d5 3 ♘d2

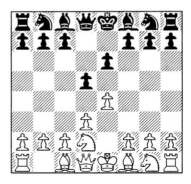

In this section we look at lines where Black refrains from playing ...c7-c5. The most promising alternatives to this move are lines with an early ...b7-b6 (A) or lines with ...♘c6 and ...e6-e5 (B), although this second approach does effectively lose a tempo.

3...♘f6

Alternatively

a) 3...♘c6 4 ♘gf3 ♘f6 transposes to Variation B, as does 4...e5 5 c3 ♘f6.

b) 3...dxe4 (Black does better to delay this exchange) 4 dxe4 e5 5 ♘gf3 (White has gained a significant tempo) 5...♗c5 6 c3 ♕e7 7 ♕c2 a5 8 ♘c4 ♘c6 9 ♘e3 ♘f6 10 ♗b5 0-0 11 0-0 h6 12 a4 ♘d8 13 ♗c4 ♘g4 14 ♘d5 ♕d6 15 b4! and White was better, Galdunts-Freitag, Bad Wildbad 2000.

c) 3...b6!? 4 g3! (here White's knight is not committed to f3, so White has some more options compared to the line 3...♘f6 4 ♘gf3 b6 5 g3) 4...♗b7 5 ♗g2 and now:

c1) 5...♘f6 6 e5 ♘fd7 7 f4 (an advantage of delaying ♘f3) 7...c5 8 ♘gf3 ♗e7 9 0-0 ♘c6 10 c3 ♕c7 11 a3 and White has an edge, Varavin-Bus, Krasnodar 1991.

c2) 5...dxe4 6 ♘xe4! ♘c6 7 ♘f3 h6 8 0-0 ♘f6 9 ♘e5! ♘xe4 10 ♗xe4 ♘xe5 11 ♗xb7 ♖b8 12 ♗g2 and White is better, Xie Jun-De Wolf, Vlissingen 1997 – the bishop pair and the weak light squares on the queenside.

c3) 5...c5 6 ♘gf3 (6 ♘e2!?; 6 f4!?) 6...dxe4 (or 6...♘f6 7 0-0 dxe4 – 7...♘c6 transposes to Main Line 1 – 8 ♘g5 ♗e7 9 ♘dxe4 with an edge) 7 dxe4 ♗a6 8 c4 ♘c6 9 0-0 ♗b7 10 e5 ♘ge7 11 ♕a4 ♕c7 12 ♘e4 ♘g6 13 ♖d1 ♗e7 14 ♘d6+ ♗xd6 15 exd6 ♕d7 16 h4 and I prefer White, Davies-Raicevic, Vrnjacka Banja 1988.

4 ♘gf3

Now we shall look at two main possibilities for Black

A: 4...b6

B: 4...♘c6

4...dxe4 is likely to transpose to lines similar to B1.

A)

4...b6

A move favoured by French Defence stalwarts Alexei Dreev and Evgeny Bareev. Black's play is very much directed towards punishing an early g2-g3 from White. Indeed, in this position 5 g3 dxe4! 6 dxe4 ♗b7 looks fine for Black, for example 7 ♗g2 ♘xe4 8 ♘e5 ♘c3! or 7 ♕e2 ♗a6 8 c4 ♘c6 9 e5 ♘d7 10 ♗g2 ♘c5 11 0-0 ♗b7 12 ♖d1 ♕d3, as in Zhang Zhong-Dreev, Shenyang 1999. Instead of 5 g3, I'm advocating two different approaches here for White.

A1: 5 e5

A2: 5 c3!?

A1)

5 e5 ♘fd7 6 d4 c5 7 c3

7...♗e7

A good waiting move. After 7...♗a6 8 ♗xa6 ♘xa6 we reach a position which can also be reached via a French Tarrasch after 1 e4 e6 2 d4 d5 3 ♘d2 ♘f6 4 e5 ♘fd7 5 ♗d3 c5 6 c3 b6 7 ♘gf3 ♗a6 8 ♗xa6 ♘xa6, where White's space advantage gives him a small plus. One example here is 9 0-0 ♗e7 10 a3!? (10 ♕e2 ♘c7 11 dxc5 bxc5 12 c4 0-0 13 ♖d1 f6 14 cxd5 exd5 15 e6 ♘e5 16 ♘xe5 fxe5 17 ♕xe5 ♗d6 18 ♕h5 ♕f6 was unclear in Frolov-Moskalenko, Simferopol 1990) 10...♘c7 11 ♖e1 ♘f8 12 ♘f1 ♘g6 13 ♘g3 h5 14 h3 h4 15 ♘f1 c4 16 a4 a6 17 ♘3h2 b5 18 ♕g4 ♕d7 19 axb5 axb5 20 ♖xa8+ ♘xa8

21 f4 ♘c7 22 ♘e3 b4 23 f5! and White went on to convert his advantage, Dolmatov-Rakic, Frunze 1983.

8 ♗b5!

A clever move, anticipating ...♗a6 from Black. After 8 ♗d3 ♗a6 Black gains a tempo on the line we were discussing in the previous note.

8...♗a6

After 8...a6 9 ♗a4 b5 10 ♗c2! the bishop has found its best diagonal, while its black counterpart is stuck on c8.

Another possibility is 8...a5 9 0-0 ♗a6 10 a4 ♕c8 11 c4! ♘c6 12 cxd5 exd5 13 dxc5 bxc5 14 ♘b3 ♘b4 15 ♗d2 0-0 16 ♘xa5 c4 17 ♗xb4 ♗xb4 18 ♘c6 and White was better, Turner-Conquest, British Championship 1997.

9 a4

The point of White's previous move. White is only willing to exchange bishops at a cost; following a recapture on b5 the pawn cramps Black and makes it difficult for him to develop his queenside.

9...0-0

Despite the statement above, it doesn't make sense for Black to opt out of exchanging bishops with 9...♗b7, for example 10 0-0 ♘c6 11 ♖e1 cxd4 (or 11...♖c8 12 ♘f1 c4 13 ♘g3 h5 14 b4 cxb3 15 ♕xb3 ♘a5 16 ♕c2 ♘c4 17 ♘d2 h4 18 ♘gf1 h3 19 g3 a6 20 ♗xc4 dxc4 21 ♘e4 0-0 22 ♕e2 b5 23 axb5 axb5 24 ♕g4 and White was clearly better, Anand-Dreev, London {rapid} 1995) 12 ♘xd4 ♕c7 13 ♘2f3 0-0 14 ♗xc6 ♗xc6 15 ♗g5 ♗d8 16 ♗xd8 ♖axd8 17 b4 and White has a typical 'good knight versus bad bishop', Anand-Dreev, London (rapid) 1995.

10 0-0 cxd4

This is an improvement over the previously played 10...♕c8 11 ♕e2 ♗xb5 12 axb5 a6 13 c4 ♕b7 14 cxd5 ♕xd5 15 dxc5 ♘xc5 16 ♘c4, when White has a good initiative, Psakhis-Raicevic, Moscow 1986.

11 cxd4 ♕c8

Preparing to play ...♘c6.

12 ♖e1 ♘c6 13 ♖e3! ♕b7

In a later game Bareev diverged with 13...♗xb5, and after 14 axb5 ♘b4 15 ♖c3 ♕b7 16 ♘f1 a6 17 bxa6 (17 ♗g5!?) 17...♖xa6 18 ♖xa6 ♘xa6 an equal position was reached, Adams-Bareev, Frankfurt 2000.

14 ♘f1 ♖fc8 15 ♗d2 ♗xb5 16 axb5 ♘a5

Adams-Bareev, Sarajevo 1999, continued 17 b3 a6 18 bxa6 ♖xa6 and now White finally began operations on the kingside with 19 h4!.

A2)
5 c3!?

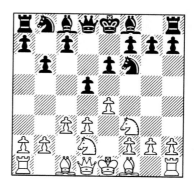

A tricky move, which perhaps gives Black more to think about than 5 e5.

5...♗e7

Black has various other tries:

a) 5...♗b7 6 e5 ♘fd7 7 d4 ♗e7 (7...c5 8

Ґb5!) 8 Ґd3 c5 9 0-0 Ґa6 transposes to the note to the seventh move in Variation A1 (with both sides having played an extra move).

b) 5...c5 6 ♕a4+!? ♕d7 (after 6...Ґd7 7 ♕c2! the bishop misplaced on d7, while 6...♘bd7 7 e5! ♘g8 8 d4 is also good for White) 7 ♕c2 ♕c7 8 Ґe2 Ґe7 (8...♘c6!? 9 0-0 Ґd6 10 ♖e1 0-0 11 ♘f1 h6 12 ♘g3 dxe4 13 dxe4 Ґb7 was roughly level in Bauer-Bareev, Cannes 2001) 9 0-0 0-0 10 ♖e1 Ґa6 11 ♘f1 ♘c6 12 ♘g3 dxe4 13 dxe4 Ґxe2 14 ♕xe2 and White has a small plus, Nevednichy-Matlak, Odorheiu Secuiesc 1995. The rest of the game is worth quoting: 14...♖fd8 15 e5 ♘d7 16 h4 h6 17 Ґf4 ♖ac8 18 h5 Ґf8 19 ♖ad1 ♘db8 20 ♘e4 ♖xd1 21 ♖xd1 ♖d8 22 ♖xd8 ♘xd8 23 Ґxh6! f5 24 exf6 gxh6 25 ♘h4 ♘bc6 26 ♕g4+ ♔h7 27 f4 ♕f7 28 ♘g6 c4 29 ♕e2 b5 30 g4 ♔g8 31 g5 ♕d7 32 ♕g4 ♘f7 33 gxh6 ♘xh6 34 ♘e7+ ♔h8

35 ♕g8+!! (what a move!) 35...♘xg8 36 ♘g6+ ♔h7 37 ♘xf8+ 1-0.

c) 5...Ґa6 6 Ґe2 Ґe7 7 0-0 0-0 (7...dxe4 8 dxe4 Ґxe2 9 ♕xe2 0-0 10 e5 ♘d5 11 ♘e4 gives White a pleasant space plus) 8 e5 ♘fd7 9 ♖e1 c5 10 ♘f1 ♘c6 11 Ґf4 ♖b8 12 ♕a4 (or 12 g3, with the idea of h2-h4 and ♘1h2-g4) 12...♕c8 13 Ґg3 c4 14 d4 b5 15 ♕c2 b4 16 Ґh4 ♖e8 17 Ґxe7 ♖xe7 18 ♕d2 f6 19 exf6 ♘xf6 20 ♘g3 with an edge to White, Yudasin-Gelman, Chicago 1997 – Black's bishop on a6 is out of the game.

6 ♕a4+

6 e5 ♘fd7 7 d4 c5 transposes to Variation A1.

6...c6 7 Ґe2

It's also possible to swing the queen over to the kingside after 7 e5 ♘fd7 8 ♕g4. Davies-Komarov, Saint Vincent 2000, continued 8...0-0 9 d4 c5 10 ♘b3 f5 11 ♕g3 Ґa6 12 h4 Ґxf1 13 ♔xf1 a5 with an unclear position.

7...0-0 8 0-0 ♕c7!?

Alternatively:

a) 8...Ґa6 9 ♖e1 ♕c7 10 ♘f1 ♘fd7 11 ♘g3 Ґd6 12 exd5 cxd5 13 ♕h4! ♘c6 14 ♘h5 and Black is lacking defenders on the kingside. Oratovsky-Kalinitschev, Fuerth 1998, continued 14...♘de5 15 ♘xg7! ♔xg7 16 Ґh6+ ♔g8 17 ♘xe5 Ґxe5 18 d4 Ґg7 19 Ґxg7 ♔xg7 20 ♕g5+ ♔h8 21 ♕f6+ ♔g8 22 ♕g5+ ♔h8 23 ♕f6+ ♔g8 24 Ґxa6 and White was a clear pawn ahead.

b) 8...b5 9 ♕c2 c5 10 d4 ♕b6 11 dxc5 Ґxc5 12 Ґd3! ♘c6 13 exd5 exd5 14 ♘b3 Ґg4 15 ♘xc5 ♕xc5 16 Ґe3 was Bologan-Bunzmann, Biel 1999. Here White's bishop pair and the weak pawn on d5 gives White a clear advantage.

9 ♖e1 ♘bd7

see following diagram

9...c5 10 Ґf1 ♘c6 11 a3 a5 12 ♕c2 a4 13 g3 ♖a7 14 Ґg2 ♖d8 15 exd5 ♘xd5 16 ♘e4 h6 was equal in Todorcevic-Itkis, Yugoslav Team Championship 1994, but perhaps White can play more ambitiously with 11 e5!?, for example 11...♘d7 12 d4 Ґb7 13 a3 a5 14 Ґd3 Ґa6 15 Ґb1!, intending ♕c2.

After 9...♘bd7 the game Orlov-Kruppa, St Petersburg 2000, continued 10 ♕c2 Ґb7 11 ♘f1 c5 12 ♘g3 Ґd6 13 Ґf1 h6 and Black had equalised. Perhaps retreating the queen on move 12 is not the right idea. Possible is 10 Ґf1!? (intending e4-e5), for example 10...Ґb7 11 e5 ♘e8 12 ♕g4! c5 13 d4, 10...e5 11 d4!?, or 10...♘c5 11 ♕c2 Ґa6 12 e5, all of which look interesting for White.

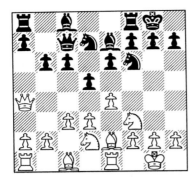

B)
4...♘c6

Black plans to play an early ...e6-e5 and perhaps ...dxe4.

5 c3!

5 g3 dxe4 6 dxe4 ♗c5 7 ♗g2 e5 looks equal. If Black plans to exchange on e4 and play ...e6-e5, it makes more sense for White to keep his light-squared bishop on the f1-a6 diagonal. A Philidor arises, with colours reversed and White having two extra tempi.

After 5 c3 Black must make a choice between:
B1: 5...dxe4
B2: 5...a5

Or 5...e5 6 ♗e2 (6 b4!?) 6...♗e7 (6...a5! transposes to B2) 7 0-0 0-0 8 b4! a6 9 ♗b2 ♗g4 10 a3 ♕c8 11 ♖e1 ♖d8 12 ♕c2 and White was better in Lobron-Reyes, New York 1988.

B1)
5...dxe4 6 dxe4 ♗c5

Or 6...e5 7 ♗b5! ♗d6 8 0-0 0-0 9 ♕c2 ♘e7 10 ♖e1 c6 11 ♗f1 ♘g6 12 ♘c4 ♗c7 13 a4 ♗g4 14 ♘fd2 b6 15 ♘e3 ♕c8 16 ♘dc4 a6 17 ♘f5 b5 18 ♘ce3 ♗xf5 19 ♘xf5 and White was better, Shchekachev-Schuette, Bad Zwesten 1999.

7 ♗b5 ♗d7 8 0-0 0-0 9 ♕e2

Dvoretsky also suggests 9 b4 ♗b6 10 ♕e2.

9...a6 10 ♗d3 e5 11 b4 ♗a7 12 ♘c4 ♖e8 13 ♗g5 h6 14 ♗h4 ♗g4 15 ♖ad1 ♕e7 16 h3 ♗h5 17 a4 ♕e6 18 ♘e3

We are following the game Dvoretsky-Orlov, Moscow (rapid) 1984, which continued 18...g5 19 ♗g3 g4? (19...♗xe3 restricts White's advantage) 20 hxg4 ♘xg4 21 ♘d5 ♖ac8 22 ♗c4 ♕g6 23 ♖d3 ♘e7 24 ♘h4 ♘xf2? 25 ♘xe7+ ♖xe7 26 ♗xf2 ♗xe2 27 ♘xg6 1-0.

B2)
5...a5

A useful restraining move; Black makes it harder for White to achieve the liberating b2-b4.

6 ♗e2 e5

Also possible is 6...g6 7 0-0 ♗g7 8 ♖e1 (8 e5 ♘d7 9 d4 0-0 10 ♖e1 b6 11 ♘f1 ♗a6 12 ♗xa6 ♖xa6 13 h4 b5 14 h5 with a slight plus, Reinderman-Tondivar, Leeuwarden 1993) 8...0-0 9 ♗f1 b6 10 e5 ♘d7 11 d4 f6

12 exf6 ♕xf6 13 ♗b5! ♘cb8 14 ♘f1 c6 15 ♗a4 ♕f7 16 ♗g5 ♗a6 17 ♗h4 h6 18 ♗g3 and White held the advantage in Ansell-Sarkar, London 2000.

7 0-0

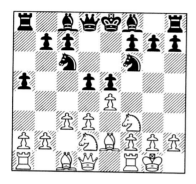

7...♗c5!?

A major alternative here is the more restrained 7...♗e7 and now:

a) 8 ♖e1 0-0 9 ♕c2 (9 b3 ♗c5 10 ♕c2 d4! 11 ♗b2 dxc3 12 ♗xc3 ♖e8 13 a3 ♕e7 14 ♕b2 ♗g4 15 h3 ♗xf3 16 ♘xf3 ♖ad8 was equal in Bates-N.Pert, British League 1998) 9...h6 10 ♗f1 ♖e8 11 b3! (with the plan of a2-a3, ♗b2 and b3-b4) 11...♗g4?! (11...d4! looks critical) 12 h3 ♗h5 13 a3 ♗d6?! 14 ♗b2 ♘b8? 15 exd5 ♘xd5 16 c4 ♘f4 17 g3 ♘e6 18 ♘xe5 and White was just a clear pawn up, Dvoretzky-Ek, Wijk aan Zee 1975.

b) 8 b3 (I think this is more the point – it's not clear whether White needs the rook on e1) 8...0-0 9 ♗b2 (9 a3 ♗e6 10 ♗b2 dxe4 11 dxe4 ♘d7 12 ♕c2 ♕e8 13 ♗c4 ♗c5 14 b4 ♗xc4 15 ♘xc4 was slightly better for White in Maiwald-Moor, Bern 1996) 9...♖e8 10 a3 ♗f8 11 b4 (11 ♕c2!?) 11...axb4 12 axb4 ♖xa1 13 ♕xa1 b6 14 ♗d1 (14 b5!?) 14...♗b7 15 ♗b3 ♕d7 16 ♖e1 b5 and the players agreed a draw in Visser-Psakhis, Groningen 1993, although White can still claim an edge after 17 ♕a2 ♖a8 18 ♕b1 ♖e8 19 exd5 ♘xd5 20 d4!.

8 b3 0-0

8...d4 9 cxd4 ♘xd4 10 ♗b2 looks better

for White, for example 10...♗g4 11 ♘xd4 ♗xd4 12 ♗xd4 ♗xe2 13 ♕xe2 ♕xd4 14 ♘f3 ♕d6 15 d4!.

9 ♗b2

There's also something to be said about leaving the bishop on c1, especially if White is going to block the centre with c3-c4 (after the advance ...d5-d4). So White should consider 9 a3 d4 (or 9...♖e8 10 ♖b1!?) 10 c4!?, followed by ♘e1-c2 and ♖b1.

9...♖e8

This looks better than 9...♕e7 10 a3! ♖d8 11 b4 dxe4 12 dxe4 ♗b6 13 ♕c2 and I prefer White. Jakupovic-N.Pert, Yerevan 1999, continued 13...axb4 14 axb4 ♖xa1 15 ♗xa1 ♗g4 16 h3 ♗xf3 17 ♗xf3 ♘b8 18 ♘c4 and White's advantage was evident.

The game Lastin-Gavrilov, Moscow 1996, continued 10 ♕c2 ♘h5! (10...d4 11 cxd4 ♘xd4 12 ♗xd4 ♗xd4 13 ♘xd4 exd4 14 ♖ac1 ♖e7 15 ♗f3 looks better for White) 11 ♖fe1 ♘f4 12 ♗f1 dxe4 13 ♘xe4 ♗a7 14 ♗c1 ♘g6 15 ♗e3 ♗g4 16 ♗xa7 ♘xa7 with a roughly level position.

As well as 10 ♕c2, White can consider 10 a3!? d4 11 cxd4 (11 c4!?) 11...♘xd4 12 ♖c1 b6 13 ♘xd4 ♗xd4 14 ♗xd4 exd4 15 f4.

Main Line 3:
Black plays ...c7-c5, but not ...d7-d5

1 e4 e6 2 d3 c5

2...c5 is actually a popular choice for

French players who would rather play Sicilian type set-ups without ...d7-d5 against the KIA. There are many games and much theory on the line 3 ♘f3 ♘c6 4 g3 g6 (or 4...♘ge7 5 ♗g2 g6), which is one of Black's most respected lines against the King's Indian Attack, and can obviously arise from both the French Defence and the Sicilian Defence. I must confess that rather than striving to find an advantage for White in these lines, I've taken something of a shortcut, but I hope you'll agree that this is a good practical decision, which makes full use of our repertoire.

3 g3!?

Keeping White's options open.

3...♘c6

Naturally Black can still advance his d-pawn; 3...d5 4 ♘d2 ♘c6 5 ♘gf3 transposes to Main Line 1.

4 ♗g2 g6

4...d5 5 ♘d2 will once again transpose to Main Line 1, while 4...♘f6 5 ♘c3 (5 f4!?) 5...d5 transposes to the Closed Sicilian.

5 ♘c3! ♗g7 6 ♗e3

and suddenly we are back in the Closed Sicilian, in a line where Black is committed to an early ...e7-e6 (see Variation A, Main Line 1 of the Closed Sicilian).

Rare Moves for Black

We'll finish off this section by looking at a few rare second moves Black has.

A: 2...♘c6
B: 2...b6

Or:

a) After 2...b5 White should just develop sensibly, for example 3 g3 ♗b7 4 ♗g2 c5 5 f4 ♘f6 6 ♘f3.

b) 2...f5?! can be met in a few ways. 3 ♘f3 fxe4 4 dxe4 ♘f6 5 e5 ♘d5 6 ♗c4 ♘b6 7 ♗d3 looks good for White.

A)

2...♘c6

Or 2...e5 3 ♘f3 ♘c6, although White should also consider playing a souped-up King's Gambit with 3 f4.

3 ♘f3 e5!?

3...d5 4 ♘bd2 ♘f6 leads to Main Line 2.

With 3...e5 Black is trying to play a king's pawn opening, claiming that White's extra d2-d3 is of no real consequence.

4 ♘c3!

Black was equal after 4 g3 ♗c5 5 ♗g2 d6 6 0-0 ♘f6 (6...f5!?) 7 c3 a6, Shirov-Ivanchuk, Novgorod 1994. 4 ♘c3 is Shirov's improvement.

4...♘f6 5 g3

This is Shirov's point. Now White is playing the so-called 'Glek system' (1 e4 e5 2 ♘f3 ♘c6 3 ♘c3 ♘f6 4 g3), but with an extra tempo.

5...♗c5 6 ♗g2 d6 7 0-0 a6 8 ♗e3 ♗g4 9 h3

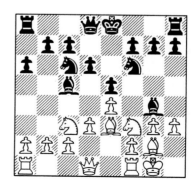

Shirov-Short, Yerevan Olympiad 1996, continued 9...♗xe3 10 fxe3 ♗xf3 and here Shirov recommends 11 ♕xf3 with a slight advantage to White.

B)

2...b6 3 g3 ♗b7 4 ♗g2 f5!?

This gives the variation its own character. For 4...d5 5 ♘d2 and 4...♘f6 5 ♘d2 d5 see Main Line 2.

5 ♘f3

5 ♘d2 ♘f6 6 ♘gf3 is possible, as 6...fxe4 7 dxe4 ♘xe4? 8 ♘h4! d5 9 ♘xe4 dxe4 10 ♕h5+ ♔d7 11 ♗g5 looks very strong for White.

5...fxe4

5...♘f6 is less accurate, as after 6 e5 ♘d5? 7 ♘h4! Black has big trouble dealing with the treats of c2-c4 and ♕h5+, for example 7...♕c8 8 ♕h5+ ♔d8 9 ♗xd5 ♗xd5 10 ♗g5+ ♗e7 11 ♘g6!.

6 ♘g5 ♘f6 7 0-0 ♗e7 8 ♘c3 0-0 9 dxe4 e5 10 ♗e3

White should also consider the immediate 10 f4!?.

10...♘a6 11 f4

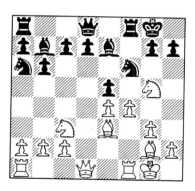

The game Benko-Sills, USA 1967, continued 11...exf4 12 gxf4 h6 13 e5! ♗xg2 14 ♔xg2 hxg5 15 exf6 ♖xf6 16 ♕d5+ ♔h8 17 fxg5 ♘b4 18 ♕d1 ♖xf1 19 ♕h5+ ♔g8 20 ♖xf1 ♘xc2 21 ♗d2 ♗xg5 22 ♗xg5 ♕e8 23 ♕xe8+ ♖xe8 24 ♖d1 d6 25 ♘d5 1-0

Important Points

Main Line 1

1) Think carefully before advancing with e4-e5; this lunge is usually more effective once Black has committed himself to castling kingside, or when White can easily support the advanced pawn.

2) If you play e4-e5, be wary of undermining attempts from Black, including the advance ...g7(g6)-g5.

3) Be aware of exd5 ideas, which can be advantageous to White in some lines, especially if Black is lagging behind in development. This motif is especially important in Variation B.

4) If White has played e4-e5 and Black pressures the pawn with ...♕c7, White should look out for tricks involving ♗f4 and then capturing on d5 with a piece (see Variation A22).

5) In Variation A242, White often plays the move a2-a3, to prevent Black playing ...a4-a3. This idea was first adopted by Bobby Fischer.

6) Bear in mind ideas of h4 for White. In Variation B Black often meets this with ...h7-h6, preparing to meet h4-h5 with ...g6-g5. Similarly, White often meets and unprovoked ...h7-h6 with ...h2-h4, making Black think twice about playing ...g6-g5.

Main Line 2

1) If Black exchanges too early on e4, White can consider deploying his light-squared bishop on the f1-a6 diagonal.

2) If Black plays an early ...b7-b6, White often plays e4-e5, following up with d3-d4.

CHAPTER FOUR

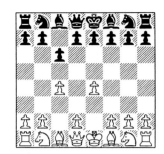

Attacking the Caro-Kann: 2 c4

1 e4 c6 2 c4

The Caro-Kann has a reputation of being a very solid defence and is a favourite of, amongst others, Anatoly Karpov. All the main lines have withstood the test of time; they are unbelievably hard to break down (I should know – I've done my fair share of trying!).

2 c4, however, is a deceptively tricky move, which may simply be used as another way of reaching the popular Panov-Botvinnik Attack (1 e4 c6 2 d4 d5 3 exd5 cxd5 4 c4) after 2...d5 3 exd5 cxd5 4 d4. However, by delaying the move d2-d4 White gives himself extra options; he can try to force Black into transpositions that may not be comfortable for the second player (this will become apparent when we study the theory and the numerous transpositions). It's true that Black also has extra options after 2 c4, but the white player has no need to fear these. In any case, the majority of Caro-Kann players will be attempting to steer the game back into a normal path with 2...d5, and it's here where White can adopt some devious move orders!

We shall concentrate on Black's two main replies to 2 c4. These are:

A: 2...d5
B: 2...e5!?

2...e6!? is a strange looking move, but it's not so bad. In the game Gulko-Shabalov, Bern 1992, White kept the advantage after 3 ♘f3 d5 4 cxd5 exd5 5 exd5 cxd5 6 ♗b5+ ♘c6 7 ♕e2+! ♕e7 8 ♘e5 ♗d7 9 ♗xc6 bxc6 10 0-0 ♔d8 11 b3! ♕e6 12 ♗b2 f6 13 ♕f3 ♗d6 14 ♘xd7 ♔xd7 15 ♘c3 ♘h6 16 ♘a4!.

A)
2...d5

This is by far the most popular choice for Black; on my database, games with 2...d5 outnumber games with 2...e5 by more than three to one.

3 cxd5

With our repertoire it really doesn't matter which way you capture first, as 3 exd5 cxd5 4 cxd5 comes to the same thing. Be wary of 3 exd5 ♘f6!?, though. Now 4 dxc6 ♘xc6 is known to give Black good play for the pawn, so White should react with 4 ♘c3 cxd5 5 cxd5, transposing to the main line.

3...cxd5

Again Black could offer a pawn with 3...♘f6!?, but White can simply decline with 4 ♘c3.

4 exd5

Now Black must make a decision concerning the d5-pawn: whether to capture it with the queen or try and capture it with the g8-knight.

A1: 4...♘f6
A2: 4...♛xd5

A1)
4...♘f6

This move is more popular than 4...♛xd5.
5 ♘c3

White has various other playable moves here, including 5 ♗b5+ and 5 ♛a4+, both of which try to hang onto the d5-pawn (for the time being at least). It's probable that an opponent will feel less prepared for 5 ♘c3, which on first sight appears less critical. After all, Black can simply win his pawn back immediately.

After 5 ♘c3 Black has another decision to make. The possibilities are:
A11: 5...♘xd5
A12: 5...g6!?

Other moves are less important:
a) 5...♘bd7!? 6 ♘f3 a6 7 d4 ♘b6 8 ♘e5 ♘bxd5?? (Oh dear! – 8...♘fxd5 is playable, but better for White) 9 ♛a4+ ♗d7 10 ♘xd7! 1-0 Lautier-Bologan, Enghien-les-Bains 1999; 10...♛xd7 loses material to 11 ♗b5. So even grandmasters have trouble getting to grips with 5 ♘c3!

b) 5...a6?! 6 d4 g6 7 ♛b3 (now we have a ...g6 variation of the Panov-Botvinnik Attack, where Black's ...a7-a6 is a bit irrelevant) 7...♗g7 8 g3 0-0 9 ♗g2 ♘e8 10 ♘f3 ♘d6 11 0-0 ♗f5 12 ♘e5 ♛c8 13 ♖e1 ♗h3 14 ♗h1 h5 15 ♗f4 and White has a clear advantage, Keitlinghaus-Schuste, Bad Wörishofen 1997 – Black has no chance of regaining his pawn.

A11)
5...♘xd5 6 ♘f3

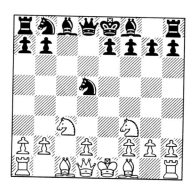

Again we have a further split:
A111: 6...♘c6
A112: 6...e6
A113: 6...♘xc3

6...g6!? looks risky after 7 ♛b3! ♘b6 (7...♘xc3 8 ♗c4! e6 9 ♛xc3 or simply 8 ♛xc3 is good for White) 8 ♗b5+! and now:
a) 8...♘8d7 9 ♘e5 e6 10 ♘e4! ♗e7 11 d4 0-0 12 ♗h6 ♖e8 (or 12...♘xe5 13 ♗xf8 ♔xf8 14 dxe5 ♛d4 15 ♘c3 ♛xe5+ 16 ♗e2 ♗d7 17 0-0 and White converted his material advantage, Thesing-Trzaska, Dortmund 1992) 13 0-0 a6 14 ♗xd7 ♘xd7 15 ♖fe1 and

Black is rather tied up.

b) 8...♗d7 9 ♘e5 e6 10 ♘e4! ♗e7 11 d4 ♘c6 (11...♗xb5 12 ♕xb5+♘8d7 13 ♗h6 a6 14 ♕e2 ♗b4+ 15 ♔f1 – White is already doing well here – 15...♘d5? 16 ♘xf7! ♔xf7 17 ♘g5+ ♔e8 18 ♕xe6+ ♕e7 19 ♕xd5 and White won, Illescas-Kamsky, Manila 1990) 12 ♘xd7 ♕xd7 13 ♗e3 0-0 14 ♘c5 ♕c7 15 0-0 ♘d5 16 ♖ac1 a6 17 ♗e2 ♖ab8 18 ♗f3 ♖fd8 19 ♕a4! ♗xc5 (19...♕b6?! 20 ♘xb7 ♕xb7 21 ♖xc6 ♕xb2 22 ♗xd5 ♖xd5 23 ♕xa6 and White is a clear pawn up, Miljanic-Todorovic, Niksic 1991) 20 ♖xc5 and White has an edge, according to the Czech GM Pavel Blatny.

A111)
6...♘c6

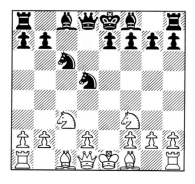

7 ♗b5!?

7 d4 would reach one of the main lines of the Panov-Botvinnik Attack (Black will be ready with 7...e6, 7...♗g4 or 7...g6!?), but this move forces Black to think for himself.

7...e6

Another possibility for Black is to exchange on c3 immediately with 7...♘xc3!? 8 bxc3 and now:

a) 8...♗g4!? 9 h3 (9 ♕e2 a6 10 ♗xc6+ bxc6 11 ♕e4 ♗xf3 12 ♕xf3 ♕d5 13 ♕xd5 cxd5 was equal in Lalic-Hodgson, Aberdeen 1996; 9 ♖b1!? looks interesting) 9...♗d7?! (9...♗h5 is the logical follow-up, after which White could try 10 ♖b1!?) 10 0-0 e6 11 ♖b1

♗d6 12 d4 and White was better in Conquest-Astolfi, French League 1992.

b) 8...g6 9 0-0 ♗g7 10 ♖e1 0-0 11 ♗a3 ♗f6 12 ♗xc6 bxc6 13 ♕a4 ♕c7 14 d4 ♗f5 15 ♘e5 ♖fc8 16 ♗c5 and White has a pleasant bind on the position, Tkachiev-Van der Werf, Wijk aan Zee 1995.

8 0-0 ♗e7 9 d4 0-0

9...♘xc3 10 bxc3 0-0 11 ♗d3 b6 12 ♖e1 transposes to Variation A11222.

10 ♖e1

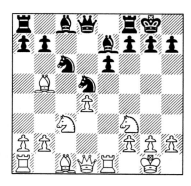

Normally White's light-squared bishop is on either c4 (see Variation A1122) or d3. The position with the bishop on b5, however, is still very playable for White.

10...♗d7

Alternatively:

a) 10...♘xc3 11 bxc3 ♗d7 (11...♗f6 12 ♖b1 ♘e7 13 ♕c2 ♕c7 14 ♘g5 g6 15 ♕d3 a6 16 ♗a4 ♕a5 17 ♘e4 ♗g7 18 ♗a3 was very unpleasant for Black in Forster-Palat, Geneva 1996) 12 ♕e2 ♖e8 13 ♗d3 ♖c8 14 h4 (14 ♖b1!? looks like a good alternative) 14...♕a5 (14...♗xh4 loses to 15 ♕e4!, hitting h7 and h4) 15 ♖b1 ♕xc3 16 ♖xb7 and White is very active, Belikov-Filipenko, Moscow 1998.

b) 10...♘f6 11 ♗f4 ♘b4 12 ♘e5 a6 13 ♗e2 ♘bd5 14 ♗g3 ♘xc3 15 bxc3 ♘e4 16 ♕d3 ♘xg3 17 hxg3 ♕c7 18 a4 and again White has an active position, Korchnoi-Serper, World Team Championship, Lucerne 1993.

c) 10...a6?! 11 ♗xc6! (weakening Black's pawn structure – White will target the isolated c-pawn and the weak dark squares around it) 11...bxc6 12 ♘e5 ♗b7 (12...c5? 13 ♘c6 ♘xc3 14 bxc3 ♕d7 15 ♘xe7+ ♕xe7 16 ♗a3! – Lukacs) 13 ♘a4 a5!? (13...♖c8? 14 ♘d3! left Black in a very passive position in Karpov-Dreev, Cap d'Agde 2000) 14 ♘c5 ♗xc5 15 dxc5 ♕e7 16 ♕g4 ♖fd8 17 ♗h6 f6 18 ♘c4 e5 19 ♘d6 ♗c8 20 ♕g3 and White is better – Lukacs.

11 ♗d3!?

Also promising, and perhaps more consistent, is 11 ♘xd5!? exd5 12 ♕b3 and now:

a) 12...♗g4?! 13 ♗xc6 bxc6 14 ♘e5 ♖b8 15 ♘xc6 ♖xb3 16 ♘xd8 ♖d3 17 ♘c6 ♗f6 18 ♗e3 and White is a clear pawn ahead, Damaso-Silva, Portuguese Championship 1996.

b) 12...a6 13 ♗xc6 ♗xc6 14 ♗f4 (14 ♘e5!?) 14...f6 15 ♗d2 a5 (to prevent the positionally desirable ♗b4) 16 ♘h4 ♖e8 17 ♘f5 ♗f8 18 ♖xe8 ♕xe8 19 ♖e1 ♕d7 20 ♕h3 ♔h8 21 ♕g4 g6 22 ♘e3 f5 23 ♕f3 with an unclear position, Peptan-Maric, European Women's Team Championship, Batumi 1999.

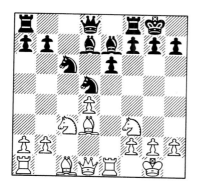

11...♗f6

Or:

a) 11...♘cb4 12 ♗b1 ♖c8 13 a3 ♘xc3 14 bxc3 ♘d5 15 ♕d3 ♘f6 16 ♗g5 g6 17 c4 and White is better, Kiik-Maki Uuro, Vantaa 1994.

b) 11...♖c8?! (this looks natural, but...) 12 ♘xd5 exd5 13 ♘e5! ♘xe5?! (13...♘xd4 is probably stronger, although I still prefer White after 14 ♗xh7+ ♔xh7 15 ♕xd4) 14 ♖xe5, ♗e6?! (perhaps Black should give up the d-pawn with 14...♗f6!?) 15 ♕h5! and now:

b1) 15...h6? 16 ♗xh6! gxh6 17 ♕xh6 gives White a winning attack.

b2) 15...g6 16 ♕h6

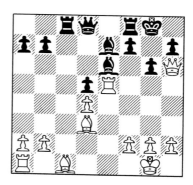

Black is in some trouble, for example 16...♗g4? (16...♗f6 17 ♖h5 ♖xc1+! 18 ♖xc1 ♖e8 19 ♖e1 was better for White in Belikov-Guliev, Moscow 1998) 17 h3! f6 18 ♗xg6! hxg6 19 ♕xg6+ ♔h8 20 ♖e3! and Black resigned in Vaganian-Serper, Groningen 1993, on account of 20...♗d7 21 ♖g3.

12 ♗e4 ♖e8 13 ♕d3

13 ♘xd5 exd5 14 ♗xd5 ♕a5! 15 ♗xc6 ♗xc6 16 ♖xe8+ ♖xe8 gives Black good

counterplay for the pawn.

The game Balashov-Yandemirov, Moscow 1998, continued 13...h6 (13...g6!?) 14 ♘e5 (but not 14 ♘xd5 exd5 15 ♗xd5?? ♖xe1+ 16 ♘xe1 ♕a5 17 ♕e4 ♖e8 and Black wins – Blatny) 14...♘db4 15 ♗h7+, ♔f8 16 ♕e4 ♘xe5 (Blatny suggests 16...♖c8!? as an improvement) 17 dxe5 ♗e7 18 ♕g4 g5 19 h4! and White had a strong attack.

A112)
6...e6

A popular and solid move. With 6...e6, Black is inviting White back into a main line of the Panov-Botvinnik Attack again.

7 ♗c4!?

But White is not so accommodating! After 7 d4 we have the Panov-Botvinnik Attack, against which Black can play 7...♗e7 or 7...♗b4. For the record, against the latter line White has been struggling to find an advantage, both after 8 ♗d2 0-0 9 ♗d3 ♘c6 10 0-0 ♗e7 (Karpov has used this line effectively with Black), and 8 ♕c2 ♘c6 9 ♗d3 ♗a5! 10 a3 ♘xc3 11 bxc3 ♘xd4.

With 7 ♗c4, White is making use of the fact that the d-pawn hasn't yet moves, so Black has no ...♗b4 pin at his disposal. This means we can simply bypass a lot of unwanted theory!

7....♗e7

Or:

a) 7...♘xc3 8 bxc3 ♗e7 9 0-0 0-0 10 d4 transposes to Variation A1121.

b) 7...♘b6 8 ♗b3 ♗e7 9 d4 0-0 10 0-0 ♘c6 11 a3 is a nice isolated queen's pawn (IQP) position for White – Black misses his defensive knight on f6. Kiik-Ovetchkin, St Petersburg 1999, continued 11...♗f6 12 ♗e3 ♘a5 13 ♗a2 ♘ac4 14 ♘e4 ♗e7 15 ♕e2 ♘xe3 16 fxe3 ♗d7 17 ♘e5 and White had very active pieces.

8 0-0 0-0 9 d4

In this position Black has a choice:
A1121: 9...♘xc3
A1122: 9...♘c6

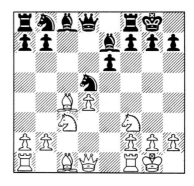

A1121)
9...♘xc3

After this move Black generally plays ...b7-b6, ...♗b7 and ...♘bd7(-f6).

10 bxc3 ♕c7

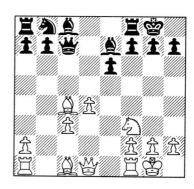

Alternatively:

a) 10...♘c6 11 ♖e1 transposes to A11222.

b) 10...♘d7 11 ♗d3 ♕c7 12 ♕e2 ♖e8 (grabbing on c3 looks very risky) 13 c4 g6 14 c5 ♘f6 15 ♘e5 ♗d7 16 ♗f4 ♕c8 17 ♖ab1 and White was better, Anand-Adams, FIDE World Championship, Groningen 1997.

c) 10...b6!? 11 ♗d3 ♗b7 12 ♖e1 ♘d7 13 c4 and White has an edge, according to the Danish IM Jacob Aagaard.

11 ♕e2

Also enticing is the pawn offer with 11 ♗d3!?. Onischuk-Liang Chong, Beijing 1998, continued 11...♕xc3 12 ♗g5 ♘c6 13 ♖c1 ♕a3 14 ♖e1 g6 15 ♗b5 ♗xg5 16 ♘xg5 ♕a5

17 ♕d3 a6 18 ♗xc6 ♕xg5 19 ♗f3 ♖b8 20 ♖c7 ♕a5 21 ♖ec1 ♕xa2 22 ♕e3 ♕b2 23 h4 and White had unmistakable pressure.
11...♘d7 12 ♗b2

White plans to drop his bishop back to d3 and play c3-c4. Here are two examples:

a) 12...♘f6?! (it looks natural to defend the kingside, but perhaps the knight is better on d7) 13 ♗d3 b6 14 ♘e5! ♗b7 15 f4 g6 16 c4 ♖ad8 17 ♖ae1 (17 ♖ad1!?) 17...♗b4 18 ♖d1 ♕e7 19 ♕e3 20 a4 ♗a8 21 ♔h1 ♕b7 22 ♕h3 ♖d6 23 ♖f3 and White's position is beginning to look threatening, Psakhis-Porper, Israeli Championship 1996.

b) 12...b6 13 ♗d3 ♗b7 14 c4 ♖fe8 15 ♕e3 ♗xf3 16 ♕xf3 ♗f6 17 ♖fe1 ♖ad8 18 ♖ad1 ♘c5 19 ♗c2 ♘b7 20 ♗a4 and White's bishop pair compensate for the weakness of the hanging pawns on d4 and c4, Alterman-Khlian, Rostov 1993.

A1122)
9...♘c6

The most popular choice.
10 ♖e1

We have now officially transposed into the Semi-Tarrasch Defence! *ECO* gives the route via 1 d4 d5 2 c4 e6 3 ♘c3 ♘f6 4 ♘f3 c5 5 cxd5 ♘xd5 6 e3 ♘c6 7 ♗c4 cxd4 8 exd4 ♗e7 9 0-0 0-0 10 ♖e1, but there are seemingly endless ways of reaching this position. The important thing to remember is that White has very good chances of keeping

an advantage in this line. On my database White has scored a healthy 64% from this position.

The following moves are Black's most popular choices:
A11221: 10...a6!?
A11222: 10...♘xc3
A11223: 10...♗f6

Firstly, let's look at a couple of less important moves:

a) 10...b6?! (this is only playable after an exchange on c3) 11 ♘xd5! exd5 12 ♗b5 (now ...b7-b6 has merely created weaknesses in the black camp) 12...♗d7?! (12...♗b7 more resilient, although White kept a clear positional advantage after 13 ♗f4 ♗d6 14 ♗xd6 ♕xd6 15 ♖c1 a6 16 ♗xc6 ♗xc6 17 ♘e5, Comas Fabrego-Pomes Marcet, Platja d'Aro 1994) 13 ♕a4 ♘b8 14 ♗f4 ♗xb5 15 ♕xb5 a6 16 ♕a4 ♗d6 17 ♗xd6 ♕xd6 18 ♖ac1 ♖a7 19 ♕c2 ♖e7 20 ♖xe7 ♕xe7 21 ♕c7 ♕xc7 22 ♖xc7 and White's activity gives him a virtually winning ending, Botvinnik-Alekhine, AVRO 1938.

b) After 10...♘f6 it's another transposition! This position can also be reached via the Queen's Gambit Accepted, and it's known to be somewhat better for White. One powerful example of White's attacking prospect is seen in the following line: 11 ♗g5 b6 12 a3 ♗b7 13 ♕d3! ♖c8 14 ♖ad1 ♖e8 15 h4!

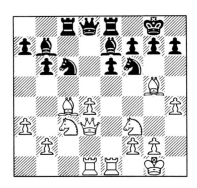

15...g6?! (15...♘d5 16 ♗xd5 exd5 17 ♗xe7 ♘xe7 keeps White's advantage to something more bearable for Black) 16 d5 ♘xd5 17 ♗xd5 exd5 18 ♘xd5 ♗xg5 19 hxg5 ♖xe1+ 20 ♖xe1 ♕f8 21 ♘f6+ ♔h8 22 ♕d7 ♗a8 23 ♕h3 h5 24 g4 and Black was forced to resign, Ribli-Wells, Szeged 1997.

A11221)
10...a6 11 ♗b3!?

11 ♕e2!? is an interesting suggestion from Aagaard. Grabbing a pawn with 11...♘b6 12 ♗b3 ♘xd4 is very risky; White has plenty of compensation after 13 ♘xd4 ♕xd4 14 ♗e3 ♕d8 15 ♖ed1. Instead Black should play 11...b5, after which 12 ♘xd5 exd5 13 ♗d3 ♗g4 14 ♗xh7+ ♔xh7 15 ♕c2+ ♔g8 16 ♕xc6 ♗xf3 17 gxf3 is unclear, while White could also simply drop back with 12 ♗d3.

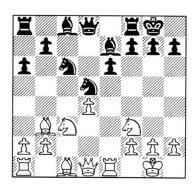

11...♘f6

After this retreat, we step back into Queen's Gambit Accepted territory. Instead Black can keep an independent flavour with 11...♘xc3 12 bxc3 b5 and now:

a) 13 ♕d3 ♗b7 14 ♗c2 g6 15 ♗h6 ♖e8 (Matveeva-Anand, Frunze 1987), and here Anand likes White after 16 a4!.

b) 13 ♗c2 (shifting to the more dangerous diagonal) 13...♗b7 14 h4! with a further split:

b1) 14...♗xh4 15 ♘xh4 ♕xh4 16 ♖e3 gives White a strong attack (compare with Variation A11222).

b2) 14...♗f6 15 ♘g5 g6 (or 15...h6? 16 ♕d3 g6 17 ♘xe6! fxe6 18 ♕xg6+ ♗g7 19 ♗xh6 ♕f6 20 ♕h7+ ♔f7 21 ♗xg7 ♕xg7 22 ♗g6+ ♔f6 23 ♖xe6+ and White wins) 16 ♕g4 and White will continue with h4-h5, An.Sokolov-Kharitonov, Moscow 1990.

b3) 14...♘a5!? is an untried suggestion from *ECO*.

b4) 14...♕d5 15 ♗g5 ♖fe8 16 ♕d3 g6 17 ♗b3 ♕d6 18 h5 ♗xg5 19 ♘xg5 ♕f4 20 hxg6! hxg6 (or 20...♕xg5 21 gxf7+ ♔xf7 22 ♕xh7+ ♕g7 23 ♗xe6+ ♖xe6 24 ♕xg7+ ♔xg7 25 ♖xe6) 21 ♘xe6 fxe6 22 ♕xg6+ ♔f8 23 ♖e4 ♕f5 24 ♕h6+ ♔e7 25 ♖f4 ♕d3 26 ♕xe6+ ♔d8 27 ♕d6+ ♔c8 28 ♗e6+ ♖xe6 29 ♖f8+ 1-0 Muhutdinov-Nenashev, Swidnica 1997.

Another idea is 11...♖e8 12 ♕d3 ♘xc3 (Aagaard criticises this; perhaps Black should try 12...♘cb4!?) 13 bxc3 ♗f6 14 ♕e4 ♗d7 15 h4 ♘e7 16 ♘g5 ♗xg5 17 ♗xg5 and White is clearly better, An. Sokolov-Burger, Reykjavik 1990.

12 ♗f4 ♘a5

Or:

a) 12...♘b4 13 ♘e5 ♘bd5 14 ♗g3 ♗d7 15 ♗xd5 ♘xd5 16 ♘xd5 exd5 17 ♕b3 ♗c8 18 ♖ac1 and Black is very passive, Christiansen-Kaidanov, Seattle 2000.

b) 12...b5 13 d5! exd5 14 ♘xd5 ♘xd5 15 ♕xd5 ♗b7 16 ♕h5 ♗f6 17 ♖ad1 and White's rooks are posted powerfully in the centre, Epishin-Jonkman, Amsterdam 2000.

13 d5!?

A new try. White got nothing after 12 ♗c2 b5 13 d5 exd5 14 ♕d3 ♘c6 15 ♗c7 ♕d7 16 ♘e5 ♘xe5 17 ♗xe5 g6 18 ♗xf6 ♗xf6 19 ♘xd5 ♗g7, Kasparov-Anand, Wijk aan Zee 1999.

13...♘xb3 14 ♕xb3 exd5

Or:

a) 14...♘xd5 15 ♖ad1 (15 ♘xd5!?) ♘xf4 15 ♖xd8 ♖xd8 16 ♖d1 and White has an edge, Gelfand-Shirov, FIDE World Championship, New Delhi 2000.

b) 14...♗d6 15 ♗xd6 ♕xd6 16 ♖ad1 exd5 17 ♘xd5 ♘xd5 18 ♖xd5 ♕f6 19 ♘d4 and Black has problems developing his c8-bishop, Kaidanov-D.Gurevich, Seattle 2000.

15 ♖ad1

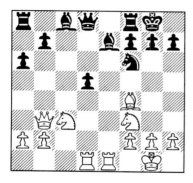

We are following the game Kramnik-Anand, Monaco (rapid) 2001. White kept an edge after 15...♗e6 16 ♕xb7 ♗c5 17 ♗e5 ♕a5 18 ♘d4 ♗xd4 19 ♖xd4 ♘d7 20 ♗d6 ♘c5 21 ♕c7 ♕xc7 22 ♗xc7 ♖fc8 23 ♗g3.

A11222)
10...♘xc3 11 bxc3 b6

After 11...♗f6 12 ♗d3, I can see nothing better for Black than 12...b6, after which White continues with 13 h4!.

12 ♗d3!

An important move. White quickly focuses his attention on the kingside, where Black is missing his normal defensive knight on f6.

12...♗b7

13 h4!

White has scored very well with this move (70% on my database). The idea is to start a quick attack with ♘g5.

13...♘a5!

Alternatives leave Black struggling:

a) 13...♕d5 14 ♖b1 ♖ac8 15 ♖b5 and the b5-rook can swing over to help the kingside attack, Anand-Timman, Moscow 1992.

b) 13...♗xh4 14 ♘xh4 ♕xh4 15 ♖e3! g6 16 ♖h3 ♕f6 17 ♗h6 ♖fe8 18 ♕g4 ♖ac8 19 ♗g5 ♕g7 20 ♕h4 f5 21 ♖e1 ♘a5 22 ♖he3 ♕f7 23 ♗b5 ♗c6 24 ♗xc6 ♘xc6 25 c4 ♕d7 26 ♗f6 and Black has major dark-squared weaknesses around his king, Kasparov-Gonda, Cannes simultaneous 1988.

c) 13...♗f6 14 ♘g5 g6 15 ♕g4 h5 (or 15...♘e7 16 h5! ♘f5 17 hxg6 hxg6 18 ♖xe6! fxe6 19 ♘xe6 and White wins – Nunn) 16 ♕g3 ♕d7 (16...♘e7 17 ♗a3 ♖c8 18 ♘xe6! fxe6 19 ♖xe6 ♖c7 20 ♖ae1 ♖f7 21 ♗xg6 ♖d7 22 ♗xf7+ ♔xf7 23 ♖xf6+ ♔xf6 24 ♕e5+ ♔f7 25 ♕e6+ ♔f8 26 ♕f6+ was the grisly conclusion to C.Hansen-Ki.Georgiev, Kiljava 1984) 17 ♘e4 ♗g7 18 ♗g5 ♘e7 19 ♕d6! and White has a decisive advantage, Onischuk-Magem Badals, New York 1998.

14 ♘g5

The natural follow-up, although Aagaard also suggests 14 h5!? and 14 ♗c2!?.

14...♗xg5

This is virtually forced. After 14...h6 we have:

a) 15 ♕h5? ♖c8! (15...♗d5? 16 ♘h7 ♖e8 17 ♗xh6 gxh6 18 ♕xh6 f5 19 ♖e3 led to a quick win in Razuvaev-Farago, Dubna 1979) 16 ♗h7+ (16 ♘h7 ♖xc3! is unclear) 16...♔h8 and now, according to Nunn, White should repeat with 17 ♗b1 ♔g8 18 ♗h7+.

b) 15 ♘h7! ♖e8 16 ♕g4 ♔h8 17 ♘g5! ♖f8 18 ♘xe6! fxe6 19 ♕g6 ♖f5 (or 19...♔g8 20 ♕h7+ ♔f7 21 ♗g6+ ♔f6 22 ♗h5) 20 ♖xe6 and White wins – Nunn.

14...g6 is only marginally stronger. Nunn gives the winning line 15 ♕g4! ♖c8 16 h5 ♖xc3 17 hxg6 ♖xd3 18 gxf7+ ♔h8 19 ♘xe6.

15 ♗xg5

After 15 hxg5!? Black should play 15...f5! (Pachman) 16 gxf6 (not 16 ♖xe6?? ♕d5!) 16...♕xf6 17 ♕e2 ♖ac8, which is unclear.

15...♕d5 16 ♕g4 f5 17 ♕g3

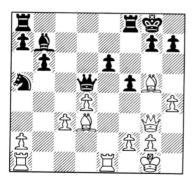

Both sides have weaknesses, but I prefer White's position. The game Poluljahov-Balashov, St Petersburg 1998, continued 17...♖ac8 18 ♖e5 ♕d7 and now 19 ♖c1!? ♘c4 20 ♖e2 ♗d5 21 h5 keeps White's initiative going.

A11223)
10...♗f6 11 ♘e4

Also interesting is 11 ♗b3 ♘ce7 12 ♘e4 b6 13 ♘xf6+ ♘xf6 14 ♗g5 ♘g6 15 ♘e5 ♕d6 16 ♗xf6 gxf6 17 ♕f3 and White was better, Shavtvaladze-Bystron, Herculane 1994.

11...b6

11...h6, avoiding a later ♗g5, is not very common, but it certainly has something to said for it. In Kokkila-Karttunen, Tampere 1998, White kept an advantage after 12 a3 b6 13 ♕d3 ♗b7 14 ♗d2 ♘ce7 15 ♖ad1 ♘f5 16 ♘e5.

12 ♘xf6+ ♘xf6

Or 12...♕xf6 13 ♗g5 ♕g6 14 ♖c1 ♗b7 15 ♗d3 ♕h5 16 ♖e4 f5 17 ♖xe6 ♘xd4 18 ♘xd4 ♕xg5 19 ♘f3 ♕d8 20 ♕a4 ♔h8 (Sokolovs-Schlosser, German Bundesliga 1999), and now I like the move 21 ♖d1.

13 ♗g5

Normally an exchange of a pair of minor pieces helps Black in an IQP position, but here Black suffers as he has no good way to break the pin on the f6-knight and is reduced to allowing his kingside pawns to be broken.

13...♗b7 14 a3! ♕d6

Israeli IM Ilya Tsesarsky gives the line 14...h6 15 ♗h4 ♖c8 16 ♗a2 ♘b8 17 ♘e5 g5 18 ♗g3 ♘e4 19 ♕f3 ♕xd4 20 ♘xf7! and Black is in trouble.

15 ♗xf6 gxf6

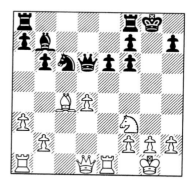

Black's apparent weakness on the kingside gives White a promising position. In the game S.Ivanov-Hillarp Persson, Stockholm 2000, White increased his advantage after 16 d5! ♘a5 17 ♗a2 ♗xd5 18 ♕d4 ♘c6 19 ♕xf6 ♗xa2 20 ♖xa2 ♕d3 21 b4 ♕g6 22 ♕h4.

A113)

6...♘xc3

With this move Black immediately gives White the 'hanging' c- and d-pawns.

7 bxc3

7...g6

Logically Black follows up by fianchettoing his f8-bishop, thus securing a safe kingside. 7...e6 is not so good: 8 d4 ♗e7 9 ♗d3 0-0 10 0-0 ♘d7 11 ♖e1 ♕c7 12 c4 b6 13 ♗b2 ♗f6 14 ♕d2 ♗b7 15 ♘g5 g6 16 h4 and White has a powerful attack, Sher-Ferguson, Hastings 1995.

8 d4

Or:

a) 8 h4?! is in some ways quite logical, but it's probably a little too ambitious. 8...♗g7! 9 h5 ♘c6 10 ♖b1 ♕c7 11 ♗a3 ♗f5 left Black with a good position in An.Sokolov-Karpov, Linares (11th matchgame) 1987.

b) 8 ♗b5+!? (this looks quite promising – White keeps the d-pawn at home for the moment) 8...♗d7 (8...♘c6 transposes to Variation A111, note to Black's seventh move) 9 a4! ♗g7 10 0-0 0-0 11 ♗a3 (11 ♖e1!? a6 12 ♗f1 is another idea) 11...a6 (11...♘c6 12 ♖e1 ♖e8 13 d4 a6 14 ♗f1 ♕c7 15 ♘g5 h6 16 ♘e4 was better for White in Balashov-Lastin, Elista 2000) 12 ♗xd7 ♕xd7 (Dautov gives 12...♘xd7 13 d4 ♖c8 14 ♕b3 with an edge to White) 13 ♖e1 ♘c6 14 ♖b1 ♖fd8 15 ♗c5! ♕f5? (Black should play 15...e5! – Dautov) 16 d4 ♖d7 17 ♕e2 and

White has strong pressure down both b- and e-files, Christiansen-Dautov, Essen 1999.

8...♗g7 9 ♗d3 0-0 10 0-0 ♘c6 11 ♖e1 ♗g4

Black has quite a few alternatives here:

a) 11...♖e8 12 ♗g5 ♗e6 13 ♖xe6!? (this move is fun, especially in a blitz game!) 13...fxe6 14 ♗c4 ♕d6 15 ♕e2 ♘d8 16 ♖e1 ♖c8 17 ♘d2 ♔h8 18 ♘e4 ♕c7 19 ♗b3 e5 20 h4 exd4 21 h5 gxh5 22 ♕xh5 ♖f8 23 ♗c2 ♕e5 24 ♘g3 ♕xe1+ 25 ♔h2 h6 26 ♗xh6 ♔g8 27 ♗xg7 ♖xf2 28 ♕h7+ ♔f7 29 ♕g6+ ♔g8 30 ♗h6+ 1-0 Tal-Karpov, Brussels (blitz) 1987. Don't be surprised if Black has improvements in this last line, but certainly 13 ♖xe6 is interesting.

b) 11...b6!? 12 ♗g5 (12 ♗e4 ♗b7 13 ♗f4 e6 14 ♖c1 ♕d7 15 h4 ♖ad8 16 h5 ♘e7 was equal in Thesing-Gipslis, Pardubice 1995) 12...♖e8 13 ♕d2 ♗g4 14 ♕f4 ♗xf3 15 ♕xf3 ♕d6 16 ♗c4 was roughly level, Fernandez Garcia-Magem, Spanish Championship 1998.

c) 11...♕a5 12 ♗d2 ♗g4 13 ♗e4 e5 14 d5 ♘e7 15 c4 ♕d8 16 ♕b3 f5 17 d6! and the complications favour White, Korneev-Evseev, Novgorod 1997.

12 ♗e4 ♖c8

Or 12...♕d7 13 ♖b1 ♖ac8 14 h3 ♗xf3 15 ♗xf3 ♘a5? 16 ♗g4 e6 17 d5! f5 18 dxe6 ♕xd1 19 ♗xd1 ♗xc3 20 ♖e2 a6 21 ♖c2 b5 22 ♗a3 1-0, Korneev-Oms Pallise, Linares 1998, on account of 22...♖fe8 23 ♖bc1.

13 ♗g5 ♕d7 14 h3 ♗xf3 15 ♕xf3

Winants-C.Hansen, Wijk aan Zee 1994. White's bishop pair promises him a slight edge.

A12) 5...g6

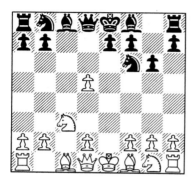

This move's a bit cheeky. Black forgets about recapturing the d5-pawn for the time being and concentrates on developing the kingside. White should aim to punish Black by hanging onto his pawn as long as possible.

6 ♗c4!?

6 ♕b3 ♗g7 7 d4 would transpose to the ...g6 variation of the Panov-Botvinnik Attack. After 6 ♗c4 White can aim to use the fact that the d-pawn is still on d2.

6...♗g7 7 ♘f3 0-0 8 0-0 ♘a6

Planning to increase the pressure on the d5-pawn with ...♘c7. Alternatives are less testing:

a) 8...♘bd7 9 d3! (in this line the pawn is better on d3, where it supports the bishop) 9...♘b6 10 ♕b3 ♗f5 11 ♗f4 ♖c8 12 ♖fe1 ♘fd7 13 ♗g5 ♘c5 14 ♕a3 and Black is in trouble, Kalinichev-Tischbierek, Berlin 1986.

b) 8...b6?! 9 d4 ♗b7 10 ♕b3 ♘a6 11 ♘e5 ♕d6 12 ♘b5 ♕b8 13 d6 e6 14 ♗g5 ♖e8 15 d7 ♖f8 16 ♖fe1 and White has a dominating position, Balashov-Skatchkov, Novgorod 1998.

9 d4 ♘c7 10 ♕b3

Black answers 10 ♖e1 with 10...♘fxd5!, after which 11 ♘xd5 ♘xd5 12 ♗xd5 ♕xd5 13 ♖xe7 ♗g4 gives Black good compensa-

tion for the pawn.

10...a6!

10...♘fe8 is too slow. White is better after 11 ♗f4 ♘d6 12 ♗d3 b6 13 ♖fe1 ♗b7 14 ♘e5 e6 15 ♘c6 ♗xc6 16 dxc6 ♗xd4 17 ♖ad1, P.Claesen-Rogers, Wijk aan Zee 1996.

11 ♘e5 b5 12 ♗e2

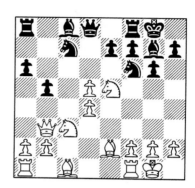

In the game Korneev-Alavkin, Novgorod 1997, White kept an edge after 12...♗b7 (12...♘cxd5!?) 13 ♘c6 ♕d6 14 ♗f3 e6 15 ♗g5 ♘fxd5 16 ♘a5 ♗c8 17 ♖ac1 ♗d7 18 ♘b7 ♕b6 19 ♘c5 ♗c6 20 ♖fd1.

A2)
4...♕xd5

With this move Black immediately recaptures the pawn, but White can now gain time by attacking the black queen.

5 ♘c3

5...♕d6

The most popular retreat, but there are alternatives:

a) 5...♕e5+?! (now White can gain further time with d2-d4) 6 ♗e2 ♗g4 7 d4 ♗xe2 8 ♘gxe2 ♕a5 9 ♕b3 ♕b6 10 ♘d5! ♕xb3 11 axb3 ♘a6 12 ♖xa6 bxa6 13 ♘c7+ and White went on to win in Kiik-Nykanen, Jyvaskyla 1999.

b) 5...♕d8 6 d4 ♘f6 7 ♘f3 e6 8 ♗c4 ♗e7 9 0-0 0-0 10 ♖e1 ♘c6 transposes into Variation A122, note to Black's tenth move, while 10...a6 11 ♗b3 ♘c6 transposes to A1221.

c) 5...♕a5 6 d4 ♘f6 7 ♘f3 e6 8 ♗d3! ♗e7 9 0-0 ♘c6 10 ♕e2 0-0 11 a3 ♖d8 12 ♖d1 g6 13 ♗e3 a6 14 b4 ♕c7 15 ♖ac1 ♗d7 16 ♗b1 ♗e8 17 ♗a2 and I prefer White, Finkel-Payen, Cannes 1996.

6 d4 ♘f6 7 ♘f3

It's time for those transpositions again! This particular position can also be reached via the c3 Sicilian after 1 e4 c5 2 c3 d5 3 exd5 ♕xd5 4 d4 cxd4 5 cxd4 ♘f6 6 ♘c3 ♕d6 7 ♘f3. I'll stick my neck out a little and say that this is a good version of the c3 Sicilian – Black has given White extra options by exchanging early on d4.

7...e6

I can find no example of 7...♗g4!? in this actual position, even though I believe White has nothing better than to reach a slightly favourable variation of the c3 Sicilian after 8 ♗e2 e6 9 h3 ♗h5 10 0-0 ♘c6 11 ♕b3! (11 ♗e3 ♗e7 is known to be okay for Black)

11...♕b4 (11...♗xf3 12 ♗xf3 ♘xd4 13 ♕a4+ ♕d7 14 ♕xd7+ ♘xd7 15 ♗xb7 gives White an endgame edge due to the bishop pair) 12 ♗e3 and now:

a) 12...♕xb3 13 axb3 ♗e7 14 g4 ♗g6 15 ♘e5 ♘b4 (15...0-0 transposes to the next note) 16 ♗b5+ ♔f8 17 ♖fc1 a6 18 ♗e2 ♘fd5 19 ♘xd5 ♘xd5 20 ♗f3 and Black's king is misplaced, Ravi-Neelotpal, Calcutta 1996.

b) 12...♗e7 13 g4 ♗g6 14 ♘e5 0-0 15 g5

White has scored well from this position:

b1) 15...♘h5 16 ♘xc6 bxc6 17 ♕d1! ♕xb2 18 ♖c1 ♗b4 19 ♘b1 c5 20 a3 ♗xa3 21 ♗xh5 ♗xh5 22 ♕xh5 cxd4 23 ♗xd4 ♕xc1 24 ♖xc1 ♗xc1 25 ♘c3 left White with a winning position in Sermek-V.Georgiev, Cannes 1996.

b2) 15...♘d5 16 ♘xd5 exd5 17 ♘xc6 bxc6 18 ♕xb4 ♗xb4 19 ♖fc1 ♗f5 20 a3 ♗e7 21 ♖xc6 ♗xh3 22 b4 ♖fd8 23 b5 and White has a dangerous queenside pawn majority, Smagin-Paschall, Bad Wiessee 1999.

b3) 16 axb3 ♘d5 17 ♘xd5 exd5 18 ♖fc1 ♗f5 19 ♘xc6 bxc6 20 ♖xc6 20...a5 21 ♗f3 ♖fd8 22 ♗d2 ♗e6 23 ♖xa5 ♖ab8 24 ♗g4! and White went on to win, Sermek-Sher, Bled 1993.

8 ♗c4

8 g3!? is interesting, for example 8...♗e7 9 ♗g2 ♘c6 10 0-0 0-0 (Down-Emms, Cambridge 1993) and now 11 a3 ♖d8 12 ♗f4 ♕d7 13 ♘e5 ♘xe5 14 dxe5 favours White.

8...♗e7 9 0-0 ♘c6

After 9...0-0 White has the chance to play 10 ♕e2! ♘c6 11 ♖d1 ♘b4 12 ♗g5 ♘bd5 13 ♘e5 a6 14 ♕f3, with strong pressure on d5, Stoica-Przewoznik, Timisoara 1987.

10 ♗g5

White has two enticing alternatives here:

a) 10 ♘b5!? ♕d8 11 ♗f4 0-0 12 ♗c7 ♕d7 13 ♘e5 ♘xe5 14 dxe5 ♘e8 15 ♗a5 b6 16 ♗d2 a6 17 ♘c3 ♗b7 18 ♕e2 b5 19 ♗b3 ♗c5 20 ♘e4 ♗e7 21 ♖fd1 was better for White in Blatny-Muse, Poznan 1986.

b) 10 ♕e2!? ♘xd4 11 ♘xd4 ♕xd4 12 ♘b5 looks dangerous, while the alternative 10...0-0 transposes to the note to Black's ninth move.

10...0-0 11 ♖e1

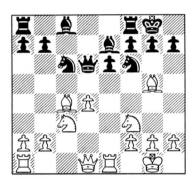

Black must play accurately to solve his problems here:

a) 11...a6?! 12 d5! ♘a5 (12...exd5 13 ♘xd5 ♘xd5 14 ♕xd5 ♕xd5 15 ♗xd5 gives White a favourable ending) 13 ♗d3 ♖d8 (13...♘xd5? 14 ♗xe7 ♕xe7 15 ♘xd5 and 13...exd5? 14 ♘xd5! ♕xd5 15 ♗xf6 are winning for White) 14 ♕c2 exd5 15 ♗xh7+ ♔f8 16 ♖ad1 and Black's in some trouble, Godena-Lazarev, Cannes 1992.

b) 11...♖d8! 12 ♘b5 ♕b4! (12...♕d7 13 ♘e5 ♘xe5 14 dxe5 ♘d5 15 ♗xe7 ♕xe7 16 ♘d6 is unpleasant for Black) 13 ♖c1 ♕a5 14 ♗f4 ♘d5 15 ♗xd5 ♕xb5 and Black was okay in the game Guseinov-Speelman, Baku 1983.

2...e5!?

Black takes advantage of the fact that White didn't play 2 d4. This is not such a popular choice for Black, perhaps because Caro-Kann players prefer to play 2...d5, rather than learning lines of the Old Indian or Kings Indian (more transpositions, I'm afraid!).

3 ♘f3

Attacking the e5-pawn, and making use of the fact that Black doesn't have the c6-square for his knight.

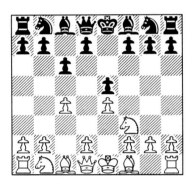

Now we shall take a look at Black's choices:

B1: 3...♕a5!?
B2: 3...d6

Alternatively:

a) 3...f5 (a kind of Latvian Counter Gambit!) 4 ♗e2! fxe4 5 ♘xe5 and now:

a1) 5...♘f6 6 0-0 ♗e7 7 ♘c3 d6 (7...d5 8 cxd5 cxd5 9 ♗b5+ ♗d7 10 ♘xd7 ♘bxd7 11 ♘xd5! won a pawn in Gofshtein-Hector, Manila Olympiad 1992) 8 ♘g4 ♗xg4 9 ♗xg4 d5 10 cxd5 cxd5 11 d3 and Black will be left with a weak pawn in the centre.

a2) 5...♕h4 6 ♘c3 d6 7 ♗g4! ♘a6 8 ♗xc8 ♖xc8 9 ♘g4 ♘c5 10 0-0 ♘f6 11 ♘xf6+ gxf6 12 g3 ♖g8 13 ♖e1 and Black's king has no safe place to hide, Sher-Hector, Vejle 1994.

b) 3...♕c7 4 ♘c3 ♗b4 5 g3!? (5 a3 ♗xc3

6 dxc3!? also looks like a promising way to play) 5...♘f6 6 ♗g2 ♗xc3 7 bxc3 ♘xe4 8 ♕e2 d5 9 ♗a3! ♗e6 10 0-0 ♘d7 11 cxd5 cxd5 12 ♖fe1 ♘df6 13 ♖ab1 0-0-0 14 ♘xe5! ♕xe5 15 d3 and White has a strong attack, An.Sokolov-Glek, Vilnius 1984.

c) 3...♘f6 4 ♘xe5! (this is a good version of the Petroff Defence – the insertion of c2-c4 and ...c7-c6 helps White) 4...d6 5 ♘f3 ♘xe4 6 ♘c3 and now:

c1) 6...♘g5 7 d4 ♗e7 8 ♘xg5 ♗xg5 9 ♕e2+ ♗e7 10 ♗g5 ♗e6 11 ♗xe7 ♕xe7 12 d5 was better for White in Fernandez Garcia-Gil, Cala d'Or 1986.

c2) 6...♗f5 7 ♗d3! ♘xc3 8 dxc3! (the d6-pawn is vulnerable) 8...♕e7+?! 9 ♗e3 ♗xd3 10 ♕xd3 ♘d7 11 0-0-0 ♘e5 12 ♘xe5 dxe5 13 ♖he1 g6 14 ♗xa7! ♗g7 15 ♕e3 ♕e6 16 ♕c5 ♗f6 17 ♗b6 ♖xa2

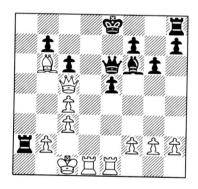

18 ♖xe5! 1-0 Beliavsky-Tavadian, Yaroslav 1982.

c3) 6...♘xc3 7 dxc3 ♗e7 8 ♗e2 (8 ♗f4 is more ambitious; after 8...0-0 White plays 9 ♕c2 and 0-0-0) 8...♘d7 9 0-0 0-0 10 ♗f4 and White has an edge, Kuporosov-Meduna, Lazne Bohdanec 1994.

B1)
3...♕a5!?

A rather extravagant way of dealing with the threat to the e-pawn. Black's idea is to keep the f8-a3 diagonal free so that the dark-squared bishop can develop to an active post.

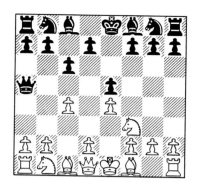

4 ♗e2 ♘f6

4...f5?! is too ambitious, for example 5 exf5 e4 6 ♘g5! ♕xf5 7 d3 ♗b4+ 8 ♘c3 exd3 9 ♗xd3 ♕e5+ 10 ♗e3! ♘f6 (or 10...♗xc3+ 11 bxc3 ♕xc3+ 12 ♔f1 and White has a strong attack – 12...♘f6 runs into 13 ♗d4!) 11 0-0 0-0 12 ♘ce4 ♘xe4 13 ♗xe4 h6 14 ♗h7+! ♔h8 15 ♗c2 and Black's kingside is full of weaknesses, M.Gurevich-Hector, Taastrup 1992.

5 0-0 ♘xe4

5...d6 is inconsistent. Following 6 ♘c3 ♗e7 7 d4 it's not clear what the black queen is doing on a5.

6 ♖e1 d6 7 d4 ♘f6 8 ♗d2 ♕c7 9 dxe5 dxe5 10 ♘xe5 ♗e7 11 ♗f4

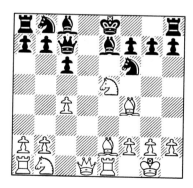

In the game Lautier-Kuczynski, Polanica Zdroj 1991, White kept a useful edge after the moves 11...♕b6 12 ♕c2 0-0 13 ♘c3 ♗e6 14 ♖ad1.

B2)
3...d6 4 d4

Now we will look at:
B21: 4...♗g4
B22: 4...♘d7

4...♕c7 5 ♘c3 ♗g4 6 ♗e2 ♘f6 7 ♗e3 ♘bd7 8 h3 ♗xf3 9 ♗xf3 ♗e7 10 0-0 0-0 11 g3 gave White a comfortable edge in Hübner-Bachmann, Berlin 1999.

B21)
4...♗g4 5 dxe5! ♗xf3 6 gxf3 dxe5 7 ♕xd8+ ♔xd8 8 f4!

It makes sense to open the position, as White has the bishop pair and Black's king is misplaced.
8...f6
Or:

a) 8...♗b4+ 9 ♔e2! (9 ♘c3 ♘f6 10 f3 ♘bd7 11 ♗e2 ♗d6 12 fxe5 ♗xe5 13 0-0 g5! was equal in Nevednichy-Becerra Rivero, Yerevan Olympiad 1996) 9...♘d7 10 ♗h3! is better for White, according to the Yugoslav IM Vojinovic.

b) 8...♘d7 9 fxe5 ♘xe5 10 f4 ♘f3+ 11 ♔f2 ♘d4 12 ♘c3 ♔e8 13 ♗h3 and White will follow up with ♗e3, Gheorghiu-Malich, Romania 1983.

9 ♘c3 ♗d6
Or 9...♔c7 10 fxe5 fxe5 11 f4!.
10 fxe5
Also possible is 10 ♖g1!? g6 11 fxe5

♗xe5?! (11...fxe5! transposes to the text) 12 f4 ♗xc3+ 13 bxc3 ♘d7 14 ♗a3 and Black will have a hard time coping with the power of White's bishops.

10...fxe5 11 ♖g1 g6 12 ♗g5+ ♔c7
After the alternative 12...♘e7 13 0-0-0 ♔c7 14 ♗h3, White has the awkward threat of ♖xd6.
13 ♗h3

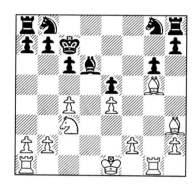

White has a very active position. Here are some examples:

a) 13...♘d7 14 0-0-0 ♘gf6 15 ♖g3! (threatening ♖gd3) 15...♗c5 16 ♖f3 ♖af8 17 ♗h6! ♖fg8 18 ♗xd7 ♘xd7 19 ♖f7 ♗d4 20 ♘e2 c5 21 ♗g7 and White wins an exchange.

b) 13...h6 14 ♗e3 g5 15 0-0-0 ♘f6 16 ♗f5! (Kaidanov-Blocker, Washington 1994), and here Kaidanov gives 16...♘bd7 17 ♘a4 as better for White.

c) 13...♘a6 14 0-0-0 ♖f8 15 ♖g3! ♗c5 16 ♖gd3 ♗d4 17 ♖xd4! exd4 18 ♖xd4 gave White a very strong attack against the black king in Berkovich-Vainshtein, Israel 1994. The rest of the game is of some interest: 18...♘b8 19 ♗h4! ♖e8 20 ♗g3+ ♔b6 21 ♘a4+ ♔a5 22 ♘c5 b6 23 ♘b7+ ♔a6 24 ♘d6 ♖f8 25 ♖d3 b5 26 c5 ♔a5 27 f3! b4 (or 27...♔b4 28 ♘b7 ♔c4 29 ♖d6 ♖xf3 30 ♗e6+ ♔b4 31 ♖d4 mate) 28 ♖a3+! bxa3 29 ♗e1+ and Black resigned on account of mate after either 29...♔a4 30 b3, or 29...♔a6 30 ♗f1.

B22)
4...♘d7 5 ♘c3 ♘gf6 6 ♗e2

Black must now make a decision as to where to develop his dark squared bishop
B221: 6...♗e7
B222: 6...g6

Variation B221 leads to a line of the Old Indian Defence, while B222 reaches a line of the King's Indian Defence!

B221)
6...♗e7

7 0-0 0-0
After 7...a6 White has scored very well with 8 ♘h4!:

a) 8...♘xe4? 9 ♘xe4 ♗xh4 10 ♘xd6+ is obviously bad news for Black.

b) 8...0-0 9 ♘f5 ♖e8 10 ♘xe7+ ♕xe7 11 f3 and White will follow up with b2-b3 and ♗a3 – Ribli.

c) 8...exd4 9 ♕xd4 ♕b6 10 ♕xb6 (10 ♘f5 and 10 ♗e3 also promise an edge) 10...♘xb6 11 ♗e3 and Black has to worry about his weak d6-pawn, V.Ivanov-Shchukin, St Petersburg 1999.

d) 8...g6 (preventing ♘f5, but weakening the dark squares on the kingside) 9 ♗h6 ♗f8 (against 9...♕b6?! Ribli gives 10 dxe5!? dxe5 11 ♖b1, intending b2-b4) 10 ♗xf8 ♔xf8 11 ♕d2 ♔g7 12 f4 and White has an impressive looking pawn centre, Dreev-Serper, Tunja 1989.

8 ♗e3

Now we have a further split. Black can play:
B2211: 8...♖e8
B2212: 8...a6

B2211)
8...♖e8

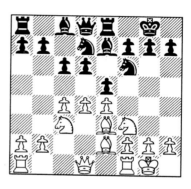

9 d5 c5
Closing the centre. Black's other options include:

a) 9...a5!? (trying to secure the c5-square for the knight) 10 a3 ♘g4 11 ♗d2 ♘c5 12 ♕c2 (12 b4 axb4 13 axb4 ♖xa1 14 ♕xa1 ♘b3 15 ♕a7 ♘xd2 16 ♘xd2 ♗g5 was unclear in Z.Polgar-De Armas, Thessaloniki Olympiad 1988) 12...a4 13 h3 ♘f6 14 ♗e3 ♘fd7 15 ♖ad1 ♕a5 16 ♘d2 ♕d8 17 ♗g4! ♘b6?! (17...♗g5!?) 18 ♘f3 ♗xg4 19 hxg4 ♕c8 20 ♗xc5 dxc5 21 d6 and White was clearly better, Atalik-Vorobyov, Bled 2001.

b) 9...cxd5 10 cxd5 a6 11 a4 b6 12 ♘d2 ♗b7 13 f3 ♘h5 14 g3 g6 15 ♘c4 ♖b8 16 f4 exf4 17 gxf4 ♘g7 18 ♗f3 and Black was passively placed in Psakhis-Escobar Forero, Linares 2001.

After 9...c5 White has three possible plans: to play for b2-b4, to play for f2-f4, or a mixture of both.

10 ♘e1
The knight comes to d3, where supports both b2-b4 and f2-f4.

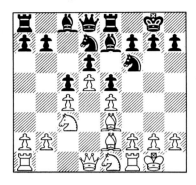

10...♘f8

Or 10...♗f8 11 ♖b1 h6 12 a3 g6 13 b4 b6 14 ♘d3 ♘h7 15 ♕d2 h5 16 ♔h1 h4 17 h3 ♗g7 18 f4! and White has succeeded in his plan, Lukacs-Zhang Pengxiang, Budapest 1999.

11 ♘d3 ♘g6 12 a3 ♗d7

12...a5?! 13 b4 axb4 14 axb4 ♖xa1 15 ♕xa1 b6 16 ♖b1 gives White a quick attack on the queenside.

13 b4 b6 14 ♖b1

Preparing to open the b-file.

14...♖f8

This looks strange, but Black wants the e8-square for his knight.

15 bxc5 bxc5

Another option is 15...dxc5, planning ...♘e8-d6. White should reply with 16 a4, intending a4-a5.

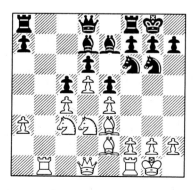

In the game Ilincic-Tosic, Subotica 2000,

White broke through with the typical pseudo-sacrifice 16 ♘xc5! dxc5 17 d6, and now Illincic gives the variation 17...♖e8 18 dxe7 ♕xe7 19 ♘d5 ♘xd5 20 cxd5, assessing the position as better for White.

B2212)
8...a6

Preparing queenside counterplay with ...b7-b5.

9 d5 cxd5

Or 9...c5 10 ♘e1 ♘e8 11 ♕d2 (preventing ...♗g5) and now

a) 11...h6 12 g3! (preparing to meet ...bg5 with f2-f4) 12...♘df6 13 f4 ♘g4 14 ♗xg4 ♗xg4 15 fxe5 dxe5 16 ♘d3 ♕c7 17 ♕g2 ♘f6 18 h3 ♗h5 19 g4 ♗g6 20 ♖ad1 and White is harmoniously placed, Wells-Martin, British Championship 1998.

b) 11...g6 12 ♘d3 ♘g7 13 ♗h6 ♔h8 14 ♔h1 ♘f6 15 f4 and again White has achieved the desired pawn break, Rowson-Summerscale, British Championship 1998.

10 cxd5

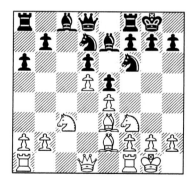

10...b5

This is consistent with Black's eighth move. Another idea is to harass e3-bishop first with 10...♘g4 11 ♗d2 b5 12 ♘e1 ♘gf6 13 ♘c2 and now:

a) 13...♘b6?! 14 ♘b4! ♗b7 15 ♖c1 ♖c8 16 b3 and White is better – Stohl.

b) 13...♘c5 14 f3 ♗d7 (after 14...b4 White can safely play 15 ♘xb4!, as 15...♕b6 16

♘c6 ♘cxe4+ 17 ♔h1 wins material for White) 15 b4 ♘a4 16 ♘xa4 bxa4 17 ♘a3! and White has a clear advantage, Chekhov-Hickl, German Bundesliga 1992.

11 ♘d2 ♘b6

Or:

a) 11...♘xe4 12 ♘cxe4 f5 13 a4 b4 14 a5 fxe4 15 ♘xe4 ♘f6 16 ♘xf6+ ♗xf6 17 ♗b6 and Black's queenside pawns are vulnerable, Psakhis-Zapata, Manila Olympiad 1992.

b) 11...♘e8 12 b4 ♗g5 13 ♗xg5 ♕xg5 14 a4 and again White is making headway on the queenside, Psakhis-Herndl, Vienna 1998.

12 a4 bxa4

12...b4 is answered by 13 a5!.

13 ♘xa4

13...♘xa4 14 ♖xa4 ♗d7! 15 ♖a3!

15 ♖xa6 ♖xa6 16 ♗xa6 ♘g4! exchanges off the dark-squared bishop and promises Black counterplay.

After 15 ♖a3 White can make good use of his extra space on the queenside, for example:

a) 15...♕b8 16 ♖b3 ♕e8 17 ♖b6 ♖b8 18 f3 ♖xb6 19 ♗xb6 ♕b8 20 ♘c4 ♗b5 21 ♗f2 ♗xc4 22 ♗xc4 ♕xb2 23 ♕a1 ♕xa1 24 ♖xa1 and Black faces a nightmare ending, S.Ivanov-Shchukin, St Petersburg 1998; a6 is dropping and Black will have to grimly defend the d6-pawn.

b) 15...♗b5 16 f3 ♘h5 17 ♗xb5 axb5 18 ♖xa8 ♕xa8 19 ♕b3 ♖b8 20 ♖c1 ♘f4 21 ♔f1 and White was better in Yakovich-

Kremenietsky, Moscow 1996.

B222)
6...g6

With this move Black aims for a King's Indian set-up, although it's one where he is already committed to the moves ...♘bd7 and ...c7-c6.

7 0-0 ♗g7 8 ♗e3 0-0

Black's main alternative is 8...♘g4!? 9 ♗g5 f6 10 ♗c1 0-0 11 h3! ♘h6 12 ♗e3 and now:

a) 12...♘e7 13 ♕c2 ♘f7 14 ♖ad1 ♖e8 15 ♖fe1 ♗h6 16 ♗xh6 ♘xh6 17 b4 and White begins activity on the queenside, Miles-Zapata, Manila 1990.

b) 12...♘f7 13 ♕c2 ♗h6 14 ♗xh6 ♘xh6 15 ♖fd1 ♕e7 16 c5! 17 d5! f5 (or 17...♘b6!? 18 dxc6 bxc6 19 ♘a4! ♘xa4 20 ♕xa4, followed by ♖ac1) 18 dxc6 bxc6 19 ♕d2 ♔g7 20 ♕d6! ♕xd6 21 ♖xd6 and Black's queenside pawns are extremely weak, Nogueiras-Zapata, La Habana 1991.

9 d5 c5

Or:

a) 9...cxd5 10 cxd5 ♘g4 11 ♗d2 transposes to the next note.

b) 9...♘g4 10 ♗d2 f5 (or 10...cxd5 11 cxd5 ♗h6 12 ♖c1 a6 13 a4 f5 14 exf5 gxf5 15 h3 ♗xd2 16 ♕xd2 ♘gf6 17 ♘g5! and White's better, Chekhov-Casper, Leipzig 1988) 11 ♘g5 ♘df6 12 b4 cxd5 13 cxd5 ♕e7 (13...fxe4? 14 ♘e6! ♗xe6 15 dxe6 ♘h6 16 g4! left Black in total disarray in Ivanchuk-

Piket, Wijk aan Zee 1996) 14 ♕b3! ♘xe4 15 ♘cxe4 fxe4 16 ♘xe4 and the white knight has an excellent outpost on e4.

10 ♘e1

Preventing ...♘g4 and preparing ♘d3.

10...♘e8

Preparing ...f7-f5. 10...a6 11 a3 ♔h8 12 b4 b6 13 ♘d3 ♘g8 14 a4 f5 15 a5! attacked the base of Black's pawn chain in Shumiakina-Kovalevskaya, Chisinau 1998.

11 g4!

Anticipating ...f7-f5. White wishes to attack along the g-file!

11...f5

11...♕h4? proved to be a waste of time in Gelfand-Ivanchuk, Kramatorsk 1989, after 12 ♔h1 ♔h8 13 ♖g1 ♕e7 14 a3 ♘df6 15 b4.

12 exf5 gxf5 13 gxf5 ♘b6

Or 13...♘df6 14 ♗d3 and now:

a) 14...e4 15 ♘xe4 ♘xe4 16 ♗xe4 ♗xb2 17 ♖b1 ♗g7 18 ♔h1 ♕h4 19 ♕c2 ♕h3 20 ♘g2 and White went on to win in Michaelsen-Lane, Wijk aan Zee 1995.

b) 14...♕e7 15 ♕f3 ♕f7 16 ♔h1 ♘h5 17 ♖g1 ♗xf5 18 ♗xf5 ♕xf5 19 ♕xf5 ♖xf5 20 ♘e4 and White has a very favourable ending, C.Hansen-Djurhuus, Reykjavik 1996; The d6-pawn is weak and the knight on e4 is a monster.

14 ♘f3! ♗xf5 15 ♘g5

White uses both the g-file and the e4-square for the basis of an attack.

15...♕e7 16 ♔h1 ♘f6

16...h6?! is met by 17 ♘ge4, while 16...e4 17 ♖g1 ♘d7 18 ♖g3! is also good for White.

17 ♖g1

We are following the game Kramnik-Knaak, Dortmund 1992, which continued

17...♔h8 18 ♕d2 (18 ♖g3!?, intending ♕g1-g2 and ♖g1, is also promising) 18...♗g6 19 ♖af1 ♘h5 20 ♘e6 ♖f7 21 b3 and White was in total control.

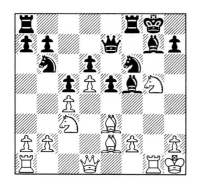

Important Points

Variation A

1) Be aware of all the transpositional possibilities here. It may be very easy to lure your opponent into unfamiliar territory.

2) There are many attacking possibilities discussed in this chapter for White in IQP and 'hanging pawns' positions. Familiarise yourself with these.

Variation B

1) Don't feel too concerned about having to face a 'King's Indian' set-up. It's only one line, which is meant to be quite favourable to White. Anyway, it's very possible that your opponent will feel less comfortable than you!

2) The manoeuvre ♘f3-e1-d3 is seen quite often once the position is closed with d4-d5 and ...c6-c5. From c3 the knight support both the f2-f4 and b2-b4 breaks.

CHAPTER FIVE

Attacking the Pirc: The 150 Attack

1 e4 d6 2 d4 ♘f6 3 ♘c3 g6

The Pirc Defence appeals to the black player who likes to fianchetto his dark-squared bishop. This gives Black security on the kingside, where the bishop is used as a solid defender to the castled king. The Pirc is similar to the more popular King's Indian (1 d4 ♘f6 2 c4 g6) in another way; Black allows White to occupy the centre with pawns and generally only strikes back in the centre once his forces are co-ordinated. The Pirc is well suited to players who like to counter-attack, and its famous adherents include former Russian Champion Peter Svidler and Slovenian number one Alexander Beliavsky.

The way to attack the Pirc Defence that I'm advocating is with a very simple, but frighteningly effective system. White plays an early ♗e3 and ♕d2, lining up the two pieces along the c1-h6 diagonal. Then White often plays ♗h6, in order to exchange the dark-squared bishops. This is sometimes augmented by shoving the h-pawn down the board to attack Black's castled king. Then, in Fischer's words, 'pry open the h-file, sac, sac... mate!'

In recent years White's system has been dubbed 'the 150 Attack', a reference to the idea that this way of attack would be the first thing a club player would think of (a British grade of 150 is roughly equivalent to an Elo rating of 1800). I can still remember a comment from my Pirc playing days when, after having been checkmated by ♕g7, I was told that this was exactly what I should have expected, after having weakened myself with ...g7-g6 as early as move three! Experience of playing both sides of the Pirc has taught me that many black players feel uncomfortable playing against the 150 Attack, and more generally, when their 'Pirc bishop' is exchanged. The 150 Attack is an excellent weapon at club level, but it's also very popular at the highest levels: Gary Kasparov, Vishy Anand, Michael Adams and Nigel Short have all used it to good effect.

Before we move onto the theory, I should also point out that, to be comprehensive, as well as 3...g6 (the Pirc), we shall also be looking at less popular third move choices for Black, including 3...e5 and 3...c6.

After **1 e4 d6 2 d4 ♘f6 3 ♘c3**, Black's has the following choices:
A: 3...e5!?
B: 3...c6
C: 3...g6

3...♘bd7 4 f4 e5 5 ♘f3 transposes to Line A.

A)
3...e5!?

This move is not particularly common. Black's main idea is that 4 ♘f3 ♘bd7 transposes to the Philidor Defence (1 e4 e5 2 ♘f3 d6 3 d4 ♘f6 4 ♘c3 ♘bd7), without giving us the option to play the our beloved Bishop's Opening!
4 f4!?

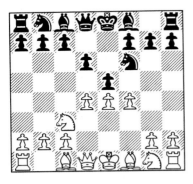

4...exd4
Black's alternatives include:

a) 4...♗g4 5 ♕d3 exd4 6 ♕xd4 d5 (6...♘c6 7 ♗b5 ♗d7 transposes to main text) 7 ♘xd5 ♘xd5 8 exd5 c6 9 ♕e5+ ♕e7 10 d6 ♕xe5+ 11 fxe5 ♘d7 12 ♗f4 and White has a favourable ending, Leko-Zetocha, Hungarian League 1998.

b) 4...♘bd7 5 ♘f3 exd4 6 ♕xd4 c6 7 ♗e3 d5!? (this leads to great complications) 8 exd5 ♗c5 9 ♕d3 ♕e7 10 ♘d4 and now:

b1) 10...♘b6 11 dxc6 bxc6 (11...0-0? 12 0-0-0 bxc6 13 ♗g1! ♕c7 14 g3 ♖d8?? 15 ♘db5! led to two quick victories for Judit Polgar in the same year – J.Polgar-Rivas Pastor, Dos Hermanas 1993 and J.Polgar-Khalifman, Seville 1993; White wins after 15...♖xd3 16 ♘xc7 ♖xd1+ 17 ♘xd1 ♗xg1 18 ♘xa8) 12 ♗e2 ♗a6 13 ♕d2 ♘bd5 14 ♘xd5 ♘xd5 15 ♘f5 ♗xe3 16 ♘xe7 ♗xd2+ 17 ♔xd2 ♔xe7 18 ♗xa6 ♘xf4 19 ♖ae1+ and White has a slight advantage in this ending – the bishop is superior to the knight on the open board.

b2) 10...♘xd5 11 ♘xd5 cxd5 12 0-0-0 0-0 13 g3 ♘f6 14 ♗g2 ♘e4 15 ♖he1 ♗d7 16 ♗g1 and I prefer White, Galissot-Verheyen, Artek 2000.

5 ♕xd4 ♘c6 6 ♗b5 ♗d7 7 ♕f2 ♗e7
Also possible is 7...g6!?, for example 8 ♘f3 ♗g7 9 ♗d2 0-0 10 0-0-0 a6 11 ♗xc6 ♗xc6 12 ♖he1 ♖e8 13 e5 ♘g4 14 ♕g3 ♘h6 15 ♘e4 ♘f5 16 ♕f2 ♗xe4 17 ♖xe4 dxe5 18 ♗c3 ♘d6 19 ♖xe5 and White has an edge, Kotronias-Jansa, Gausdal 1995.
8 ♘f3 0-0 9 0-0 a6 10 ♗d3 ♘b4 11 ♗d2

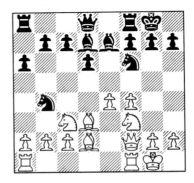

White has a nice space advantage. The game Hector-Zagorskis, Roskilde 1998 continued 11...c5!? 12 e5 ♘xd3 13 cxd3 ♘e8 14 ♘d5 ♗b5 15 ♗a5 ♕d7 16 ♘b6 ♕d8 17 b4 ♖b8 18 ♖fd1 dxe5 19 bxc5 exf4 20 d4 ♘f6 21 a4 and White has excellent compensation for the pawn.

B)
3...c6
This is a relatively new defence, utilised by the Russian Anatoly Ufimtsev, and then popularised by some leading Czech players in the late eighties. Black very much keeps his options open and waits to see how White proceeds.
4 f4!
The most aggressive way to play against this system.
4...♕a5

With the obvious threat of ...♘xe4, winning a pawn.

5 e5 ♘e4 6 ♕f3

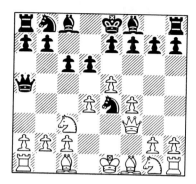

Now Black has a choice of moves:

B1: 6...d5

B2: 6...♘xc3

B1)

6...d5 7 ♗d3 ♘a6!

This is an interesting idea from Julian Hodgson. Otherwise 7...♘xc3 8 ♗d2 gives White a big lead in development, while 7...c5 8 ♗xe4 dxe4 9 ♕xe4 cxd4 10 ♕xd4 ♗f5 11 ♕d5 ♘c6 12 ♕xa5 ♘xa5 13 ♘b5 0-0-0 14 c3 ♘c6 15 ♗e3 worked out well for White in D.Ledger-Summerscale, British Championship 1999.

8 ♘ge2

One of the points of Black's idea is seen after 8 ♗xe4 dxe4 9 ♕xe4 g6!, planning ...♗f5; Black has good pressure on the light squares.

8...♗b4 9 0-0

But not 9 ♗xe4? dxe4 10 ♕xe4 f5! 11 exf6 ♗f5! (unfortunately it was me who fell for this trick in the stem game against Hodgson).

9...♘xd3 10 cxd3 ♘xc3 11 bxc3 g6

Black must prevent White from steamrollering with f4-f5.

12 a4!?

12 g4?! h5 13 h3 hxg4 14 hxg4 ♗d7 15 f5 gxf5 16 gxf5 0-0-0 gives Black unwanted

counterplay, according to Scottish GM Jonathan Rowson.

12...h5 13 h3 h4 14 ♗a3 ♗f5 15 ♖fb1

White also kept an edge after 15 ♔h2 e6 16 ♕e3 ♖c8 17 ♗xf8 ♔xf8 18 ♖fc1 ♔g7 19 c4 c5 20 dxc5 ♖xc5 21 ♘d4 dxc4 22 dxc4 ♖cc8 23 ♘b5 a6 24 ♘d6 ♖c7 25 ♖a3 b6 26 ♖cc3 ♕c5 27 ♕xc5 ♖xc5 28 ♖cb3, Krizsany-Morrison, Koszeg 1999; White's knight certainly overshadows Black's bishop.

15...♕c7

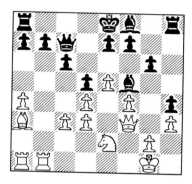

We are following the game Motwani-Summerscale, Scottish Championship 1999. Now, instead of Motwani's 16 ♕e3, White should play 16 a5! e6 17 ♗c5!, when the two weaknesses on b7 and h4 give White a clear advantage – Motwani.

B2)

6...♘xc3 7 ♗d2 ♗f5

Also possible here is 7...♕d5!? 8 ♕xc3! and now:

a) 8...♕e4+ 9 ♔f2 dxe5 10 fxe5 e6 11 ♘f3 and White will follow up with ♗d3.

b) 8...dxe5 9 dxe5 ♗f5 10 ♘f3 e6 11 ♗c4 ♕e4+ 12 ♔d1 ♗g4 13 ♖e1 ♗xf3+ 14 gxf3 ♕g6 15 ♕b3 b6 16 ♗d3 ♕h5 17 f5 ♕xf3+ 18 ♔c1 ♘d7 19 ♗e4! ♕xb3 20 axb3 and White has a strong initiative – Beliavsky.

c) 8...♗f5!? 9 ♘f3 dxe5 (9...♕e4+ 10 ♔d1 ♗g4 11 ♗d3 ♗xf3+ 12 ♔c1 ♕d5 13 gxf3 ♕xf3 14 ♖f1 ♕h5 15 ♕b3 b6 16 d5 gives White a strong attack, while 9...b5 10 ♗e2 e6

11 0-0 &e7 12 a4 dxe5 13 ♘xe5 b4 14 ♕e3 0-0 15 &f3 ♕d6 16 c3 was good for White in Palliser-Hickman, Port Erin 1998) 10 &c4! and now:

c1) 10...♕e4+ 11 ♔d1 &g4 12 ♕b3 e6 13 ♕xb7 &xf3+ 14 ♔c1 ♕xd4 (or 14...&xg2 15 ♕c8+ ♔e7 16 &b4+ ♔f6 17 ♕d8+ ♔f5 18 ♕g5 mate) 15 gxf3 ♕xc4 16 ♕c8+ ♔e7 17 fxe5 f6 18 ♕b7+ ♘d7 19 ♕xa8 and White has a winning advantage.

c2) 10...♕d8 11 ♕b3 e6 12 ♕xb7 (Beliavsky-Bezold, Portoroz 1996) 12...♘d7 13 ♘xe5 ♘xe5 14 dxe5 &e4 15 0-0-0 ♖b8 16 ♕xa7 ♖a8 17 ♕e3 &d5 18 &b3 &xb3 19 ♕xb3 and White has a clear advantage – Beliavsky.

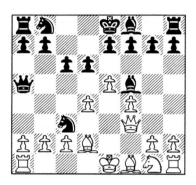

8 &d3 &xd3

8...g6 9 bxc3 ♕d5 10 ♕e2 &xd3 11 cxd3 c5 12 c4 ♕xd4 13 ♖b1 dxe5 14 ♘f3 ♕d7 15 ♘xe5 ♕c7 16 ♕e4 gave White a strong attack for the pawn in Kengis-Hausner, Luxembourg 1990.

9 cxd3 ♕d5 10 bxc3 dxe5

10...♘d7 may be more resilient. Black was okay in Beaumont-Lund, British League 1999, after 11 ♕xd5 cxd5 12 ♖b1 (12 a4!?) 12...b6 13 ♘f3 e6 14 ♔e2 dxe5 15 fxe5 f6 16 a4 &e7 17 ♖hc1 ♖c8.

11 fxe5 ♕xf3 12 ♘xf3

White has an impressive centre and is ahead on development. The game Motwani-Adams, Moscow Olympiad 1994, continued 12...e6 13 ♔e2 ♘d7 14 ♖hb1 b6 15 a4 &e7

16 a5 b5 17 c4 a6 18 ♖c1! 0-0 19 cxb5 cxb5 20 ♖c7 ♖fd8 21 ♖ac1 ♔f8

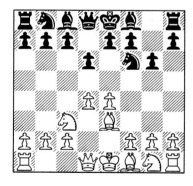

22 d5! exd5 23 e6! ♘f6 24 ♘g5 h6 25 ♖xe7! hxg5 and now Motwani points out that the quickest win is 26 ♖cc7 ♘e8 27 &b4! ♘xc7 28 exf7! ♖e8 29 ♖xe8+ ♔xf7 30 ♖e7+.

C)
3...g6

Reaching the starting position of the Pirc Defence.

4 &e3!

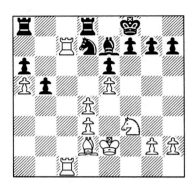

It's pretty straightforward stuff: White prepares ♕d2, followed possibly by &h6 and 0-0-0. Now Black has a decision. Black now generally develops his bishop with 4...&g7, but this can also be delayed. The choices are:
C1: 4...&g7
C2: 4...c6

C1)

4...♗g7 5 ♕d2

And immediately we have another intersection. Black can play the following:

C11: 5...0-0
C12: 5...c6

Lesser alternatives are:

a) 5...♘c6 6 ♗b5 (6 f3!?) 6...0-0 7 ♘f3 a6 8 ♗xc6 bxc6 9 ♗h6 ♗g4 10 ♗xg7 ♔xg7 11 ♕f4 ♗xf3 12 ♕xf3 ♘d7 13 0-0 (White's already a little better) 13...e5 14 ♖ad1 exd4 15 ♖xd4 ♖e8 16 ♕d1 ♕b8 17 b3 ♕b6 18 ♔h1 ♕a5 19 ♕a1! ♕e5 20 ♘c4 c5 21 f4 ♕f6 22 e5! dxe5 23 ♘e4 ♕e7 24 f5 and White has a very strong attack, Hebden-Beikert, France 1993.

b) 5...♘g4 (White used to play the cautious 5 f3 to prevent this move, but more recently players have realised that 5...♘g4 isn't such a threat at all) 6 ♗g5 h6 7 ♗h4 and now:

b1) 7...c6 8 h3 ♘f6 9 f4! b5 10 ♗d3 b4 11 ♘ce2 a5 12 ♘f3 0-0 13 0-0 d5? (13...♗a6 is stronger, although White keeps an edge – Piket) 14 ♗xf6 (Piket-Epishin, Dortmund 1994), and now 14...♗xf6 15 e5 ♗g7 16 a3 and 14...exf6 15 f5 are both promising for White.

b2) 7...g5 8 ♗g3 e5 9 dxe5 ♘xe5 10 0-0-0 ♘bc6 11 f4 gxf4 12 ♗xf4 ♗e6 13 ♘d5 a6 14 ♘f3 was better for White in Millican-Davis, correspondence 1990; Black can hardly contemplate castling kingside here.

C11)

5...0-0

Black 'safely' castles before developing queenside counterplay. This is not as popular as 5...c6 and, by committing his king early, Black has given White an obvious target to aim at.

6 0-0-0

The good news for white players is that, according to my database, White has scored a massive 74% from this position!

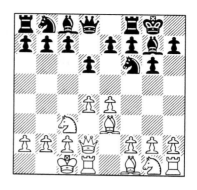

6...c6

Or:

a) After 6...♘c6 White can simply continue the attack with 7 ♗h6.

b) 6...♘g4 (preventing ♗h6) 7 ♗g5 h6 8 ♗h4 ♘c6 9 h3 ♘f6 10 f4! a6 11 g4 b5 12 e5 dxe5 13 dxe5 ♕xd2+ 14 ♖xd2 ♘h7 15 ♗g2 and White has an excellent position, Yudasin-Janjgava, Lvov 1987.

7 ♗h6!

White plays in a very direct manner. Black's defensive bishop must be exchanged!

7...b5

Black has to get going on the other side of the board. Here's a example of what can happen to Black if he plays too slowly: 7...♖e8?! (planning ...♗h8, but the horse has bolted long ago...) 8 ♗xg7 ♔xg7 9 f4 ♕a5 10 ♘f3 ♗g4 11 ♗e2 ♘bd7 12 h3 ♗xf3 13 ♗xf3 e5 14 g4 (White's kingside attack is automatic) 14...♘b6 15 ♗e2 exf4 16 ♕xf4 h6 17 h4 g5 18 ♕f3 ♖e7 19 e5! dxe5 20 hxg5 hxg5 21 ♕f5 ♖e6 22 ♕xg5+ ♔f8 23 ♖df1 ♔e7 24 ♖xf6! and Black resigned in Hübner-Nautsch, Germany 1981, on account of 24...♖xf6 25 dxe5.

8 f3!

Protecting the e4-pawn and thus taking much of the sting out of ...b5-b4.

8...♕a5

8...♗xh6 just seems to speed up White's attack, for example 9 ♕xh6 b4 10 ♘ce2 ♕a5 11 ♔b1 ♗e6 12 ♘c1 (the knight does a great defensive job here; Black's attack is going nowhere) 12...♖c8 13 h4 ♕d8 14 ♘ge2 ♕f8 15 ♕d2 a5 16 ♘f4 ♘bd7 17 h5 ♕g7 18 g4 ♘f8 19 g5 ♘e8 20 hxg6 hxg6 21 ♖h4! c5 22 d5 ♗d7 23 ♗c4

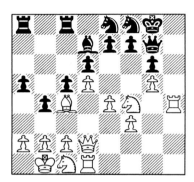

23...f6 24 ♖g1 fxg5 25 ♖xg5 ♘f6 26 e5! ♘6h7 27 ♖g1 ♗f5 28 e6 ♕d4? 29 ♘xg6!! ♕xg1 30 ♘xe7+ ♔h8 31 ♘xf5 ♖c7 32 ♖g4 ♕h1 33 ♕f4 ♕e1 34 ♘xd6 a4 35 ♘f7+ ♖xf7 36 ♕xf7 and Black resigned, Efimov-Sarno, Reggio Emilia 1998.

An even quicker disaster befell Black in the game Hamdouchi-Battikhi, Dubai 1995, which continued 8...♕c7 9 h4 ♘bd7 10 h5! (there's no point hanging around!) 10...e5 11 g4 exd4 12 ♗xg7 dxc3 13 ♕h6 cxb2+ 14 ♔b1 ♕d8 15 g5 and Black resigned, as 15...♘xh5 16 ♖xh5 gxh5 17 ♗f6 leads to mate.

9 ♔b1 b4

After 9...♗e6 White has the clever retort 10 ♘d5! (Oratovsky) and now:

a) 10...♕a6 11 ♘xe7+ ♔h8 12 ♗xg7+ ♔xg7 13 d5 and White is simply a pawn up.

b) 10...♕xd2 11 ♘xe7+ ♔h8 12 ♗xd2 (but not 12 ♗xg7+?? ♔xg7 13 ♖xd2 ♖e8 14 ♘xc6 ♘xc6 15 d5 ♗xd5! with a back rank mate trick) 12...♖e8 13 ♘xc6 ♘xc6 14 d5 and White regains the piece with some advantage – Black's pawns will be weak in the ending.

c) 10...♕d8 11 ♘xf6+ exf6 12 d5 and White will continue with h2-h4-h5.

10 ♘ce2 ♘bd7

Or 10...♗e6 11 ♘c1, and White will continue the attack with g2-g4 and h2-h5.

11 h4 c5 12 h5

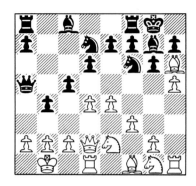

White's attack is quicker than Black's. The game Matikozian-Minasian, Yerevan 1999, continued 12...c4 (12...♘xh5?? loses to the standard 13 ♖xh5! gxh5 14 ♕g5) 13 hxg6 fxg6 14 ♗xg7 ♔xg7, and now White missed the very strong continuation 15 ♕h6+ ♔f7 (or 15...♔g8 16 ♘f4 ♗a6 17 ♘xg6) 16 ♘h3 c3 17 ♘g5+ ♔e8 18 ♘xh7!.

C12)
5...c6

This is Black's most sensible approach. He keeps his king in the centre, for the time being at least, and prepares queenside counterplay.

6 ♘f3

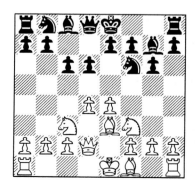

Also very playable are 6 f3 and the immediate 6 ♗h6, although I believe the latter line has lost a bit of its sting since Black players discovered the line 6 ♗h6 ♗xh6 7 ♕xh6 ♕a5 8 ♗d3 c5!.

After 6 ♘f3, it's decision time again for Black. His main choices in this position are the following:

C121: 6...0-0
C122: 6...b5
C123: 6...♕a5

Alternatively:

a) 6...♘g4 7 ♗g5 h6 8 ♗h4 0-0 9 h3 ♘f6 10 ♗d3 ♕c7 11 ♗xf6!? (normally White wouldn't consider this exchange, but here Black is forced to capture with the e-pawn) 11...exf6 12 0-0 ♘d7 13 ♘e2 ♖e8 14 c3 and White has a slight advantage, Hebden-Strikovic, Oviedo (rapid) 1993; Black will find it hard to activate his dark-squared bishop.

b) 6...♗g4 (Black often waits for White to commit his bishop to d3 before doing this) 7 ♗e2 (the more aggressive 7 ♗d3!? is also promising, for example 7...♗xf3 8 gxf3 ♘bd7 9 0-0 ♕a5 10 ♔b1 b5?! 11 ♗h6 ♗xh6 12 ♕xh6 ♘b6 13 ♖he1 ♘a4 14 ♘xa4 ♕xa4 15 e5! dxe5 16 dxe5 ♘d5 17 ♕g7 ♖f8 18 e6! and White broke through, Gallagher-Ramseier, Zurich 1999) 7...0-0 8 h3 ♗xf3 9 ♗xf3 ♘bd7 10 0-0 (on this occasion White chooses a quieter life) 10...♖e8 11 ♖fd1 ♕c7 12 a4 ♖ad8 (12...a5 13 ♕e2 e5 14 d5 cxd5 15 ♘xd5 ♘xd5 16 ♖xd5 ♖a6 17 ♖b5 was nice for White in Emms-Belov, German Bundesliga 1995) 13 g3 e5 14 d5!? ♘b6 15 ♕d3 a5 16 ♖ab1 with an slight edge for White as in Gallagher-C.Hansen, Reykjavik 1998.

C121)
6...0-0 7 ♗h6

There's no reason to delay this move any longer; White wants to get rid of Black's defensive bishop.

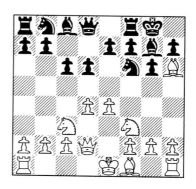

7...♗g4

Black has some other moves here:

a) 7...b5 8 ♗d3 transposes to Variation C1222.

b) 7...♘bd7 8 0-0-0 b5 9 ♗xg7 ♔xg7 10 e5! (this lunge in the centre, forcing Black to move his defensive knight, is usually very desirable) 10...♘e8 11 h4 h5 12 ♗d3 ♘b6 13 ♖he1 with lots of pressure down the central files, Corvi-De Luca, Palocco 1998.

c) 7...♕a5 8 h4 (8 0-0-0 ♗g4 transposes to the note White's eighth move) 8...♗g4 9 ♗xg7 ♔xg7 10 e5 dxe5 11 ♘xe5 h5 12 f3 ♗e6 13 ♗c4 ♗xc4 14 ♘xc4 ♕c7 15 0-0-0 with a slight advantage to White, Stripunsky-Vulicevic, New York 1998.

8 ♗xg7

8 0-0-0!? is also dangerous:

a) 8...♕a5 9 h3 (American GM Joel Benjamin suggests the line 9 ♗xg7 ♔xg7 10 e5 dxe5 11 dxe5 ♘fd7 12 ♕d4 ♗xf3 13 e6+ ♘f6 14 gxf3 fxe6) 9...♗xf3 10 gxf3 ♗xh6 11 ♕xh6 ♘bd7 12 h4 ♘h5 13 ♖g1 ♔h8 14 f4 ♘df6 15 f5 and White's attack is very quick, Emms-Spraggett, Paris 1990.

b) 8...b5 9 ♗xg7 ♔xg7 10 h3 ♗xf3 11 gxf3 ♘bd7 12 h4 b4 13 ♘e2 ♕a5 14 ♔b1 h5 15 ♖g1 ♖h8 16 ♗h3 and White has the initiative, Reefat-Nikolic, Istanbul Olympiad 2000.

c) 8...♗xf3 9 gxf3 ♘bd7 10 ♗xg7 ♔xg7 11 f4 and White can look to push with e4-e5.

d) 8...♘bd7!? (this may be best) 9 ♗xg7

♔xg7 10 e5 ♘d5 11 exd6 exd6 (11...♘xc3?
12 ♕xc3 exd6 13 d5+ is good for White) 12
♘xd5 cxd5 13 ♕f4 ♗xf3 14 ♕xf3 ♕g5+ 15
♔b1 ♘f6 (Speelman-Piket, Tilburg 1992),
and here White should play 16 h4 ♕g4 17
♗e2 ♕xf3 18 ♗xf3, which is roughly level.

8...♔xg7 9 ♘g5!

We will frequently come across this idea.
In the 150 Attack, Black's light-squared
bishop is a often a problem piece for him, as
it has no useful role. Black sees it as an
achievement if it can be exchanged. White,
on the other hand, is often prepared to go
out of his way to avoid such a trade. In this
instance the bishop is left hitting thin air, and
it will soon have to retreat after h2-h3.

9...h6 10 h3 ♗c8

10...♗h5?! is answered by 11 ♘xf7! ♖xf7
12 g4, and White regains the piece with some
advantage.

11 ♘f3

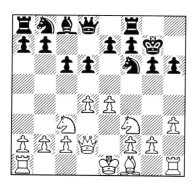

We are following the game Degraeve-
Ponomariov, Belfort 1998, which continued
12 e5 dxe5 13 ♘xe5 ♘bd7 14 ♘g4 ♘xg4 15
hxg4 ♖h8 16 f3 ♘f6 17 ♗c4 b5 18 ♗b3
♗b7 19 0-0-0 and White was better.

C122)

6...b5

A popular choice. Black delays castling for
another move, expands on the queenside and
threatens ...b5-b4. On the other hand, this
also gives White a target on the queenside.

Often in this variation White abandons a
direct kingside attack in favour of striking
back on the queenside with a2-a4. The trick
is to know when to do this!

7 ♗d3

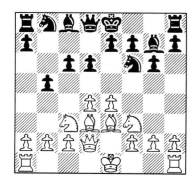

Now Black's main moves are:

C1221: 7...♗g4
C1222: 7...0-0

Alternatively:

a) 7...♘g4!? 8 ♗g5 f6 (or 8...h6 9 ♗h4 g5
10 ♗g3 e5 11 dxe5 ♘xe5 12 ♗e2 ♗e6 13
0-0 0-0 14 ♖fd1 and Black has problems with
his vulnerable d-pawn, Spraggett-Mezcua
Coronil, Cala Galdana 1994) 9 ♗h4 e5 10 h3
♗h6 11 ♕e2 exd4 12 ♘xb5 ♘e5 13 ♘bxd4
with an extra pawn, Ermenkov-Popchev,
Ikaros 1999.

b) 7...a6 (this is too slow; the rest of the
game is a severe example of what can happen
to Black if he is not careful) 8 ♗h6 0-0 9 e5
dxe5 10 dxe5 ♘d5 11 h4 ♘b4 12 h5 ♘xd3+
13 cxd3 ♗f5 14 ♗xg7 ♔xg7 15 0-0-0 b4 16
hxg6 ♗xg6 17 ♕h6+ ♔g8 18 ♘h4 1-0
Spraggett-McTavish, Toronto 1995.

c) 7...♘bd7 8 ♗h6 ♗xh6 (8...0-0 transposes to note 'b' to Black's eighth move in
Variation C1222) 9 ♕xh6 e5 10 dxe5 dxe5
11 0-0 ♕e7 12 ♖fe1 ♘g4 13 ♕d2 0-0 14 a4
b4 15 ♘d1 ♔g7 16 b3 a5 17 ♘b2 and the
white knight will find a nice home on c4,
Beliavsky-Marangunic, Slovenian Team
Championship 1998.

C1221)

7...♗g4

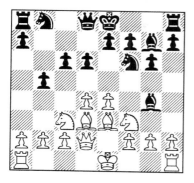

Black looks to exchange his problem piece.

8 e5!?

This idea is fairly new. Instead of this, 8 ♘g1!? is an amusing retreat, which certainly prevents the exchange, and leaves Black's bishop 'hanging' on g4; White will regain lost time with h2-h3 (for those not liking the aesthetic value of this move, 8 ♘h4 probably comes to the same thing). Following 8...e5 9 dxe5 dxe5 10 h3 ♗e6!? (10...♗c8 11 ♘f3 ♘bd7 actually reaches Variation C2, note 'b' to Black's ninth move) 11 ♘f3 ♘bd7 12 ♘g5!? ♕e7 13 ♘xe6 ♕xe6 14 a4 b4 15 ♘e2 a5 16 0-0 0-0 17 c3 ♖ab8 18 ♘g3 bxc3 19 ♕xc3 ♕b3 20 ♖fc1 ♖fc8 21 ♗a6 ♕xc3 22 ♖xc3 ♖c7 23 ♗b5 White was better in Ramesh-Hendriks, Amsterdam 2000.

8 0-0-0 looks natural, but Black achieves good counterplay after 8...♘bd7 9 h3 ♗xf3 10 gxf3 a5 11 f4 b4 12 ♘a4 ♘b6 13 ♘xb6 ♕xb6, Adams-Hodgson, Dublin 1993.

8...b4

8...♘fd7!? 9 ♗h6 0-0 10 ♗xg7 ♔xg7 was unclear in Beckemeier-Tischbierek, German Bundesliga 1999. Perhaps White should settle here for 11 exd6 exd6 12 ♕f4 ♖e8+ 13 ♘e2.

9 ♘e4

Also interesting is 9 ♘e2!? ♘d5 10 ♗h6 0-0 11 h4 and now:

a) 11...♗xf3 12 gxf3 dxe5 13 ♗xg7 (13 h5

♗f6! 14 hxg6 hxg6 15 ♗xf8 ♕xf8 and Black has good compensation for the exchange, Apicella-Hickl, Kaufbeuren 1996) 13...♔xg7 14 h5 transposes to the next note.

b) 11...dxe5 12 ♗xg7 ♔xg7 13 h5 ♗xf3 14 gxf3 ♘d7 15 hxg6 hxg6 16 ♕h6+ ♔f6 17 ♖g1 and Black is living very dangerously, S-B.Hansen-Yrjola, Reykjavik 2000.

9...♘xe4

After 9...♘d5?! 10 ♗h6! White has all the makings of a successful attack. Short-Irzhanov, Elista Olympiad, continued 10...0-0 11 h4! ♗xf3?! 12 gxf3 dxe5 13 h5 ♗f6 14 ♘xf6+ exf6 15 hxg6 fxg6 16 ♗xf8 ♕xf8 17 dxe5 and Black didn't last much longer.

10 ♗xe4 d5

Or:

a) 10...♗xf3 11 ♗xf3 dxe5 12 0-0-0 a5 13 ♗h6! and White has a strong attack; one possible line is 13...♗xh6 14 ♕xh6 exd4 15 ♕g7 ♖f8 16 ♖xd4 ♕b6 17 ♖hd1 ♘a6 18 ♖d6!.

11 ♗d3 ♗xf3 12 gxf3 ♕b6

12...a5?! looks a bit irrelevant. The game Leko-Beliavsky, Madrid 1998, saw a large White advantage after 13 h4! ♘d7 14 h5 ♕b6 15 c4! bxc3 16 bxc3 e6 17 ♖b1 ♕c7 18 ♗h6.

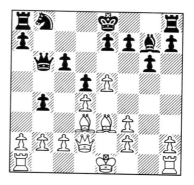

An important position for the evaluation of this line. Here are two practical examples:

a) 13 h4 ♘d7 14 h5 c5 15 dxc5 ♘xc5 16 ♗e2 0-0?! (16...e6 looks stronger) 17 ♕xd5

罝ac8 18 hxg6 hxg6 19 豐d4! and White was better, Deep Junior 6-Khalifman, Dortmund 2000.

b) 13 a3!? bxa3 14 b4! ②a6 15 c3 ②c7 16 罝xa3 0-0 17 罝a5 豐b7 18 罝g1 and I prefer White, who can attack on either side, Nguyen Anh Dung-Postny, Budapest 2000.

C1222)
7...0-0 8 魚h6
White wishes to trade bishops.

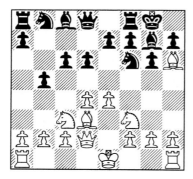

8...魚g4
Again Black is looking to exchange his problem piece. Alternatively:

a) 8...b4?! (this unprovoked lunge just drives the knight to where the action is – the kingside) 9 ②e2 a5 10 ②g3 豐c7 11 魚xg7 含xg7 12 e5 dxe5 13 dxe5 ②g4 14 豐f4 豐b6 15 0-0 f6 16 罝ae1 罝a7 17 e6 and White has a clear advantage, Dunnington-Fabris, Cappelle la Grande 1994.

b) 8...②bd7!? 9 a4!? (after 9 e5!? dxe5 10 dxe5 ②g4 11 魚xg7 含xg7 12 豐f4 Black has a little trick: 12...②dxe5! 13 ②xe5 豐d6 14 ②xg6 fxg6 15 豐xd6 exd6 with an equal position) 9...b4 10 ②e2 a5 and now:

b1) 11 ②g3!? e5 12 dxe5 ②xe5 13 ②xe5 dxe5 14 h4 豐d4 15 魚xg7 含xg7 16 0-0-0 h5 17 豐g5 魚e6 is unclear (but not 17...②h7?? 18 ②xh5+ 含h8 19 ②f6! 豐xf2 20 ②xh7 含xh7 21 罝df1 豐a7 22 h5 and Black resigned in Gaulin-Leygue, Bescanon 1999).

b2) 11 魚xg7 含xg7 12 e5 (12 ②g3!?)

12...dxe5 13 dxe5 ②g4 (13...②d5 14 h4!, intending h4-h5, gives White a very quick attack) 14 豐f4 ②c5 15 魚c4 f6 16 e6 f5 (or 16...②h6 17 ②ed4 豐b6 18 b3 魚a6 19 魚xa6 ②xa6 20 0-0-0 ②c7 21 豐e4 罝a6 22 ②e2 ②d5 23 ②fd4 and White's better, Kaidanov-Bishop, Las Vegas 1997) 17 h3 ②f6 18 豐e3 with a complex position, Ansell-Koneru, London 1999.

9 魚xg7
Interesting is 9 a4!?, which is more to gain a tempo for kingside action rather than the start of an attack on the queenside. After 9...b4 10 ②e2 (now the b-pawn needs to be defended) 10...a5 11 ②g3 ②bd7 12 h4! White has the makings of a successful kingside offensive. The game Zapata-Schussler, Santa Clara 1996, continued 12...e5 13 dxe5 dxe5 14 h5! 魚xh5 15 0-0-0 ②c5 16 魚xg7 含xg7 17 豐g5! and Black was unable to resist White's assault.

9...含xg7 10 ②g5
Once again White avoids the exchange on f3. 10 e5!? is probably a bit premature, but still playable. After 10...dxe5 11 dxe5 ②fd7 12 豐e3 豐c7 13 e6 魚xe6 14 ②g5 豐e5 15 ②xe6+ fxe6 16 a4 豐xe3+ 17 fxe3 b4 18 ②e4 White has some compensation for the pawn, Adams-Shirov, Dos Hermanas 1995.

10...e5
Or:

a) 10...h6 (obviously this is the critical test of 10 ②g5) 11 h3! 魚h5 (or 11...b4 12 hxg4! bxc3 13 ②e6+! fxe6 14 豐xh6+ 含f7 15 e5!) 12 ②xf7! 罝xf7 13 g4 and White regains the piece with some advantage. This trick associated with ②g5 is worth remembering.

b) 10...b4!? 11 ②e2 豐b6? (Black should play 11...h6) 12 f3 魚c8 13 h4 e5 14 h5 and White's attack plays itself. De la Riva Aguado-Iruzubieta, Spanish Team Championship 1998, concluded 14...h6 15 dxe5 dxe5 16 hxg6 hxg5 17 豐xg5 c5 18 豐h6+ and Black resigned.

11 dxe5 dxe5 12 h3 魚c8 13 a4! b4 14 ②e2

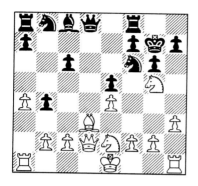

White can combine play on the kingside with threats to Black weaknesses on the other wing. Here are two practical examples:

a) 14...a5 15 f4 ♘bd7 16 0-0 ♕e7 17 ♖f2 ♘e8 18 ♘f3 f6 19 ♘g3 exf4 20 ♕xf4 ♘d6 21 ♖e1 ♖e8 22 ♘d4 ♘e5 23 ♗f1 with an edge for White, Sadler-Szmetan, Buenos Aires 1995.

b) 14...c5 15 ♕e3 ♕e7 16 0-0 ♘c6 17 c3 ♗b7 18 a5! a6 19 ♘g3 h6 20 ♘f3 ♘e8 21 ♘d2 ♘c7 22 ♘b3 ♘e6 23 ♗c4 and Black has pawn weaknesses on c5 and a6, Yagupov-Irzhanov, Nizhnij Novgorod 1998.

C123)
6...♕a5

A solid choice that has been a favourite of grandmasters Julian Hodgson and Colin McNab. By moving the queen to a5, Black puts White off castling queenside; White may have to look for another way forward.

7 h3

With this move, preventing both ...♗g4 and ...♘g4, White signals his intentions of playing in a more positional manner. For those with more aggressive intentions there's 7 ♗d3!?, with the following variations:

a) 7...0-0 8 ♗h6 (8 h3 transposes into the text) 8...♗g4 9 0-0-0 ♘bd7 10 ♗xg7 ♔xg7 11 ♗e2 e5 12 h3 ♗xf3 13 ♗xf3 ♖ad8 14 g4 ♘b6 15 ♗e2 exd4 16 ♕xd4 ♖fe8 17 f4 with an unclear position, Khalifman-Bogdanovski, Paide 1999.

b) 7...♗g4 8 e5!? dxe5 (or 8...♘fd7 9 exd6 ♗xf3 10 gxf3 exd6 11 ♘e4! ♕xd2+ 12 ♔xd2 ♔e7 13 ♖ae1!) 9 ♘xe5 ♘bd7 10 f4 ♖d8 (10...♘xe5 11 dxe5 ♘d5 12 ♘xd5 ♕xd2+ 13 ♔xd2 cxd5 14 h3 ♗d7 15 ♗d4 was slightly better for White, Stripunsky-Vulicevic, New York 1998) 11 h3 ♗f5 12 ♗xf5 gxf5 13 0-0-0 h5 14 ♔b1 ♘b6 15 ♕d3 e6 with a small plus for White, Gadjily-Bogdanovski, European Team Championship, Batumi 1999.

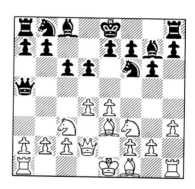

7...0-0

Or 7...♘a6!? and now:

a) 8 a4 b5 (8...♘b4!?) 9 ♗d3 b4 10 ♘e2 c5 11 c3 bxc3 12 bxc3 0-0 13 0-0 ♖b8 and probably White's a bit better, Kinsman-Hodgson, British League 1998

b) 8 a3 b5 9 ♗d3!? ♘b4 10 0-0 ♘xd3 11 cxd3 0-0 12 ♗h6 ♕b6 13 e5 ♘e8 (13...♘d5 looks stronger) 14 ♘e4 ♗e6 15 ♕f4 f6 16 exf6 ♘xf6 (Emms-Vigus, British Championship 2000), and now instead of my 17 ♕h4? ♗xh6! 18 ♕xh6 ♘xe4 19 dxe4 ♖xf3! 20 gxf3 ♕xd4, when Black was better, I should have played 17 ♗xg7 ♔xg7 18 ♕h4 ♗f5 19 ♖fe1, with an edge to White.

8 ♗d3 ♘bd7 9 0-0 e5

9...b5 is met by 10 ♘d5! ♕d8 11 ♘xf6+ ♘xf6 12 a4, and White begins to probe on the queenside.

10 a4

Gaining space on the queenside. English GM Mark Hebden has preferred the slightly more restrained 10 a3, and he has an ongoing theoretical debate with the Scottish Grandmaster and Pirc expert Colin McNab in this line. So far I can count three battles between the two (there may well be more). The latest encounter continued 10...♖e8 (10...♕c7 11 a4!? b6 12 a5 b5 13 dxe5 dxe5 14 ♘e2 a6 15 c4 bxc4 16 ♗b1 ♖b8 17 ♘c3 ♘h5 18 ♖a4 ♖d8 19 ♖d1 ♗b7 20 ♕e2 c5 21 ♕xc4 was better for White in Hebden-McNab, London 1994) 11 ♗c4 exd4 12 ♘xd4 ♕c7 13 ♘f3 ♘e5 14 ♘xe5 dxe5 15 ♖fd1 ♗e6 and Black has equalised, Hebden-McNab, London 2000.

10...♖e8 11 ♖fd1

Interesting is 11 ♖fb1!?, for example 11...♕c7 12 a5 d5 13 ♖e1 dxe4 14 ♘xe4 ♘xe4 15 ♗xe4 ♘f6 (15...exd4 16 ♗xd4 is an edge for White) 16 ♗h6 ♗xh6 17 ♕xh6 exd4 18 ♗d3 ♖xe1+ 19 ♖xe1 ♕xa5 20 ♗c4 and White has a dangerous attack, Smagin-Hebert, Montreal 2000.

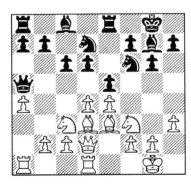

Now Black can play:

a) 11...♘f8 an now either 12 d5!? or 12 dxe5 dxe5 13 ♘d5 ♕xd2 14 ♘xf6+ ♗xf6 15 ♘xd2 gives an edge – Nunn.

b) 11...♕c7 12 a5! (gaining more space on the queenside) 12...exd4 13 ♗xd4 and White was better in Nunn-Azmaiparashvili, Wijk aan Zee 1993.

c) 11...exd4 12 ♗xd4 ♘e5 13 ♗e2 ♗e6 14 b3 (14 ♘g5!? looks more promising) 14...♖ad8 15 ♖ab1 c5 16 ♗e3 with a level

position, Summerscale-McNab, Aberdeen 1999.

C2)
4...c6!?

This is a tricky move order that may be employed by more devious opponents. Black's idea is that White will play ♗e3-h6 at some point, so why waste a move with ...♗g7 if it can exchange immediately on h6? Instead Black immediately begins queenside operations.

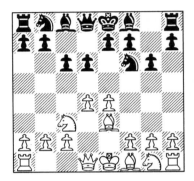

5 ♕d2

White carries on as normal.

5...b5

5...♗g7 6 ♘f3 transposes to Variation C122, while 5...♘bd7 6 ♘f3 b5 7 ♗d3 transposes to the text.

6 ♗d3 ♘bd7 7 ♘f3 e5!?

Or:

a) 7...♗g7 8 ♗h6 reaches Variation C122.

b) 7...♕c7 8 0-0 e5 (for 8...♗g7 see Chapter Six, Variation C1) 9 a4 b4 10 ♘e2 exd4 11 ♘exd4 c5 12 ♘b5! ♕c6 13 ♗c4 ♗b7 14 ♗f4 a6 15 ♗d5 ♘xd5 16 exd5 ♕b6 17 ♖fe1+ ♔d8 18 ♘g5 and White went on to win in Nunn-McNab, Walsall 1992.

8 dxe5

There's also some sense in delaying this capture with 8 0-0 and now:

a) 8...♘g4 9 ♗g5 f6 10 ♗h4 ♗h6 11 ♕d1 and Black must do something about the threat of h2-h3.

b) 8...♗b7 9 ♖ad1 (9 dxe5 dxe5 10 h3 transposes to the text) 9...a6 10 a4 ♗g7 (10...♗e7!? 11 ♗h6 exd4 12 ♘xd4 b4 13 ♘ce2 c5 14 ♘f3 ♕c7 15 ♘f4 was better for White in Gelfand-Ponomariov, Biel 2000) 11 axb5 cxb5 12 dxe5 dxe5 13 ♘xb5!? axb5 14 ♗xb5 ♗a6 15 ♗xa6 ♖xa6 16 ♘xe5 with a very unclear position, Kupreichik-Karasev, Minsk 1976.

8...dxe5

Or 8...♘xe5 9 ♘xe5 dxe5 10 h3 a6 (10...♗b7? 11 ♘xb5 cxb5 12 ♗xb5+ ♘d7 13 0-0-0 ♗c8 14 ♕d5 and White wins) 11 a4 with an edge to White – Nunn.

9 h3

9 ♗h6 ♗xh6 10 ♕xh6 ♕e7 effectively gains a tempo for Black, who will follow up with ...♕f8. With 9 h3 White signals his intentions to keep the dark squared bishops on the board (it's makes less sense to exchange bishops once Black has blocked his in with ...e7-e5). White's chances will come in the form of attacking Black's new weaknesses on the queenside.

9...♗b7

Or:

a) 9...♕e7 10 0-0-0 (Nunn prefers 10 0-0 ♘c5 11 ♖fd1) 10...a6 11 ♖he1 ♗g7 12 ♗h6 ♗xh6 13 ♕xh6 ♗b7 14 ♔b1 0-0-0 with an equal position, Tolnai-Ftacnik, Stara Zagora 1990.

b) 9...♗g7 10 a4! b4 11 ♘e2 a5 12 c3 c5 (or 12...bxc3 13 ♕xc3, intending ♘d2-c4) 13 cxb4 cxb4 14 0-0 0-0 15 ♖fd1 and White has a promising position, Nunn-Gelfand, Munich 1991.

10 0-0 ♗g7

It makes good sense for Black to complete his development. The game Adams-Bisby, Hastings 1995 is a graphic example of what can happen to Black if he fails to do so: 10...a6 11 a4 ♕e7?! 12 axb5 cxb5 13 ♘xb5! axb5 14 ♖xa8+ ♗xa8 15 ♖a1 ♕d8 16 ♗xb5 ♗e7 17 ♘xe5! ♗xe4 18 ♘xd7 ♘xd7 19 ♖a7

♗f5 20 ♗xd7+ ♗xd7 21 ♗b6 ♕c8 22 ♕d4 f6 23 ♖c7 ♕d8 24 ♖c3! ♕a8 25 ♖e3 ♕c6 26 ♕c5! and Black resigned – White regain the piece and keeps a decisive two-pawn advantage.

11 a4 a6 12 ♘e2 0-0 13 ♘g3 ♕e7

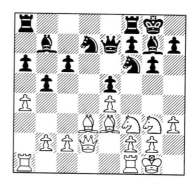

After 14 c4 b4 15 c5 a5 16 ♕c2 ♖fd8 17 ♖fd1 ♘e8 18 ♗c4 h6 19 ♖d2 White was slightly better, Palac-Ftacnik, Ljubljana 1998.

Important Points

1) If you see a promising kingside attacking idea, go for it! The 150 Attack is specifically geared for this.

2) Useful attacking ideas include: exchanging bishops with ♗h6, forcing the defensive knight to move with e4-e5, and opening the h-file with h2-h4-h5.

3) Black will often try to exchange his light-squared bishop for your knight on f3, with ...♗g4xf3. Be aware of opportunities when this can and should be avoided.

4) If Black lunges too quickly on the queenside with ...b7-b5, sometimes it's better for White to adopt a different plan involving striking back with a2-a4.

5) Black sometimes keeps delays developing his bishop to g7, preferring to keep it on f8. Be aware that the exchange of bishops with ♗h6 now effectively loses a tempo.

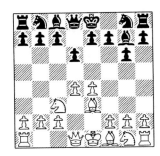

CHAPTER SIX

Attacking the Modern: The 150 Attack

1 e4 g6 2 d4 ♗g7 3 ♘c3 d6 4 ♗e3

The Modern Defence is very closely related to the Pirc Defence. Indeed, one often transposes into the other. There are subtle differences, however. From Black's point of view, one of the advantages of the Modern Defence move order is that he has not committed his knight to f6 so early. This piece can be kept on g8, so that the g7-bishop is not blocked, and so that White is not able to exchange bishops quickly with ♗h6. Black can begin queenside operations early on, only finishing development on the kingside when it suits him.

So why doesn't everyone play the Modern move order rather than the Pirc? Well, there's some good news for White as well. With the knight on g8, Black is still two moves from castling, and this can be hazardous if the position suddenly opens up. Another factor is that White can consider a very early pawn lunge with h2-h4-h5, making use of Black's lack of control over h5. One final factor is that White doesn't have to worry so much about the possibility of ...♘g4. Of course there are other reasons outside the 150 Attack as to why Black chooses the Pirc over the Modern, or vice-versa (playing the Modern mover-order allows 3 c4, for instance).

As well as the main move (3...d6), we shall also be having a quick look at third move alternatives for Black.

1 e4 g6 2 d4 ♗g7 3 ♘c3

Black now has three main choices:
A: 3...c5
B: 3...c6
C: 3...d6

A)
3...c5

This move is seen from time to time. Black is offering White the chance to transpose into a Benoni or an Open Sicilian. There *is* a third option...
4 dxc5! ♕a5 5 ♗d2 ♕xc5 6 ♘d5!

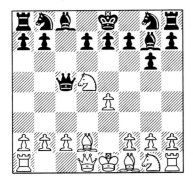

6...♘a6

Or:

a) 6...b6 7 ♗b4! ♕c6 8 ♗b5 ♕b7 9 ♗c3 f6 10 ♕f3!? a6 11 ♗d3 ♘c6 12 0-0-0 and White is better – Bangiev.

b) 6...♗xb2? 7 ♖b1 ♗e5 (or 7...♗a3 8 ♖b3 ♕d6 9 ♕a1 f6 10 ♖xa3 ♕xa3 11 ♘c7+ ♔d8 12 ♘xa8) 8 f4 ♗c7 9 ♖b5! ♕c6 10 ♖b3 ♗b6 11 ♖xb6! axb6 12 ♗b5 ♕c5 13 ♗b4 and the black queen is trapped.

7 ♘f3 e6 8 ♗c3 ♗xc3+ 9 ♘xc3 ♘f6 10 ♕d2 0-0 11 0-0-0

We are following Barle-Forintos, Maribor 1977. The absence of dark squared bishops leaves Black vulnerable on those squares.

B)

3...c6

The Gurgenidze System, which is a kind of cross between the Modern and the Caro-Kann. Black prepares to play ...d7-d5.

4 ♗e3

White carries on in '150 Attack' fashion.

4...d5

4...d6 transposes to Variation C1.

After 4...♕b6 5 ♖b1! White changes tack and castles kingside, leaving the black queen somewhat misplaced on b6.

5 ♕d2 dxe4

Or 5...♘f6 6 e5 ♘g4 7 ♗f4 and now:

a) 7...h5 8 h3 ♘h6 9 g4 ♕a5 (9...hxg4 10 hxg4 ♘xg4 11 ♖xh8+ ♗xh8 12 f3 traps the knight) 10 0-0-0 ♘a6 11 a3 ♘c7 12 ♗e2

♗d7 13 gxh5 gxh5 14 ♗xh5 ♘e6 15 ♗e3 ♘f5 16 ♗g4 and White has a clear plus, Gyimesi-Barczay, Hungarian league 1995.

b) 7...f6 8 exf6 ♘xf6 9 ♗h6 0-0 10 ♗xg7 ♔xg7 11 0-0-0 ♕d6 12 ♖e1 b5 13 ♘f3 b4 14 ♘d1 a5 15 ♘e5 c5 16 dxc5 ♕xc5 17 f3 ♘bd7 18 ♘f2 ♘xe5 19 ♖xe5 ♕c7 20 ♕d4 and White has a good bind on the dark squares, Kholmov-Karlik, Pardubice 1999.

6 ♘xe4 ♘d7 7 0-0-0 ♘gf6 8 ♘xf6+

8 f3 is interesting. Kupreichik-Grigorov, Lvov 1986, saw 8...♘xe4 9 fxe4 ♘f6 10 e5 ♘d5 11 ♗h6 ♗xh6 12 ♕xh6 ♗f5 13 ♘f3 ♕a5 14 ♗c4 and White has a slight edge.

8...♘xf6 9 ♘f3 0-0 10 ♘e5 ♗e6 11 ♔b1 a5 12 h4

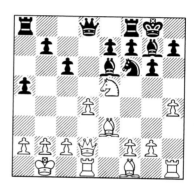

J.Polgar-Dunnington, London 1988, continued 12...h5 13 f3 a4 14 a3 ♕a5 15 ♕xa5 ♖xa5 16 ♖e1 ♖aa8 17 ♗g5 ♗f5 18 ♖g1 ♖ad8 19 g4! and White was better.

C)

3...d6 4 ♗e3

Now Black has a further choice:

C1: 4...c6

C2: 4...a6

4...♘f6 transposes into the Pirc Defence (see Chapter 5).

C1)

4...c6

Black begins operations on the queenside.
5 ♕d2

White sticks to the normal '150 Attack' plan. He is now ready to play ♗h6 once the g8-knight moves. White will simply continue developing until the opportunity arises.
5...b5

5...♘d7 6 ♘f3 b5 7 ♗d3 transposes to the text.
6 ♗d3 ♘d7 7 ♘f3

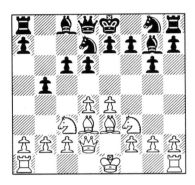

7...♕c7

At this point Black has many alternatives:

a) 7...♗b7 8 0-0 ♕c7 9 ♖fe1 a6 10 a4 b4 11 ♘e2 c5 12 ♘g3 and White is fully ready for action on the kingside. Emms-Mestel, British League 1998, continued 12...♖c8?! (12...♘f6 is stronger) 13 c3 bxc3 14 bxc3 ♘gf6 15 ♗h6 0-0 16 ♗xg7 ♔xg7 17 ♕g5 e6 18 e5! ♘g8 19 ♗e4 ♗xe4 20 ♘xe4 d5 21 ♘d6 and White had a large advantage.

b) 7...♘b6 8 0-0 ♗g4 9 ♘e1! (we've seen the idea of avoiding this exchange in the Pirc) 9...e5 10 dxe5 dxe5 11 a4 ♘c4 (11...b4 12 ♘e2 a5 13 c3 b3 14 c4 is nice for White) 12 ♗xc4 bxc4 (12...♕xd2 13 ♗xf7+! ♔xf7 14 ♗xd2 b4 15 f3 and White wins a pawn) 13 ♕xd8+ ♔xd8 14 a5 was clearly better for White in Delchev-Movsziszian, Andorra la Vella 1999 – Black's queenside pawns are very weak.

c) 7...a6 8 a4 ♗b7 9 0-0 and now:

c1) 9...♘gf6 10 e5!? dxe5 11 dxe5 ♘g4 12 e6! fxe6 13 ♘g5 is good for White.

c2) 9...♕c7 10 axb5 cxb5?! (Adams gives 10...axb5 11 ♖xa8+ ♗xa8 12 ♖a1 ♗b7 13 d5 b4 14 dxc6 bxc3 15 cxd7+ ♕xd7 16 bxc3 ♘f6 with just a small advantage for White) 11 ♘d5!

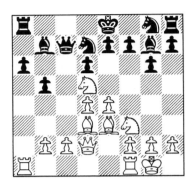

Now we have a further split:

c21) 11...♗xd5 12 exd5 ♕b8 13 ♕a5 ♘b6 14 ♗xb5+! axb5 15 ♕xb5+ ♘d7 16 ♕c6 ♖xa1 17 ♖xa1 ♘gf6 18 ♖a8 and White went on to win in Hinks Edwards-Pein, British League 1998.

c22) 11...♕d8 12 ♕a5! ♗xd5 (12...♖c8?! 13 ♕xd8+ ♔xd8 14 ♘b4 ♘gf6 15 e5 dxe5 16 ♘xe5 ♘xe5 17 dxe5 ♘d7 18 f4 g5 19 ♖fd1! left White in a winning position, Adams-Dunnington, Hastings 1995) 13 exd5 ♘b6 (Maljutin-Rashkovsky, Soviet Championship 1991), and now I like 14 b3, followed by c2-c4.

8 0-0 ♘gf6

Finally Black develops his g8-knight.
9 ♗h6

Like clockwork, the bishop goes to h6.
9...0-0 10 ♘e2 c5

It's also possible to challenge the centre with 10...e5. After 11 c3 ♘b6 12 ♘g3 ♖e8 13 ♗xg7 ♔xg7 14 ♘h4 ♘g8 15 f4 f6 16 ♖f2 White was better in Ambroz-Baum, Bad Ragaz 1993.
11 c3

This position has been reached on quite a few occasions. Here are some practical examples:

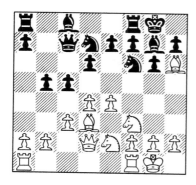

a) 11...a5 12 ♘g3 b4 13 ♗xg7 ♔xg7 14 ♕g5 bxc3 15 bxc3 e6 16 e5 ♘g8 was Hodgson-Webster, British Championship 2000. Here White played 17 exd6 ♕xd6 18 ♘e4 ♕e7 19 ♘xc5 ♕xg5 20 ♘xg5 ♘xc5 21 dxc5 and the game was eventually drawn. Instead White could consider keeping the tension with 17 h4!?.

b) 11...a6 12 ♗xg7 ♔xg7 13 ♘g3 ♖e8 (or 13...h6 14 ♖ae1 ♘b6 15 ♕f4 ♘c4 16 ♕c1 ♘b6 17 e5! dxe5 18 dxe5 ♘fd5 19 ♘h4 e6 20 ♖e4 ♘e7 21 ♖fe1 ♘f5 22 ♖g4 ♘xg3 23 ♖xg3 ♘d5 24 ♘xg6! fxg6 25 ♖xg6+ ♔f7 26 ♕xh6 ♔e8 27 ♖g7 ♗d7 28 ♕g5 1-0 Belikov-Sretenskij, Moscow 1996) 14 ♘h4 e5 15 d5 c4 16 ♗c2 ♘c5 with an unclear position, Fressinet-Tkachiev, Bordeaux 2000.

C2)
4...a6

This move is similar to 4...c6 in that Black quickly organises queenside counterplay. However, in this line Black is more likely to try and arrange ...♗b7, ...♘bd7 and ...c7-c5.
5 ♕d2 b5 6 h4!?

White angles for a quick h4-h5. Black either prepares for this or prevents it.

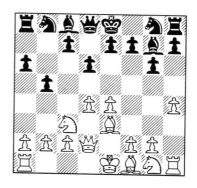

6...h5

Alternatively:

a) 6...♘f6 7 f3 ♘bd7 (7...h6!?) 8 0-0-0 ♗b7 (8...h5 transposes to the text) 9 ♗h6 ♗xh6 10 ♕xh6 e5 11 d5 ♕e7 12 g4 b4 13 ♘ce2 ♘c5 14 ♘g3 ♖c8 15 ♕d2 a5 16 h5 ♘fd7 17 ♔b1 ♖b8 18 g5 ♗a6 19 ♗xa6 ♘xa6 20 ♘h3 ♘dc5 21 b3 a4 22 ♘f2 ♘d7 23 ♘g4 ♘ac5 24 ♖h3 and White doubles on the h-file, A.Ivanov-Burnett, New York 2000.

b) 6...h6 (planning to meet h4-h5 with ...g6-g5) 7 0-0-0 ♘d7 8 f4 h5 (White now gets a very good position, so perhaps the idea of ...h7-h6 and then ...h6-h5 is just too slow; on the other hand, if Black does nothing White will be in a position to play h4-h5) 9 ♘f3 ♘gf6 10 ♗d3 ♘b6 11 f5! (a crucial move; many would be tempted to play e4-e5 instead, but that would only give Black counterplay on the light squares) 11...gxf5 12 exf5 ♘c4 13 ♕e1! (another good move; it looks dangerous to give up the dark-squared bishop, but surprisingly Black cannot take advantage of the pin along the c1-h6 diagonal) 13...♘xe3 14 ♕xe3 ♗h6 15 ♘g5 ♗b7

16 ♔b1 ♖g8 (Black could grab a pawn for his troubles, although after 16...♗xg2 17 ♖hg1 ♗b7 18 ♘ce4 White continues as in the game) 17 ♘ce4 ♗xe4 18 ♗xe4 d5 (or 18...♘xe4 19 ♕xe4 ♗xg5 20 hxg5 ♖xg5 21 ♕c6+ ♔f8 22 ♕f3 and White captures on h5) 19 ♗f3 ♕d6 20 ♖de1 ♔d7 21 ♖e2 ♘g4 22 ♕b3! ♗xg5 (22...c6 23 ♘xf7 wins) 23 hxg5 c6

24 g6! ♖af8 (24...fxg6 25 ♖e6 ♕c7 26 ♗xd5!) 25 gxf7 ♖xf7 26 ♖e6 ♕c7 27 ♖xc6! 1-0 Adams-Hodgson, Southend 2001.

7 f3 ♘f6 8 0-0-0 ♘bd7 9 ♘h3

Also interesting is 9 e5!?, for example 9...b4 10 ♘a4 ♘d5 11 ♗g5 ♗b7 12 ♗c4! a5 (12...♘7b6 13 ♘xb6 ♘xb6 14 ♕xb4 is good for White) 13 ♘h3 ♘7b6 14 ♗b3 ♕d7 15 ♘xb6 cxb6 16 e6! fxe6 (16...♕xe6? runs into 17 ♗xe7!) 17 ♕d3 0-0-0 18 ♕xg6 and White was better in Ye-Timman, Manila Olympiad. This could do with a further practical test.

9...♘b6

Or 9...♗b7 and now:

a) 10 ♗e2 ♖c8 11 ♘g5 0-0 12 g4 b4 13 ♘d5 ♘xd5 14 exd5 ♘f6 15 ♘e4 ♗xd5 16 ♘xf6+ exf6 17 gxh5 and Black's kingside is starting to open up, Schmitzer-Alber, Ger-

man Bundesliga 1991.

b) 10 ♘g5 (this is a nice outpost for the knight once Black has played ...h7-h5) 10...0-0 11 g4 c5 12 gxh5 ♘xh5 13 dxc5 b4 14 ♘d5 dxc5 15 ♗h3 ♘b6 16 ♘xb6 ♕xb6 17 ♕h2 a5 18 e5 and I prefer White, Karabalis-J.Schmidt, Bad Wildungen 1998.

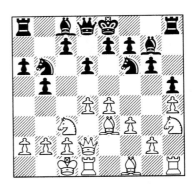

After 9...♘b6 the game Adams-Speelman, Hastings 1989/90, continued 10 ♗d3 b4 11 ♘e2 a5 12 ♘f2 (12 ♘g5!?) 12...c6 13 ♔b1 ♕c7 14 e5 ♘fd5 15 exd6 exd6 16 ♗g5 ♗e6 17 ♘e4 ♔d7! with an unclear position.

Important Points

1) Look out for opportunities to exploit the fact that Black has delayed ...♘f6.

2) When black answers h2-h4 with ...h7-h5, the g5 square becomes a useful outpost for a white knight after ♘h3-g5.

3) If Black lunges too quickly on the queenside with ...b7-b5, sometimes it's better for White to adopt a different plan involving striking back with a2-a4.

4) Look out for attacking ideas against Black's king, which often remains uncastled for a long time.

CHAPTER SEVEN

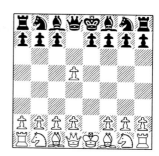

Attacking the Scandinavian

1 e4 d5 2 exd5

The Scandinavian Defence has been one of the fastest growing openings of recent years. Before then it was considered to be very much a 'second string' opening, and at grandmaster level it was only played by a few die-hards, including the Danish GM Bent Larsen and, after him, the Australian Ian Rogers. However, in the nineties a whole new generation of GMs started to appreciate that Black's chances in many of the main lines had been grossly underestimated. Suddenly the defence became very popular, and much new theory was created. At first, most of the new theory consisted of new ideas and improvements on old ones from Black's point of view, but more recently there have been fresh and important ideas for White as well. Unsurprisingly, perhaps, the Scandinavian has probably passed its peak of popularity, but it remains a far more respected defence than it did a couple of decades ago.

After 1 e4 d5 2 exd5 Black has two very different routes to choose from: 2...♘f6 and 2...♕xd5. Against 2...♘f6 I was close to advocating 3 c4 c6 4 ♘c3 cxd5 5 cxd5, transposing into the Caro-Kann chapter. However, I decided that after 3...e6!? 4 dxe6 ♗xe6 (The Icelandic Gambit), Black has far too much fun, especially at anything under

grandmaster level. Instead I've opted for the tricky 3 ♗b5+ (it's tricky in that it avoids some of Black's unusual lines against 3 d4).

Against 2...♕xd5 I've been a bit more mainstream in my recommendations, although what I suggest against the popular 3...♕a5 is quite rare, so there is still quite a bit uncharted territory here.

After 2 exd5 Black chooses between:
A: 2...♘f6
B: 2...♕xd5

A)
2...♘f6 3 ♗b5+

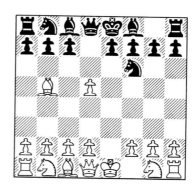

3...♗d7

Black's can offer a pawn sacrifice with 3...♘bd7 here, but instead of trying to hang on to the pawn with the theoretical 4 c4, I'm advocating the simple 4 ♘f3 ♘xd5 5 d4 and now:

a) 5...c6 6 ♗e2 (the bishop is happy to retreat now that it has forced Black to play the slightly passive ...♘bd7) 6...e6 7 0-0 ♗e7 8 c4 ♘5f6 9 ♘c3 ♕c7 10 ♖e1 0-0 11 ♗f1 a6 12 ♗g5 and White has a nice edge, Sedina-Spinelli, Turin 1998.

b) 5...e6 6 0-0 ♗e7 7 ♖e1 0-0 8 ♗f1 (White just plays simple chess) 8...c5 9 c4 ♘5f6 10 ♘c3 cxd4 11 ♘xd4 and I prefer White, Jonkman-Fernandez Barrera, Linares 2000.

c) 5...g6 6 0-0 ♗g7 7 ♖e1 0-0 8 ♘bd2 c6 9 ♗f1 ♘5f6 10 a4 c5 11 a5 cxd4 12 ♘xd4 e5 13 ♘b5 a6 14 ♘d6 and again White is better, Kogan-Carvalho, Loures 1997.

4 ♗e2 ♘xd5 5 d4

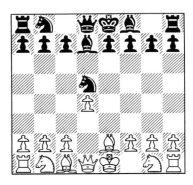

5...♗f5

Moving the bishop to a more active square is Black's most popular choice here. Alternatives are:

a) 5...g6 6 c4 ♘b6 7 ♘c3 ♗g7 (or 7...c6 8 c5 ♘d5 9 ♕b3) 8 c5! (White takes advantage of the unfortunately placing of Black's bishop) 8...♘c8 9 ♘f3 e6 10 ♗g5 ♘e7 11 ♘e4 h6 12 ♗f6 0-0 13 0-0 ♗xf6 14 ♘xf6+ ♔g7 15 ♘g4 and Black has some dark-squared weaknesses on the kingside, Honfi-Blachmann, Bad Wörishofen 1991.

b) 5...e6 6 ♘f3 ♗e7 7 0-0 0-0 8 c4 ♘f6 9 ♘c3 and White has a typical space advan-

tage, Matsuura-Silveira, Brasilia 2000.

6 ♘f3

Note that this position can also be reached via the move order 1 e4 d5 2 exd5 ♘f6 3 d4 ♘xd5 4 ♘f3 ♗f5 5 ♗e2 (with each side having played one move less). With our move order we have avoided certain possibilities for Black (the 'Portuguese Gambit' – 3...♗g4!?, as well as 4...♗g4, and the main line with 4...g6). So, in a sense, we've tricked Black into our territory.

5...e6 7 0-0 ♗e7

Or 7...♗d6 8 c4 ♘f6 (8...♘b4 9 ♘a3 0-0 10 ♗d2 ♘8c6 11 ♘b5 looks pleasant for White) 9 ♘c3 ♘e4 10 ♕b3 ♘xc3 11 bxc3 ♕c8 12 c5 ♗e7 13 ♘e5 and the players agreed a draw in Van der Weide-Reinderman, Leeuwarden 1997. They obviously had their own reasons for calling it off so soon; the final position is probably a bit for White.

8 a3

In order to prevent ...♘b4 after c2-c4. The immediate 8 c4!? is also interesting. Kupreichik-Gipslis, Aalborg 1993, continued 8...♘b4 9 ♘a3 0-0 10 ♗f4 ♘8c6 11 ♘b5 ♖c8 12 a3 a6 13 d5! axb5 14 dxc6 ♘d3 15 cxb7 ♖b8 16 ♗xd3 ♗xd3 17 ♘e5 ♗xf1 18 ♕xf1 ♕e8 19 cxb5 ♗d6 20 a4 ♖xb7 21 ♕c4 and White's powerful queenside pawns were well worth the slight material disadvantage. In this line Black should probably prevent ♘b5 with 10...a6 or 10...c6.

8...0-0 9 c4 ♘b6

With this retreat Black leaves the f6-square available for his dark-squared bishop. Also possible is 9...♘f6 10 ♘c3 c6 (10...♘e4!? may be stronger, although White was still a bit better after 11 ♗e3!? ♘xc3 12 bxc3 c5 13 d5 ♕c7 14 ♕d2 e5 15 a4 a5 16 ♘e1! ♗d6 17 f3 ♘d7 18 ♔h1 ♗g6 19 ♘c2 f5 20 ♘a3 in Skripchenko Lautier-Liardet, Cannes 1997) 11 ♘h4 ♗g6 12 ♗e3 ♘a6 13 ♘xg6 hxg6 14 ♗f3, Wang Zili-Arkell, London 1997; White has the usual advantage that comes with having more space and the bishop pair.

10 ♘c3 ♘c6

10...♗f6 11 h3 ♘c6 transposes to the text.

11 h3!?

This idea has recently risen to prominence. One idea is to prevent Black from adding pressure on the d4-pawn with ...♗g4, while there's also a sneaky trick lurking in the background. After 11 ♗e3 ♗f6 12 b3 ♕e7 13 c5 ♘d5 14 ♘xd5 exd5 15 b4 a6 Black was okay in the game Svidler-Terekhin, St Petersburg 1994.

11...♗f6 12 ♗e3

12...♕d7

Alternatively:

a) 12...♕e7? walks into 13 g4! ♗g6 14 g5 and a piece goes – another point of 11 h3.

b) 12...h6 (preparing ...♕e7) 13 b4 ♕e7 (13...a6 14 ♕b3 ♘xd4 15 ♗xd4 ♗xd4 16 ♖ad1 e5 17 ♘xe5 ♕f6 18 ♖xd4 ♕xe5 19 ♖fd1 c6 20 ♗g4 was pleasant for White, Turov-J.Ivanov, Ubeda 2000) 14 ♕b3 (14 b5 ♘a5 15 c5 ♘d5 16 ♗d2 is also good for White, Kaminski-Gipslis, Cappelle la Grande 1998) 14...♖fd8 15 ♖fd1 a5 16 c5 ♘d5 17 b5 ♘a7 18 ♘xd5 exd5 19 ♖e1 and White has a big space advantage on the queenside, Baklan-Melnik, Alushta 1999.

13 b4

13 g4?! is expansion on the wrong side. After 13...♗g6 14 g5 ♗e7 15 b4 ♖ad8 Black has reasonable counterplay, Stripunsky-Prokopchuk, Azov 1996.

13...♖ad8

After 13...♖fd8 White can play as in the main text with 14 ♕b3.

14 ♕b3!?

Also interesting is 14 ♖a2!? and now:

a) 14...♘xd4 15 ♘xd4! ♗xd4 16 ♖d2 with a further split:

a1) 16...e5 17 ♘b5 ♕e7 (17...♗xe3 18 ♖xd7 ♖xd7 19 ♕b3 is good for White) 18 ♘xd4 exd4 19 ♖xd4 and the bishop pair gives White an edge.

a2) 16...♗xe3 17 ♖xd7 ♖xd7 18 ♕b3 ♗g5 19 ♖d1 and White's queen is worth more than Black's rook, bishop and pawn, Kovalevskaya-Anisimov, St Petersburg 1999 (this isn't always the case – see note 'b1').

b) 14...a5! 15 b5 ♘xd4 and now:

b1) 16 ♘xd4 ♗xd4 17 ♖d2 ♗xe3! (17...e5 18 c5 ♘c8 19 ♗f3 ♘a7 20 a4 ♕e7 21 ♗xd4 exd4 22 ♖xd4 ♖xd4 23 ♕xd4 was good for White in Leconte-Feuvrier, French League 2000) 18 ♖xd7 ♖xd7 19 ♕b3 ♗c5 is fine for Black – the bishop is very well placed on c5.

b2) 16 ♗xd4 ♗xd4 17 ♖d2 e5 18 ♘xe5 ♗xf2+ 19 ♖xf2 ♕xd2 20 ♕xd2 ♖xd2 21 ♖xf5 ♖c2 22 c5! is very unclear.

14...♘xd4

Of course Black doesn't have to take the pawn, but after 14...♖fe8 15 ♖fd1 White has a big space advantage.

15 ♗xd4 ♗xd4 16 ♖ad1 e5 17 ♘b5 ♕e7 18 ♖fe1!?

White can keep a small advantage after 18 c5!? ♘d5 19 ♘bxd4 exd4 20 ♘xd4

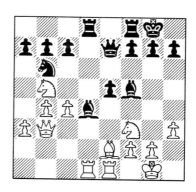

Here are a couple of practical examples from the diagram:

a) 18...c5 19 ♗f1 ♛f6 20 ♘bxd4 cxd4 21 ♖xe5 is a bit better for White, Hait-Ulko, Moscow (rapid) 1997 – Black's d-pawn is a bit vulnerable.

b) 18...♛f6 19 ♘xc7 ♗e4 (after 19...a6 White should play 20 ♘c3) 20 ♘b5 ♗c6 21 c5 ♗xb5 22 ♗xb5 ♘d5 23 ♗c4 ♘f4 24 ♘xd4 ♖xd4 25 ♖xd4 exd4 26 ♛f3! and White has a clear plus, Hait-Rasskazov, Moscow 1997.

B)
2...♛xd5 3 ♘c3

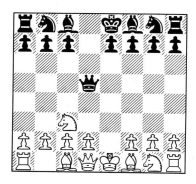

Now Black's main moves are:
B1: 3...♛d8
B2: 3...♛d6
B3: 3...♛a5

B1)
3...♛d8

This looks a bit passive, but it does have some positive points (the queen is certainly less vulnerable on this square), and recently there's been a few top level games with this move.

4 d4 ♘f6

4...g6 has been under a cloud ever since the crushing win for White in Fischer-Robatsch, Varna Olympiad 1962: 5 ♗f4 ♗g7 (5...♘h6 6 ♗e5!) 6 ♛d2! ♘f6 7 0-0-0 c6 8 ♗h6 0-0 9 h4 ♛a5 10 h5! gxh5 11 ♗d3

♘bd7 12 ♘ge2 ♖d8 13 g4 ♘f8 14 gxh5 ♘e6 15 ♖dg1 ♔h8 16 ♗xg7+ ♘xg7 17 ♛h6 ♖g8 18 ♖g5 ♛d8 19 ♖hg1 ♘f5 20 ♗xf5 1-0.

5 ♘f3 c6

Or:

a) 5...♗g4 6 h3 and now:

a1) 6...♗xf3 7 ♛xf3 c6 8 ♗e3 e6 9 ♗d3 (9 0-0-0!?) 9...♘bd7 10 0-0 ♛c7 11 ♘e2 ♘d5 12 ♗d2 ♘b4 13 ♗c4 ♘f6 14 a3 ♘bd5 15 ♗b3 b5 16 ♖ac1 and White plays for c2-c4, Tzermiadianos-Makropoulou, Greek Championship 1994.

a2) 6...♗h5 7 g4 ♗g6 8 ♘e5 e6 9 ♗g2 c6 10 0-0 (10 ♘xg6 hxg6 11 ♛d3 gives White a safe edge) 10...♘bd7 11 ♛e2 ♘xe5 12 dxe5 ♘d7 13 ♘e4!? and White has the initiative, Chandler-Santo Roman, Cannes (rapid).

b) 5...♗f5 6 ♘e5 e6 (6...c6 7 ♗c4 transposes to the text; 6...♘bd7 7 ♛f3! is good for White) 7 g4 ♗e4 (7...♗g6 8 ♗g2 c6 9 h4 with a clear edge) 8 ♘xe4 ♘xe4 9 ♗g2 ♘d6 10 ♛e2 and White will follow up with ♗f4 and 0-0-0.

6 ♗c4 ♗f5 7 ♘e5 e6

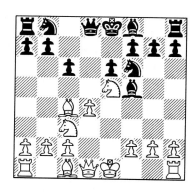

8 g4!

White can aim for a small advantage with 8 0-0, but this move promises greater rewards.

8...♗g6

Or 8...♗e4 9 ♘xe4 ♘xe4 (the exchange of these minor pieces normally helps White) 10 ♛f3 ♘d6 11 ♗b3 ♘d7 12 ♗e3!? (White is better after 12 ♗f4) 12...♘xe5 13 dxe5 ♕a5+ 14 c3 ♕xe5 15 0-0-0 ♗e7 16 ♖he1 ♗g5?! (16...♕a5 is stronger) 17 h4! ♗xe3+ 18 ♖xe3 ♕c5 19 ♗xe6! 0-0 20 ♗b3 and White has a clear advantage. Sermek-Gerencer, Pula 1999, concluded 21 ♕f4 a4 22 ♖e5 ♕a7 23 ♗c2 ♘b5 24 ♖h5 g6 25 ♕h6 1-0.

9 h4 ♘bd7

A major alternative is 9...♗b4 and now:

a) 10 h5 (this is probably good enough for an edge):

a1) 10...♗xc3+?! 11 bxc3 ♗e4 12 f3 ♗d5 13 ♗d3 b5 14 h6 g6 15 ♗g5 (Karsten Müller) – Black is in a very awkward pin.

a2) 10...♗xc2? 11 ♕xc2 ♕xd4 12 f4 ♘g4 13 ♘xg4 ♕xc4 14 h6 and White has a clear advantage – Müller.

a3) 10...♗e4 (this is Black's best move) 11 f3 ♗d5 12 ♗d3 and White follows up with ♗d2 and ♕e2.

b) 10 f3 (this leads to complications that seem favourable for White) 10...♗xc2 11 ♕xc2 ♕xd4 12 ♕e2 and now:

b1) 12...b5?! 13 ♘xf7! (13 ♗b3? ♗xc3+ 14 bxc3 ♕xc3+ 15 ♔f2 ♕xa1 16 ♖d1 ♕c3 was unclear, Herrera-Del Rio Angelis, Santa Clara 2000) 13...♗xc3+ (or 13...0-0 14 ♗xe6 ♖xf7 15 ♗xf7+ ♔xf7 16 ♗d2) 14 ♔f1 0-0 15 ♗xe6 and White is winning – Müller.

b2) 12...♗xc3+ 13 bxc3 ♕xc3+ 14 ♔f2 ♕xa1 (this is the critical test) 15 ♖d1 and now Black must do something about the threat of ♗b2.

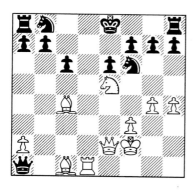

b21) 15...b5 16 ♘xf7! 0-0 17 ♗xe6 ♕c3 18 ♗b2 ♕c5+ 19 ♔g2 ♕e7 (19...♘a6 20 ♗xf6 gxf6 21 ♘g5+ ♔h8 22 ♖d7 fxg5 23 ♕b2+ mates) 20 ♘g5+ ♔h8 21 ♕c2 and White has an overwhelming attack; 21...♘a6 is answered by 22 ♖d7 and 21...♖e8, by 22 h5! and h6.

b22) 15...♕c3 16 ♗b2 ♕b4 17 ♘xf7 0-0 18 ♗xf6 gxf6 19 ♕xe6 ♕c3 (or 19...♔g7 20 h5) 20 ♖d8 ♘d7 21 ♖xa8 ♕d4+ 22 ♔g2 ♕d2+ 23 ♔h3 ♔g7 24 ♕e7 ♕f4 25 ♘g5+ 1-0 Perez-Lopez Martinez, Varadero 2000.

10 ♘xd7 ♕xd7 11 h5 ♗e4 12 ♘xe4 ♘xe4 13 ♗e3

White was still also a bit better after 13 c3 0-0-0 14 ♕e2 ♘f6 15 ♗d2 ♗d6 16 0-0-0 ♖he8 17 f4 ♕c7 18 ♕f3 c5 19 dxc5 ♗xc5 20 ♔b1 ♕c6 21 ♕xc6+ bxc6 22 ♗e2, Svidler-Adams, Frankfurt 1999.

13...0-0-0 14 ♕f3

I prefer White. The game Lutz-Adams, Frankfurt 1999, continued 14...♗b4+ 15 c3 ♘xc3 16 bxc3 ♗xc3+ 17 ♔e2 ♗xa1 18 ♖xa1 f5 19 gxf5 exf5 20 d5 cxd5 21 ♗d3 ♔b8 22 ♕f4+ ♔a8 23 ♕d4 and White kept his advantage.

B2)

3...♕d6 4 d4 ♘f6 5 ♘f3 a6

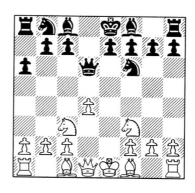

Or 5...♗g4 6 h3 ♗xf3 (6...♗h5 7 g4 ♗g6 8 ♘e5 c6 9 ♗f4 ♘d5 10 ♕d2 ♘xf4 11 ♕xf4 ♘d7 12 0-0-0 ♘xe5 13 dxe5 ♕c7 14 ♗d3 ♗xd3 15 ♖xd3 and Black's king is

stuck in the centre, Psakhis-Sygulski, Jurmala 1987) 7 ♕xf3 c6 8 ♗e3 e6 9 0-0-0 ♕c7 10 ♔b1 ♘bd7 11 ♗c1 ♘b6 12 g4 h6 13 h4 0-0-0 14 ♗h3 with a typical advantage, Bologan-Muse, Berlin 1995.

With 5...a6 Black prevents a white piece from moving to b5 and can also consider playing ...b7-b5 and ...♗b7. However, expending a tempo like this is a risky business, especially since Black has already lost time with his queen.

6 g3!?

6 ♗e2 and 6 ♗e3 are the main moves, but this move has arisen as an interesting possibility for White. One obvious point is that White prepares ♗f4, attacking the black queen.

6...♗g4

Alternatively:

a) 6...g6 7 ♗g2 ♗g7 8 0-0 0-0 9 ♖e1 ♘c6 10 ♗f4 ♕d8 11 d5! and Black is getting pushed off the board, Nevednichy-Kurajica, Ljubljana 1999.

b) 6...b5!? 7 ♗g2 ♗b7 8 0-0 e6 (8...c5 9 ♗f4 ♕b6 10 ♖e1 ♘bd7 11 d5 h6 12 a4 b4 13 ♘d2! ♕a7 14 ♘c4 ♔d8 15 ♘e4 was virtually winning for White, Tringov-Donchev, Bankia 1991) 9 ♗f4 ♕b6 10 a4 ♗d6 11 ♗e3 ♘g4 12 ♗d2 ♘f6 13 ♕e2 c6 14 ♘g5 0-0 15 ♘ce4 with an edge for White, Beshukov-Hasangatin, Koszalin 1999.

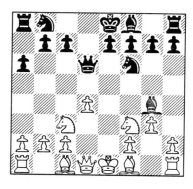

7 h3

Also interesting is 7 ♗g2 ♘c6 8 0-0 0-0-0

(Black must put pressure on the d-pawn; after 8...e6 9 ♗f4 ♕d7 10 h3 ♗xf3 11 ♕xf3 ♖d8 12 ♖ad1 ♗e7 13 d5 exd5 14 ♘xd5 ♘xd5 15 ♕xd5 ♕xd5 16 ♗xd5 White has opened up the position to his obvious advantage, Varavin-Vokarev, Ekaterinburg 1996) 9 d5 ♘b4 (after 9...♘xd5 10 ♘xd5 ♕xd5 11 ♕xd5 ♖xd5 12 ♘g5 White regains his pawn with some advantage, as 12...♖f5 runs into 13 f3) 10 h3 ♗h5 (or 10...♗xf3?! 11 ♕xf3 ♘bxd5 12 ♖d1 e6 13 ♘xd5 exd5 14 c4 with a strong attack – Müller) 11 ♗f4 ♕c5 12 ♗e3

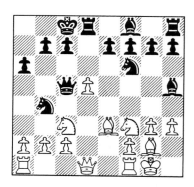

and now:

a) 12...♕a5 (Nataf-Fressinet, Vichy 2000) 13 g4! ♗g6 14 ♘d4! (threatening ♘b3) 14...♘bxd5 15 ♘b3 ♕b4 (15...♘xe3 16 ♗xb7+!) 16 ♘xd5 ♘xd5 17 ♗xd5 e6 18 a3 ♕b5 (18...♕e7 19 ♗xb7+ ♔xb7 20 ♕f3+ ♔b8 21 ♘a5 wins for White) 19 c4 ♕e8 20 ♗xb7+ ♔xb7 21 ♘a5+ ♔c8 22 ♕f3 and White is winning.

b) 12...♕d6! and I must admit that I can't find anything better than repeating with 14 ♗f4.

7...♗xf3

After 7...♗h5 8 ♗g2 ♘c6 9 0-0 0-0-0 10 g4 ♗g6 11 ♗e3 I prefer White, for example 11...h5 12 g5 ♘e4 13 ♘h4 ♘xc3 14 bxc3, or 11...e5 12 ♘xe5 ♘xe5 13 dxe5 ♕xe5 14 ♕f3.

8 ♕xf3 c6

8...♘c6 can be answered by 9 ♗e3.

9 ♗e3 ♘bd7

9...e6 10 0-0-0 ♗e7 11 g4 gives White the initiative – Glek.

10 0-0-0 e6 11 ♗f4

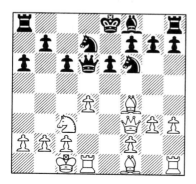

White has a small advantage, Glek-Kekelidze, Böblingen 2000.

B3)

3...♕a5

This is the main line of the Scandinavian.

4 d4 ♘f6

4...♘c6 can be met by the obvious and strong 5 d5.

The most critical alternative to 4...♘f6 is 4...e5, but this move has been under a cloud ever since the game Ivanchuk-Angelov, Varna 1987, which continued 5 dxe5 ♘c6 6 ♘f3 ♗b4 7 ♗d2 ♗g4 8 a3 ♘d4 9 ♗b5+! c6 (9...♘xb5 10 axb4 ♕xb4 11 ♖a4 ♘xc3 12 ♖xb4 ♘xd1 13 ♖xg4 ♘xb2 14 ♖b4 is winning for White) 10 0-0! ♗xf3 (10...cxb5 11 axb4 ♕xb4 12 ♘xb5! ♕xb5 13 ♘xd4 ♕d7 14 ♘f3 gives White an extra pawn) 11 axb4 ♗xd1 12 bxa5 ♗xc2 13 ♗a4 ♘e7 14 ♗xc2 ♘xc2 15 ♖a4 and White has a very favourable ending.

4...c6 5 ♘f3 ♘f6 transposes to the text.

5 ♘f3 c6

Alternatively:

a) 5...♗f5 6 ♗d2 c6 transposes to the text.

b) 5...♘c6?! 6 ♗d2! (6 ♗b5 ♗d7 7 0-0 0-0-0 8 ♕e2 a6 9 ♗xc6 ♗xc6 10 ♘e5 ♗e8 11 ♗e3 ♘d5 12 ♘xd5 ♕xd5 13 c4 was

slightly better for White in Belikov-Maljutin, Sochi 1990) 6...♗g4 7 ♘b5 ♕b6 8 c4 ♗xf3 9 ♕xf3 ♘xd4 10 ♘xd4 ♕xd4 11 ♕xb7 ♕e4+ 12 ♕xe4 ♘xe4 13 ♗e3 is known to be a very good ending for White.

c) 5...♗g4 6 h3 ♗h5 (6...♗xf3 7 ♕xf3 c6 8 ♗d2 ♘bd7 9 0-0-0 e6 10 ♔b1 gives White a typical edge – two bishops and more space) 7 g4 ♗g6 8 ♘e5 e6 9 ♗g2 c6 10 h4 ♗e4 (10...♘bd7 11 ♘xd7 ♔xd7 12 d5 exd5 13 h5 ♖e8+ 14 ♔f1 ♕a6+ 15 ♔g1 ♗e4 16 f3 ♗c5+ 17 ♔h2 ♗d6+ 18 ♔h3 and 10...♗b4 11 ♗d2 ♕b6 12 h5 ♕xd4 13 ♘f3 ♕xg4 14 hxg6 ♕xg6 15 ♗f1 are both better for White) 11 ♗xe4 ♘xe4 12 ♕f3 ♘d6 13 ♗f4 f6 14 ♘d3 and White has the advantage, Popovic-Rogers, Vrsac 1987.

6 ♗d2 ♗f5

After 6...♗g4 White should play 7 h3 ♗h5 8 g4 ♗g6 9 ♘e5.

7 ♘e4!?

7 ♗c4 e6 is the main line at the moment, but with 7 ♘e4 White keeps his options open regarding the development of the light-squared bishop.

7...♕b6

7...♕c7 8 ♘xf6+ gxf6 9 g3! (now the fianchetto is suitable; White blunts any ideas Black may have on the half-open g-file and points his bishop towards Black's kingside) 9...e6 10 ♗g2 ♘d7 11 0-0 ♗e4?! 12 ♖e1 f5? (12...♗xf3 was necessary) 13 ♘g5! ♗xg2 14 ♖xe6+! ♗e7 15 ♕h5 ♖f8 16 ♔xg2 ♘f6 17

Xxf6 Âxf6 18 ♘xh7 0-0-0 19 ♘xf8 and Black resigned, De Firmian-Owen, Las Vegas 1995.

8 ♘xf6+ gxf6

After 8...exf6!? White plays 9 ♗c4!, pointing the bishop at Black's f7-pawn.

9 ♗c4!?

White has other moves here:

a) 9 b4!? e5 10 ♗c4 ♘d7 (or 10...exd4 11 0-0, followed by Xe1 – Blatny) 11 0-0 ♗g6 12 c3 ♕c7 13 dxe5 fxe5 14 ♕b3 and I prefer White, Nijboer-Prie, Linares 1995.

b) 9 ♗c3 e6 (9...♘d7 10 g3 0-0-0 11 ♗g2 e6 12 ♘h4 ♗g6 13 0-0 ♗b4 14 ♕d2 ♗xc3 15 ♕xc3 was a touch better for White, De Firmian-Matamoros Franco, Las Palmas 1999) 10 ♕d2 h5 11 ♘h4 ♗h6 12 ♕e2 ♗h7 13 g3 ♘d7 14 ♗g2 0-0-0 15 a4! and White's attack is very quick, Galkin-Feoktistov, Novgorod 1999.

9...e6

9...♕xb2 may be more of a test, but White certainly has compensation for the pawn after 10 Xb1 ♕xc2 11 ♕xc2 ♗xc2 12 Xxb7.

10 0-0 ♗g7

10...♗d6 11 Xe1 ♘d7 12 ♘h4 ♗g6 13

♗xe6! 0-0-0 (13...fxe6 14 Xxe6+ ♗e7 15 ♕e2) 14 ♗h3 ♕xb2 15 ♗a5 b6 16 ♕f3 ♔c7 17 ♗c3 was very pleasant for White, Glek-Willemze, Utrecht 1999.

11 Xe1 0-0

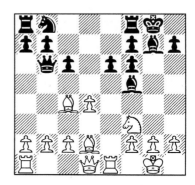

Glek-Lau, Willingen 1999, continued 12 ♘h4 ♗g6 13 ♘xg6 hxg6 and now Glek unleashed the move 14 Xxe6!. Now 14...fxe6 15 ♗xe6+ Xf7 16 ♕g4 gives White a very strong attack. Instead Lau tried 14...♕xd4, but after 15 ♕e2 ♕xb2 16 Xd1 ♕xc2 17 Xc1 ♕b2 18 Xe8! Black was under tremendous pressure.

Important Points

1) With 3 ♗b5+ against 2...♘f6, White dictates the type of position that is reached. Black has less choice than against the main line with 3 d4.

2) In Variation A White generally looks to play an early c2-c4 to get rid of the black knight on d5.

3) In the main line (B3) White plays an early ♘e4xf6+ and inflicts doubled pawn on Black.

CHAPTER EIGHT

Attacking the Alekhine: The Exchange Variation

1 e4 ♘f6 2 e5

The Alekhine is a counter-attacking defence in the same vein as the Modern or Pirc. With his first move Black actually invites White to gain time by attacking his knight with pawns. The result is that White has an impressive-looking centre after just a few moves. Black hopes that this centre will prove to be suspect to a quick attack.

For White I'm recommending the Exchange Variation (2 e5 ♘d5 3 c4 ♘b6 4 d4 d6 5 exd6), which is much easier to play than main line of 3 d4 (there's much less theory to learn), and, in my opinion, it gives White just as much chance of claiming an advantage from the opening.

The opening moves begin:
1 e4 ♘f6 2 e5 ♘d5

Or:

a) 2...♘e4 is a cheeky move which Black shouldn't really be allowed to get away with. White keeps an advantage simply by attacking the knight with 3 d3 ♘c5 4 d4 ♘e6, but 3 d4!, aiming to trap the knight in mid-board, is stronger. Then we have the following lines:

a1) 3...e6 4 ♘h3 (threatening f2-f3) 4...h6 5 ♕g4 d5 6 f3 h5 7 ♕f4 g5 8 ♘xg5 ♘xg5 9 ♕xg5 ♗e7 10 ♕g7 and White has a clear advantage – *NCO*.

a2) 3...f6 4 ♗d3 d5 5 ♘c3! and now we

have:

a21) 5...♘xc3 6 ♕h5+ ♔d7 (6...g6 7 ♗xg6+ hxg6 8 ♕xh8 ♘b5 9 ♗h6 is winning for White) 7 bxc3 e6 8 c4 and again White is clearly better – Bücker.

a22) 5...♗f5 6 ♕f3 e6 7 g4! ♗g6 8 ♘xe4 dxe4 (or 8...♗xe4 9 ♗xe4 fxe5 10 ♗d3 e4 11 ♗xe4 dxe4 12 ♕xe4±) 9 ♗xe4 ♗xe4 10 ♕xe4 ♘c6 11 exf6 ♕xf6 12 ♗e3 and White has a safe extra pawn.

b) 2...♘g8 3 d4 d6 4 ♘f3 ♗g4 5 h3 ♗h5 6 g4 ♗g6 7 ♘c3 e6 8 ♗f4 d5 9 ♗d3 and White has a good lead in development, Ernst-Welling, Copenhagen 1988.

3 c4 ♘b6 4 d4 d6 5 exd6

Now Black has a choice

A: 5...exd6
B: 5...cxd6

5...♕xd6?! 6 c5 ♕e6+ 7 ♗e2 is good for White.

A)
5...exd6

see following diagram

5...exd6 is Black's most solid choice. By keeping a symmetrical pawn structure Black is trying to keep White's opening advantage to a minimum.

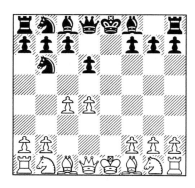

6 ♘c3 ♗e7

Black sensibly prepares to castle. Other choices are not so good:

a) 6...♘c6!? (this prevents ♗d3, but now White can take advantage of Black playing an early....♘c6) 7 ♘f3 ♗g4 8 ♗e2 ♗e7 (8...♗xf3 9 ♗xf3 ♘xc4 10 ♕e2+ ♕e7 11 ♘d5! is very good for White) 9 d5 ♗xf3 10 ♗xf3 ♘e5 11 ♗e2 0-0 12 b3 ♗f6 13 ♗b2 a5 14 0-0 ♖e8 15 ♕d2 ♘ed7 16 ♖ad1 ♘c5 17 ♕c2 g6 18 ♖fe1 ♗g7 19 ♗f1 and White has a small but secure advantage, Emms-Baburin, Port Erin 1997.

b) 6...g6 7 ♘f3! (White is no longer afraid of the pin, as Black won't be able to keep it) 7...♗g4 8 h3 ♗xf3 (obviously 8...♗h5 loses to 9 g4 – a consequence of 6...g6) 9 ♕xf3 ♘c6 10 ♗e3 ♗g7 11 0-0-0 0-0 12 h4! and White will continue in caveman fashion with h4-h5, Jepson-Westerinen, Manhems 1998.

7 ♗d3

To me this set-up with 7 ♗d3 and 8 ♘ge2 seems quite promising for White, and in practice White has scored highly. Yet it's mentioned neither by *NCO* nor *ECO*!. It's not particularly new: World Champions Alekhine and Fischer used it in their time, which serves as another recommendation.

7...♘c6 8 ♘ge2 0-0

Another important line is 8...♗g4 9 f3 ♗h5 10 0-0 ♗g6 11 ♗xg6 hxg6 12 b3 (12 d5 ♘e5 13 b3 g5 14 ♘g3 ♘bd7 15 ♘ce4 ♘f8 16 ♕d2 f6 17 ♘f5 also looks good for

White, Cicak-Freisler, Czech League 1998) 12...♗f6 13 ♘e4 (13 d5 ♘e5 14 ♗b2 0-0 15 ♘g3 ♖e8 16 ♘ge4 keeps an edge – Finkel) 13...d5 14 ♘xf6+ ♕xf6 15 c5 ♘c8 16 ♗f4 ♔d7 17 ♕d2! and suddenly Black's position looks a bit of a mess, Minasian-Nalbandian, Yerevan 1999.

9 0-0 ♗f6

Or

a) 9...♘b4 10 ♗b1 and now:

a1) 10...♘xc4? loses after the cunning 11 a3 ♘c6 12 ♕d3!. This is a useful trick to remember.

a2) 10...a5 11 b3 ♖e8 12 ♗e3 a4 13 ♘xa4 ♘xa4 14 bxa4 ♘c6 15 ♘c3 ♘a5 16 ♗d3 c6 17 ♕c2 g6 18 h3 d5 19 cxd5 cxd5 20 ♖ab1 and White's extra doubled a-pawn is of definite use, Kaminski-Baburin, Biel 1995.

b) 9...♗g4 10 f3 ♗h5 11 ♘f4 ♗g6 12 ♗xg6 hxg6 13 d5 ♘e5 14 b3 (this queenside structure is good for White) 14...♕d7 15 a4 a5 16 ♖a2 ♕f5 17 g4 ♕c8 18 ♘g2 c6 19 ♗e3 ♕c7 20 f4 ♘ed7 21 g5 ♖fe8 22 ♖d2 ♗f8 23 ♕f3 and White keeps an advantage, Djuric-Miles, Aegina 1993.

10 ♗e3

10 b3!?, preparing to answer ...♘b4 with ♗b1, is also a worthwhile possibility. White was better after 10...♖e8 11 ♗e3 ♗g4 12 h3 ♗xe2 13 ♘xe2 d5 14 c5 ♘d7 15 ♕d2 ♘f8 16 b4, Kaminski-Miroshnichenko, Vienna 1995.

10...♗g4

10...♘b4!? is an enticing alternative. Now 11 ♗b1 allows 11...♘xc4, so White must cede the bishop pair. However, following 11 b3 (11 ♘g3!?) 11...♘xd3 12 ♕xd3 ♗g4 13 f3 ♗h5 14 ♘g3 ♗g6 15 ♕d2 ♗h4 16 d5 ♖e8 17 ♖ae1 ♘d7 18 ♖e2 ♗xg3 19 hxg3 a6 20 ♖fe1 ♘f8 21 ♗d4 White kept an edge in Sermek-Zelcic, Makarska 1994. Interestingly, when the two players met again in the same line six years later, Black opted for 10...♗g4 instead.

11 h3 ♗h5 12 ♕d2 ♗g6 13 b3 ♗xd3 14 ♕xd3 d5 15 c5 ♘c8

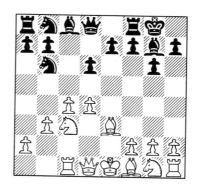

Sermek-Zelcic, Pozega 2000, continued 16 b4 ♘xb4 17 ♕b1 ♘c6 18 ♕xb7 ♘8e7 19 ♖ab1 ♕d7 20 ♕b5 ♖ad8 21 ♖fd1 and White kept an edge.

B)
5...cxd6

This is slightly more popular, and certainly more ambitious, than the other recapture 5...exd6. The structure is now asymmetrical (Black now has an extra central pawn). He will continue development with the natural moves ...g7-g6 and ...♗g7.

6 ♘c3 g6 7 ♗e3 ♗g7 8 ♖c1

This system of developing the queenside early is very ambitious, and so far White's results have been very encouraging. White is taking prophylactic measures against Black's two major pawn lunges in ...e7-e5 and ...d7-d5. Kingside development will be completed only once Black has committed himself to a certain course of action.

8...0-0

8...♘c6 9 d5 ♘e5 10 ♗e2 (an alternative is 10 f4!? ♘g4 11 ♗d4 ♘f6 12 ♘f3 0-0 13 ♗e2 e6 14 dxe6 ♗xe6 15 b3 ♘c8 16 0-0 ♘e7 17 ♘g5 which was better for White in Akopian-Minasian, Armenian Championship 1995) 10...0-0 11 b3 transposes into Variation B1.

9 b3

Protecting c4 and preparing to meet ...d6-d5 with c4-c5.

Now Black has a choice:
B1: 9...♘c6
B2: 9...f5
B3: 9...e5

White was better after 9...♗f5 10 d5 ♘a6 11 ♘f3 ♗g4 12 ♗e2 ♗xf3 13 ♗xf3 ♘c5 14 b4 ♘cd7 15 ♕b3 ♖c8 16 ♗e2 ♘f6 17 0-0, Yagupov-Petit, Ubeda 1996.

B1)
9...♘c6

This move, encouraging White's d-pawn forward, has not scored well in practice.
10 d5 ♘e5 11 ♗e2!

Preparing f2-f4. In my database White has an enormous score from this position.
11...f5

Or:

a) 11...a5 12 f4 ♘ed7 13 ♘f3 ♘c5 14 0-0 ♗g4 15 ♗d4 ♗xf3 16 ♖xf3 ♗xd4+ 17 ♕xd4 ♘bd7 18 ♗f1 ♕b6 19 ♖e1 and Black's e7-pawn is a major worry, Emms-McDonald, Hastings 1997/8.

b) 11...e6 12 f4 ♘ed7 (12...♗h6 13 ♕d2 ♘g4 14 ♗xg4 ♕h4+ 15 ♕f2 ♕xg4 16 h3 ♕f5 17 g4 ♕d3 18 ♘ge2 exd5 19 ♖d1 and the black queen is trapped – Stoica) 13 dxe6 fxe6 14 ♕xd6 e5 15 ♘f3 exf4 16 ♗xf4 ♘c5 17 0-0 ♗g4 18 h3 ♗xc3 19 hxg4 and White has a good extra pawn, V.Ivanov-Bagirov, Moscow 1995.

c) 11...h5 12 f4 ♘g4 13 ♗d4 e5 (or

13...♗h6 14 ♘h3 e5 15 dxe6 fxe6 16 ♗xg4 hxg4 17 ♕xg4 and Black is virtually lost, Howell-Trifunovic, Hastings 1995) 14 dxe6 ♗xe6 15 ♘f3 with an edge, Benjamin-Segal, New York (blitz) 1998.

12 f4 ♘g4 13 ♗d4 e5 14 dxe6 ♗xe6 15 ♘f3 ♖e8 16 ♗xg7 ♔xg7 17 0-0

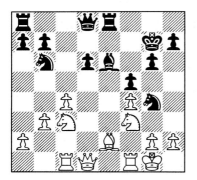

We are following the game Howell-Panchenko, Hamburg 1995. The weakness of the d6-pawn promises White a solid advantage.

B2)
9...f5

If allowed, Black plans to gain space on the kingside with ...f5-f4.

10 g3

Alternatively:

a) 10 ♘f3 f4 11 ♗d2 e5 gives Black unnecessary counterplay.

b) 10 d5!? and now:

b1) 10...e5 11 dxe6 ♗xe6 (or 11...♘c6 12 ♘h3 ♗xe6 13 ♗e2 h6 14 ♘f4 ♗f7 15 ♘fd5 and White has a nice outpost on d5, Zhao Zong Yuan-Gluzman, Gold Coast 2001) 12 ♘f3 ♘c6 13 ♕d2 ♘e5 14 ♗e2 ♕d7 15 0-0 ♖ad8 16 ♘b5 and again Black has problems with his isolated d-pawn, An.Rodriguez-Borges, Sao Paulo 1997.

b2) 10...f4 11 ♗d4 e5 12 dxe6 ♗xd4 13 ♕xd4 ♘c6 14 ♕d2 ♗xe6 15 ♘f3 ♕e7 16 ♗e2 d5 17 cxd5 ♖ad8 18 0-0 ♘xd5 with a roughly level position, Milu-Ignatescu, Ro-

mania 1995.

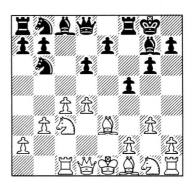

10...♘c6

A major alternative line is 10...e5 11 dxe5 dxe5 (11...♗xe5?! 12 ♘h3 and White aims for that juicy d5 outpost again) 12 ♕xd8 ♖xd8 13 c5! and now:

a) 13...♘6d7 14 ♗c4+ ♔f8 (14...♔h8 15 ♘b5!, threatening both ♘c7 and ♘d6) 15 ♘d5 ♘a6 16 ♗xa6 bxa6 17 ♘c7 ♘f6 18 ♘xa8 ♗b7 19 ♘c7 ♗xh1 20 ♘e6+ ♔e7 21 ♘xd8 ♔xd8 22 c6 and White was winning in Pavasovic-Galje, Graz 1998

b) 13...f4 14 ♗d2 ♘6d7 15 ♗c4+ and now:

b1) 15...♔h8 16 ♘b5 ♘xc5 17 ♘c7 b6 18 ♘xa8 ♗b7 19 f3 ♗xa8 20 b4 ♘e4 21 fxe4! ♗xe4 22 ♘h3 ♗xh1 23 ♘g5 and Black has problems dealing with the threat of ♘f7+, Pavasovic-Bawart, Bled 1998.

b2) 15...♔f8 16 ♘d5 ♘xc5 17 ♘c7 b6 18 ♘xa8 ♗b7 19 ♘c7! fxg3! 20 hxg3 ♗xh1 21 ♗b4! ♗h6 22 ♖c2 ♖c8 23 ♘e6+ ♔e8 24 ♗xc5! bxc5 25 f3! ♗e3 26 ♖h2 ♗xg1 27 ♖xh1!? and White is better – Ardeleanu. This final line could use a practical test.

11 d5 ♘e5 12 ♗e2 e6 13 dxe6 ♗xe6

Ardeleanu-Grunberg, Buzias 1997. Now 14 ♘h3, preparing ♘f4, looks good for White.

B3)
9...e5

This is Black's most critical response to

White's set-up.

10 dxe5 dxe5

Once again capturing with the bishop is not really what Black wants. White had a pleasant edge after 10...♗xe5 11 ♘f3 ♗g4 12 ♗e2 ♗xf3 13 ♗xf3 ♘c6 14 0-0, Raetsky-Gutkin, Riazan 1982.

11 ♕xd8 ♖xd8 12 c5! ♘6d7

It's certainly worth remembering that 12...♘d5? simply loses material after 13 ♖d1 ♗e6 14 ♗c4 (Benjamin-Johansen, Stockholm 1996).

13 ♗c4 ♘c6 14 ♘f3

Also interesting is 14 ♘e4!? ♘f8 15 ♘d6 ♘e6 16 ♘f3 ♘cd4 17 ♘g5 ♘xg5 18 ♗xg5 ♖d7, as in Yagupov-Ukolov, Moscow 1996. White probably has a slight edge here too.

14...♘a5

Or:

a) 14...h6 15 ♘e4 (15 0-0!?) 15...♘f8 (15...♘a5 16 ♗d5 ♘f6 17 ♘xf6+ ♗xf6 18 ♖d1 ♔g7 19 0-0 ♖e8 20 ♘d2 gave White something in Finkel-Drazic, Nova Gorica 1997, while Raetsky gives the line 15...♘d4 16 ♘d6 ♘xf3+ 17 gxf3 ♖f8 18 ♖g1, which is also favourable for White) 16 ♘d6 ♖d7 17 0-0 ♖e7 18 ♘xc8 ♖xc8 19 ♖fd1 ♔h7 and White must aim to advance his queenside pawn majority, Gross-Bagirov, Berlin 1996.

b) 14...♘d4 15 ♘g5 ♖f8 16 ♘ce4 ♘f5 and now:

b1) 17 ♘xf7!? ♖xf7 18 ♘g5 ♘h6 19 ♘e6 (Olsson-Zetterberg, Borlange 1995), and here Black should play 19...b5 20 ♗d5 ♘f6 21 ♗xa8 ♗xe6, which is unclear.

b2) 17 0-0 ♘f6 18 ♘d6 ♘xd6 19 cxd6 ♗d7 20 a4 ♗c6 21 ♖fd1 a6 22 f3 and White's passed d-pawn gave him an edge in Dzhindzihasvili-Alburt, US Championship 1996;

c) 14...♘f8 15 ♘g5! ♘e6 16 ♘xe6 ♗xe6 17 ♗xe6 fxe6 and White has a clear plus – Raetsky.

15 ♗e2

So far this position has been reached a few times in practice:

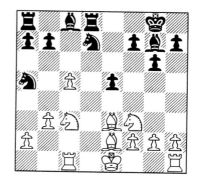

a) 15...h6 16 0-0 ♘f8 17 ♘e4 ♘c6 18 ♘d6 ♖b8 19 a3 f5 20 ♖fd1 ♗e6 21 b4 and White's queenside pawns are beginning to roll, Hunt-Schnabel, Oxford 1998.

b) 15...♘f8 16 0-0 ♘c6 17 ♖fd1 ♗f5 18 ♘b5 ♘e6 19 ♘d6 ♖ab8 20 ♘g5 ♘xg5 21 ♗xg5, Mitkov-Dischinger, Sitges 1997; the big White knight on d6 gives him a plus.

c) 15...♘c6 16 ♘b5 ♘f8 17 ♘d6 ♘e6 18 ♗c4 ♘cd4 19 ♘g5 and again White is better, Mitkov-Toth, Rio de Janeiro 2000.

d) 15...b6 16 cxb6 (16 ♘a4!? bxc5 17 0-0 c4 18 b4 ♘c6 19 ♗xc4 ♘xb4 20 a3 ♘a6 21 ♘g5 is very good for White, Kiik-Hautala, Tampere 2000) 16...♘xb6 17 ♘b5 ♗b7 18 0-0 ♘d5 19 ♖fd1 ♘c6?! (Finkel gives 19...♘xe3! 20 fxe3 e4 21 ♘fd4 ♗f8!, with equal chances) 20 ♖xd5! ♖xd5 21 ♘c7 ♖dd8 22 ♘xa8 ♗xa8 23 ♗b5! and Black's a-pawn is vulnerable, Varga-Llanos, Budapest 1999.

Important Points

1) White's set-up in Variation B is very ambitious. White prevents Black from playing ...d7-d5 and encourages only ...e7-e5.

2) After ...♘c6 (Variation B), White should normally react with d4-d5. Black, with a backward pawn on e7, is slightly worse.

3) Be wary that you are making lot of moves on the queenside in Variation B. At some point you have to stop and think of developing your kingside!

CHAPTER NINE

Other Black Defences

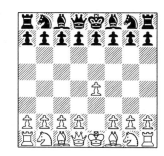

Finally we should take a look at some unusual moves that Black can play on move one. There are twenty legal moves at Black's disposal; as well as the ones we've already studied, I will draw the line with the following three:

A: 1...♘c6
B: 1...b6
C: 1...a6

Against anything else my advice is:

1) Try not to laugh (this is discourteous to your opponent).

2) Don't think for hours trying to find a quick refutation; just play normal sensible moves and enjoy the game!

A)
1...♘c6

The Nimzowitsch Defence. This is a favourite of, amongst others, England's first grandmaster Tony Miles.

2 ♘c3

This move fits in well with our repertoire, as the natural 2...e5 3 ♗c4 transposes to the Bishops Opening (see Chapter 2). Here we will deal with attempts by Black to stay strictly in Nimzowitsch territory.

2...e6

Or

a) 2...♘f6 3 d4 d5 4 e5 ♘d7 5 ♘f3 ♘b6 6 h3 is better for White according to *NCO*. Black would like to challenge with ...c7-c5, but this is difficult with Black's knight misplaced on c6.

b) 2...d6 3 d4 looks like a kind of Pirc/Modern Defence. After 3...g6 White can continue as against these openings with 4 ♗e3 ♗g7 5 ♕d2.

3 ♘f3!?

I like this tricky move. Normal is 4 d4 ♗b4, which is just a bit better for White.

3...♗b4

3...d5 should be answered by 4 ♗b5.

4 ♘e2!

A very nice idea. White deploys the knight on g3 and makes the bishop on b4 look a bit silly.

4...♗e7

4...d5 5 e5 d4 6 c3! is good for White after either 6...dxc3 7 bxc3 ♗a5 8 d4 or 6...♗c5 7 b4 ♗b6 8 b5.

5 d4 d6 6 ♘g3 ♘f6 7 c3 0-0 8 ♗d3 e5 9 0-0 ♖e8 10 h3

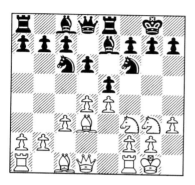

A.Ledger-Miles, British Championship 1998. I like White's position. His pieces are set up as in the Ruy Lopez, but Black has lost time with his dark-squared bishop and hasn't got the usual Lopez counterplay on the queenside.

B)

1...b6

This is Owen's Defence (otherwise known as the Queen's Fianchetto Defence). Another old favourite of Tony Miles, while more recently it's been used by the 1999 FIDE World Championship finalist Vladimir Akopian and fellow Armenian Artashes Minasian.

2 d4 ♗b7 3 ♘c3 e6 4 ♘f3 ♗b4

4...d5 5 ♗b5+! c6 6 ♗d3 is nice for White. Alekhine-Rozanov, Moscow 1908, continued 6...♘f6 7 e5 ♘fd7 8 ♘g5! ♗e7 9 ♕g4 ♘f8 10 ♘xh7! ♖xh7 11 ♗xh7 ♘xh7 12 ♕xg7 ♘f8 13 h4 ♗xh4 14 ♖xh4! ♕xh4 15 ♗g5 ♕h1+ 16 ♔d2 ♕xg2 17 ♕f6 ♕xg5+ 18 ♕xg5 and White won.

5 ♗d3 ♘f6

After 5...♘e7 White should just continue

playing natural moves, for example 6 0-0 ♗xc3 7 bxc3 d6 8 a4 a5 9 ♘e1! 0-0 10 f4 f5 11 ♕e2 ♕d7 12 ♘f3 ♘bc6 13 exf5 exf5 14 ♗c4+ ♔h8 15 ♖e1 ♘g8 16 ♗e6 ♕e8 17 d5 ♘d8 18 ♘d4 and White was better, Crouch-Basman, London 1974.

6 ♗g5 h6 7 ♗xf6 ♕xf6 8 0-0 ♗xc3 9 bxc3 d6

9...d5 10 exd5! ♗xd5 11 ♘e5 0-0 12 ♕h5 (or 12 f4!?) gives White good play on the kingside, Kramnik-Ehlvest, Moscow Olympiad 1994.

10 ♘d2 e5

Or:

a) 10...♕g6 11 f4 f5 12 ♕f3! ♕f7 13 d5! fxe4 14 ♘xe4 exd5 15 ♖ae1! gave White a strong attack in Ilincic-Filipovic, Yugoslavia 1997.

b) 10...g5!? (this looks drastic, but Black wants to stop f2-f4) 11 ♕e2 (11 ♗b5+!? may be stronger) 11...e5 12 ♕e3 ♘d7 13 ♗b5 0-0-0 14 a4 a5 15 ♖ab1 ♖he8 16 ♖fe1 ♕g6 17 ♕d3 ♔b8 18 ♗xd7 ♖xd7 19 ♕b5 ♖ee7?! (19...♖de7 is better – Minasian) 20 ♘c4 exd4 (Nikolaidis-Minasian, Panormo 1998), and now 21 cxd4 d5 22 ♘e5 is very good for White.

11 f4!

see following diagram

White has a promising attacking position. The game Dautov-Kengis, Daugavpils 1989, continued 11...exd4 12 e5! dxe5 13 fxe5! ♕g5

14 ♘f3 ♕e3+ 15 ♔h1 0-0 16 cxd4 and now best for Black is 16...♘d7 17 c3 ♗e4 18 ♗c4, and White will continue with e5-e6.

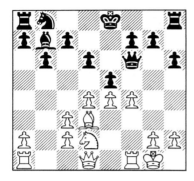

C)
1...a6

The St George Defence . This had its fifteen minutes of fame when Tony Miles used it to sensationally defeat World Champion Anatoly Karpov back in 1980. (Is this the only opening that has scored 100% at the highest level?) Despite this, Black's plan of early queenside expansion has never really caught on.

2 d4 b5 3 ♘f3 ♗b7 4 ♗d3 ♘f6

Or 4...e6 5 0-0 c5 6 c3 ♘f6 7 ♖e1 h6 8 ♘bd2 ♗e7 9 e5 ♘d5 10 dxc5 ♗xc5 11 ♘e4 ♗e7 12 a4 bxa4 13 ♖xa4 ♕c7 14 ♗b1 ♘b6 15 ♘d6+ ♗xd6 16 exd6 ♕d8 17 ♖g4 and Black is in big trouble, Hennigan-Basman, British Championship 1991.

5 ♘bd2 e6 6 0-0 c5 7 dxc5!

There are other ways to play, but this straightforward method guarantees White some advantage.

7...♗xc5 8 e5 ♘d5 9 ♘e4 ♗e7 10 a4

10 ♗g5 also looks strong.

10...b4 11 c4 bxc3 12 bxc3 0-0 13 c4 ♘b4 14 ♗b1

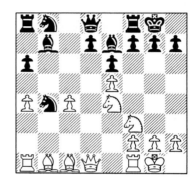

Faibisovich-Frog, St Petersburg 1993. After 14...♕c7 15 ♕b3 ♘8c6 16 c5 White is ready to jump in with ♘d6.

Important Points

1) The continued utilisation of these openings by certain Grandmasters suggests that they are not so bad. Don't look for a direct refutation; just play normal developing moves.

2) If you study the suggested lines here, your opponent's unusual choices will lose much of their surprise value.

INDEX OF VARIATIONS